MW00813771

MANAGING
Therapy-Interfering Behavior

MANAGING
Therapy-Interfering Behavior

STRATEGIES FROM DIALECTICAL BEHAVIOR THERAPY

ALEXANDER L. CHAPMAN AND M. ZACHARY ROSENTHAL

FOREWORD BY MARSHA M. LINEHAN

American Psychological Association • Washington, DC

Published by
American Psychological Association
750 First Street, NE
Washington, DC 20002
www.apa.org

To order
APA Order Department
P.O. Box 92984
Washington, DC 20090-2984
Tel: (800) 374-2721; Direct: (202) 336-5510
Fax: (202) 336-5502; TDD/TTY: (202) 336-6123
Online: www.apa.org/pubs/books
E-mail: order@apa.org

In the U.K., Europe, Africa, and the Middle East, copies may be ordered from
American Psychological Association
3 Henrietta Street
Covent Garden, London
WC2E 8LU England

Typeset in Goudy by Circle Graphics, Inc., Columbia, MD

Printer: Bang Printing, Brainerd, MN
Cover Designer: Mercury Publishing Services, Inc., Rockville, MD

The opinions and statements published are the responsibility of the authors, and such opinions and statements do not necessarily represent the policies of the American Psychological Association.

Library of Congress Cataloging-in-Publication Data

Chapman, Alexander L. (Alexander Lawrence)
  Managing therapy-interfering behavior : strategies from dialectical behavior therapy / Alexander L. Chapman and M. Zachary Rosenthal.
    pages cm
  Includes bibliographical references and index.
  ISBN 978-1-4338-2097-7 — ISBN 1-4338-2097-8 1. Dialectical behavior therapy.
2. Psychotherapy. I. Rosenthal, M. Zachary. II. Title.
  RC489.B4C43 2016
  616.89'142—dc23
                        2015014516

British Library Cataloguing-in-Publication Data

A CIP record is available from the British Library.

Printed in the United States of America
First Edition

http://dx.doi.org/10.1037/14752-000

CONTENTS

FOREWORD

MARSHA M. LINEHAN

I was so glad to hear that Alex Chapman and Zach Rosenthal were writing a book to help practitioners effectively manage therapy-interfering behavior, using principles and strategies from dialectical behavior therapy (DBT). Alex is a former postdoctoral fellow who worked in our lab for 2 years. He was fabulous then, and since then he has launched an impressive career focused on borderline personality disorder (BPD), self-injury, and emotion regulation. Alex has contributed to DBT over the years through his work as a DBT adherence coder, an outstanding DBT trainer and consultant for Behavioral Tech, LLC, a supervisor for students on my treatment development team, a member of the DBT Trainers Advisory Committee, the Exam Writing Committee for the DBT-Linehan Board of Certification, and his mentoring and teaching of graduate students and others. Alex also is one of my Zen students and a martial artist. He is a friend, colleague, and an expert in DBT and the treatment of people with complex mental health problems.

Zach Rosenthal (trained and mentored by one of the first students to learn DBT, a contributor to DBT in his own right, and my long-time collaborator, Dr. Alan Fruzzetti) was a research therapist and a research coordinator for our major National Institute on Drug Abuse randomized trial of DBT for opiate-dependent patients with BPD. It was in this trial that we rolled out our new set of DBT attachment strategies aimed specifically at keeping patients in the treatment, an important set of strategies for treating the therapy-interfering behaviors of not coming to treatment and of dropping out early. Zach's skills in DBT are outstanding, and he has developed an innovative program of research examining how to generalize treatment beyond the therapy room, as well as the use of technology to help treatment-resistant populations. As the director of Duke's Cognitive Behavioral Research and Treatment Program, Zach regularly trains interns, students, and clinicians in DBT. The authors' expertise, clinical wisdom, and experience with DBT and the treatment of complex clients shine through in this excellent book.

The bottom line is that the authors of this book are tops in their field, important enough. But even more important is that because of their wide experience with difficult-to-treat patients, they really do know how to use the DBT interventions that were designed specifically to treat therapy-interfering behaviors. I have not the slightest doubt that you will benefit from what they have to say.

ACKNOWLEDGMENTS

I (ALC) would like to express appreciation for the many people who have influenced my work in the area of dialectical behavior therapy (DBT) over the years. I went to my first DBT workshop years ago as a graduate student in Idaho, and at the time, I was so impressed that people could get to the point in their careers where they are on the workshop circuit, training others in an effective treatment. I never really imagined I would do that myself or that I would have a chance to write books to help clinicians better understand and treat their patients. Professionally, many people have been integral to my journey along this path, including my graduate mentors, Dr. Richard Farmer and Dr. Tony Cellucci; my friends; colleagues; my former internship supervisors, Dr. Tom Lynch and Clive Robins, and Dr. Marsha Linehan, who helped me learn the essence of DBT and whose continued support and guidance over the years has been invaluable. Many of what I consider to be the best suggestions and ideas in this book did not come from a book or workshop, but from my experiences with my clients, as well as the discussions I have had in my DBT consultation teams over the years. I would like to thank my current team at the DBT Centre of Vancouver for their exemplary work in helping our clients and for their support and wise advice. In addition, this book would not have been possible, or nearly as good, without my friend, colleague, and coauthor, Zach. You have a knack for breathing vitality and energy into your writing and your work, and I am so glad we had a chance to work together on this book. Finally, I would like to acknowledge the support and encouragement of my family, including my parents, my wonderful wife, and my two lovely sons (the younger of whom is, so far, the only person in my household to have read any of my books!).

* * * * *

When I (MZR) first heard about DBT as an undergraduate at the University of Kentucky, the last thing I could have envisioned was that 20 years later I would be writing this book. How in the world did I get here, to this moment, with an opportunity to translate what I have learned from past mentors, clinicians, students, and clients into a resource that might help improve how therapists respond to common things that get in the way of treatments for problems with mental health? The answer is in millions of moments, experiences, and contingencies, some guided by strategic planning, others simply dumb luck, all of which have given me the opportunities I have today to try to reach people and change lives for the better. I have been so very fortunate and am indebted to the many people who have supported me. In writing this book with Alex I have spent countless hours reflecting on the many clients I have treated and clinicians I have helped train over the years. A collage of their stories can be found in the clinical examples throughout this book, and for their trust in me I have deep gratitude.

Some of the first DBT clients I ever treated at the University of Nevada, Reno, taught me much of what I have been able to pass on in this book. Thank you, to all of you, for allowing me the privilege of trying to help you when I knew so little about DBT. It has been a long time, but our time working together is not forgotten. The same is true for the clients I have treated since coming to Duke University Medical Center. I am grateful for all that I learned from these experiences and continue to learn as time goes on and clients under my care come for treatment at our Duke Cognitive Behavioral Research and Treatment Program.

I would like to acknowledge my DBT supervisor and clinical mentor in graduate school, Dr. Alan Fruzzetti, for instilling the base of my DBT knowledge; my internship and postdoctoral mentor, Dr. Tom Lynch; the developer of DBT, Dr. Marsha Linehan, for her tireless and groundbreaking work; and all of my colleagues who have helped me refine the use of DBT strategies when treating non-DBT clients.

I also am grateful to my coauthor, Alex Chapman, for inviting me to write this book with him. It has been tons of fun! Alex, your guidance, humor, prodigious keystrokes, and level head all have been inspiring to me. Thank you.

Finally, I would like to thank my family and friends for the many ways in which they have supported me in making this book come to life. You encouraged me to keep going with this whole psychology thing when I had no clue what I was going to do with my life. How did you all know? You have and continue to keep molding me into who I am, and for that I am humbled and in awe of the special chance I have to affect others. And to my wife, Kirsten, thank you so much for giving me the selfless gift of time to write on the weekends and weeknights while parenting without me. Your support was deeply felt, and if you were resentful of being a single parent for a little while, it never once showed! I suppose that kind of acceptance is true love. Finally, thank you to my two sons, Ben and Ander, for tolerating my absent father routine when I was writing. Now I can come back outside and play street hockey with you two.

MANAGING
Therapy-Interfering Behavior

1

WHY PEOPLE GET IN THEIR OWN WAY

Clients, patients, consumers, customers, whatever your preference and training about the appropriate appellation, they are all, in a word, *people*. Like non-clients, psychotherapy clients are people with complex and long learning histories that are shaped by and that reciprocally influence their biology and environments. From the chronically mentally ill to the resilient and psychologically healthy, all our clients bring their learning history into the treatment setting. This history is an enormously important context for the therapeutic relationship. On one hand, as with the client who has learned how to trust and be vulnerable with others, it can help treatment move faster and be more effective for some clients. On the other hand, our clients' history can contribute to them doing things that function to interfere with their treatment. This is also true for clinicians, who bring their own unique learning history into the psychotherapy process. Just as our learning history sometimes gets the best of anyone in their everyday lives, it is common across psychotherapies for clients

http://dx.doi.org/10.1037/14752-001
Managing Therapy-Interfering Behavior: Strategies From Dialectical Behavior Therapy, by A. L. Chapman and M. Z. Rosenthal

and clinicians to do things that can get in the way of treatment progress. In this book, we refer to this as *therapy-interfering behavior*, or TIB.

THERAPY-INTERFERING BEHAVIOR

TIB can be intentional or unintentional, strategic or automatic, calculated or absentminded. It can include being chronically late or noncompliant with treatment, ineffectively expressing or inhibiting emotion during treatment, being overly passive or aggressive interpersonally with the clinician, and so on. Sometimes the very problem the client needs to address occurs in relation to the therapist, such as when the client has social anxiety and becomes anxious and avoidant with the clinician during treatment. At other times the TIB is something different from what is being addressed in treatment. A client may be flirtatious with the clinician, but this may not be something that is being targeted as a problem in treatment. Reduction of depressive symptoms may be the primary treatment goal, but the client may talk excessively during session about her- or himself in ways that are suggestive of narcissistic personality traits. Problems with substance use and avoidant coping may be the focus, but the client may persist in talking about various weekly problems, even crises, with little willingness to directly work on learning how to reduce substance use or change ways of coping.

If you are a clinician, it is likely you have seen TIB. If you see a lot of clients, you probably see TIB every week, maybe every day. The reason, we believe, is that it is common for clients to get in their own way. It also is common for therapists and clinicians to get in their own way of helping clients. This is not something to be upset about. With compassion and curiosity, TIB can be viewed as a predictable opportunity. However, as clinicians, we need tools to help manage the difficult moments when TIB occurs during assessment or treatment for mental health problems.

Any behavior that interferes with the client benefitting from therapy could be considered a TIB. We introduce some ways to conceptualize and manage TIBs later in the book. For now, it may help to think about some common TIBs that occur with clients: the depressed individual who is relentlessly self-judgmental during psychotherapy sessions, the client with generalized anxiety who spins a web of hopeless rumination throughout the session, or perhaps the substance user struggling after being late to the clinic to organize his or her thoughts about what to talk about during the session. The paranoid client is likely, at times, to display behavioral signs of paranoia with you. The mistrusting client at some point will likely lose trust in you. The suspicious client, naturally and inevitably, may suspect that something is amiss with treatment. Whatever the client does with others interpersonally outside the therapy setting, she or he may be likely to do with you, the clinician, inside the therapy setting. This is not unique to any one diagnosis, type of client, or model of psychotherapy. People commonly get in their own way in psychotherapy.

It is common for therapists to bemoan the client who consistently exhibits TIB during sessions. As a clinician, there are things you want to talk about and conversations you believe are more or less important to have; perhaps you even have an agenda for your therapy session. However, the client may want to share things he or she thinks are important to him or her. You are trained to listen, to be a professional ear, paid to help your clients understand, make meaning, develop insights, and change the way they live. So when the session that you expected would head in one direction now is steamrolling in another, you recognize what is happening. Each session may be a journey, you tell yourself, but you do not really know where the destination is until you get there. That stance is helpful, but it leaves you wondering how in the world you are going to help this person when he or she is so far afield from talking about what is on the treatment plan.

So you put your session agenda on hold. You feel compelled to listen intently. For the first 10 minutes you interject here and there, trying to discern where the conversation is going, but when your client's story continues to unfold, layer after layer, you end up deciding that it is better to just keep quiet. Surely the story will take the two of you somewhere. The client has all the answers inside him or her, you remind yourself, and your job is to create a safe and nurturing environment for the client to learn how to experience him- or herself and relate to others differently. You remind yourself that you cannot work harder than your client, that change is within her or him, and he or she will change when they are ready. You are meeting he or she where he or she is in that moment, being supportive, kind, gentle, and client-centered. You are a compassionate clinician, and right now, as that client continues to keep sharing his or her thoughts about what happened this week at work or at home, you choose to listen, nod, take notes, and offer brief words of support.

Eventually the session ends. You learned a great deal about how your client experienced him- or herself during some stressful situations last week. You are proud of how he or she handled certain parts of it, but see opportunities to talk about making some changes next week in your session. You are pretty sure that you listened well, reflecting, affirming, paraphrasing, and problem solving. The client seemed to feel trusting of you. He or she told you some new things about her or his past, opening up another layer of vulnerability. This is something you see as progress. Another thing that you chalk up to progress is that the client seemed to describe the events of the past week with more clarity and precision than usual. Emotions were less intense than in previous session you note in the medical record, and you attribute this to possible changes in affect regulation. The 45-minute journey is over. You did not end up where you thought you would, but it seems OK.

The next week the same client does the same thing. You drop your agenda again, although you really wanted to tie up some loose ends from the previous session. This time there is another important story for you to hear. Again, like the last one, and all of the stories that will follow, this too is a story that your client would like you to listen to. Listening will help you understand and help the client feel understood. Why in the world would you want to interrupt? This is the journey you are on together, and the process of change can take a lot of time. This may be a reasonable approach for those who can financially afford long-term psychotherapy, but for clients who cannot, or for those whose dysfunction or psychological distress is significant, change may need to move at a faster pace.

If you are a clinician and have done a lot of psychotherapy, you have seen a lot of TIB. If you have just started doing psychotherapy you have already begun to see TIB. Unless you are trained in dialectical behavior therapy, we doubt that you call it "TIB." However, every system of psychotherapy has to contend with TIB. As well they should. A central thesis of this book is that TIB can be hypothesized and conceptualized as clinically relevant. The specific behavior that interferes with therapy can represent a broader class of behavior that is common and problematic in the client's life. That is, TIB can often be what the radical behavioral treatment functional analytic psychotherapy (Kohlenberg & Tsai, 1991) labels as clinically relevant behaviors. Think of TIBs as opportunities to mine for therapeutic gold, to discover with clients how they can change with you in a way that may help them change how they express this TIB when it manifests as life-interfering behavior outside the clinic. Think of how frustrated you have been with clients who do not stop talking or who say almost nothing at all. These are moments in session when TIB can be noticed without judgment, explored collaboratively, and targeted for change using the same new ways of relating to others they are trying to learn outside the clinic. TIBs do not have to come with shock and awe, and they do not have to suddenly stun you. They are sometimes jolting (e.g., "I found a new therapist. I probably should have told you I was thinking about this."), other times subtle (e.g., "I can't remember."). They can be colorful and dramatic (e.g., "I'm only here because the court is making me, but I don't believe talking to you is going to help."), or they can be plain and common (e.g., "Sorry I forgot to tell you I would miss our session last week."). No matter your theoretical preferences, no matter your biases about what constitutes good therapy, we suggest that you expect TIB with all clients.

Chances are if you felt stumped about what to say or do in a therapy session you may have been responding to TIB. When we describe therapist TIB later in the book, we share some stories of times when one of us was treating a client and, for one reason or another, we engaged in TIB. TIBs are bumps in the road, potholes in our psychotherapy, and can at times bring relational roads extremely difficult to travel. There is nothing to fear about TIB, nothing to run from, nothing to feel ashamed about, and nothing about which to be judgmental of you or your clients. It is ordinary psychotherapy process. It is common and difficult, but clinicians who can respond well to TIB can be rewarded with extraordinary client changes.

No matter the therapeutic orientation, this book is intended to help you, the clinician, in times when things are not going quite the way you envisioned, when behavior in the therapy room, TIB, arrests and holds hostage the client's progress. Lateness to session, forgetting what was talked about in the past session, and not doing therapy homework are common TIBs. Starting the session with a story about something unrelated to treatment, extreme talkativeness, apparent disinterest in how therapy can help, serial crises, ambiguous could-be crises, and crises avoided until the last few moments of the session are also common TIBs. Other common TIBs include conflict avoidance, chitchat, long latencies to respond to questions, deftly changing the topic when emotions arise, unrelenting catharsis for 45 minutes, and deliberate efforts to inhibit emotional expression.

One reason people get in their own way in therapy is that they do not know what is expected of them. When people come to therapy for the first time, they do not know what the therapeutic process is supposed to look like. They may have expectations, desires, or assumptions. They may have been told by a friend what it is like, seen a recent movie, or read a book where they learned how a therapy client behaves. So when they walk in for the first time, curious, ambivalent, and anxious, they may be ready to follow your lead.

We ask new clients whether it is their first time doing psychotherapy or counseling. For those who are new to therapy, this is an opportunity to orient them to what is expected and most helpful in the process of talking to a therapist. This is the time to strike while the proverbial iron is hot to reduce some of the anxiety about what is expected of them, to increase a sense of controllability and predictability in a vulnerable setting. This first session is when clinicians can begin to talk about possible TIB in a nonjudgmental, compassionate, and straightforward manner.

For example, in the first appointment clients sometimes do or say things that are signs of probable TIB on the horizon. If the client expresses disinterest in attending sessions, or perhaps even disdain for therapy on the basis of past experiences, the first appointment is a wonderful time to begin attending to such feelings and experiences. This happened recently, when a young woman with borderline personality disorder (BPD) features came for an evaluation after being referred to receive dialectical behavior therapy. The client had received psychotherapy from several clinicians in the past, was suffering tremendously, and was open about her distrust of psychotherapy. It became clear during the evaluation that ignoring these comments (e.g., "I just don't trust any of you therapists") was insufficient and perhaps invalidating of her experience. Thus, the concept of TIB was introduced instead:

> If I ever say or do something to lose your trust, or to suddenly gain your trust, would you be willing to let me know? Because trust is one thing that is very important in our work together, if you lose trust in me, it is likely that you might end up doing or saying things that could get in the way of your own treatment. Think about it, if you didn't trust me, would you be as open, honest, or vulnerable than if you did have trust in me?

From our perspective, a trick to this process is not to blame or pathologize, but instead to be straightforward and humbly frame the potential TIB as completely understandable, normal, or ordinary. To begin, pick a TIB that is likely to be nonthreatening to the client. It will help keep emotional arousal in the room low enough that your message can be heard, and the client can become open to exploring TIB with you later on. Build from this example to explain that, more generally, part of treatment involves noticing and attending to TIB as needed to help the client get better faster. When TIB is expected, it can be conceptualized a priori, preparing the clinician, facilitating a strategic response with intention to help clients meet their own goals. Instead of letting TIB interfere with therapy, the planful clinician collaboratively uses TIB to help accelerate progress. Instead of TIB, it can become treatment-accelerating behavior. The very thing getting in the way becomes that which paves the way.

Expecting TIB makes it less surprising and more rewarding for both clinician and client. It may sound strange, but it can be quite useful to tell your clients who have problems with trust that you expect and hope that they have moments where they lose trust during your work together. Other therapists may not want to have to deal with suspiciousness, mistrust, and the like, and you might not want to either, but by dealing with TIB directly, you will be addressing precisely the behavior that the client struggles with outside of the session. If you have a suspicious client with relationship difficulties, how in the world can you expect him or her not to become suspicious with you? And if you accept that it is likely she or he will become suspicious with you, why not openly and compassionately plan for this behavior?

What about clients who have been in psychotherapy before? Whenever a new client who has been in therapy before comes to the clinic, it is helpful to know how the process of previous therapies was experienced. Clients may not know which brand of psychotherapy (e.g., cognitive behavior, psychodynamic) their past therapists were using, but they do remember what it was like to be in the room with the therapist. Who did most of the talking? What were the targets of change? What kinds of things did the therapist include in the treatment plan? Was there a treatment plan? Did the therapist mostly listen and give encouragement, talk about learning principles and ways to change behavior, or discuss patterns of attachment in childhood and the subsequent difficulties the client has with empathic attunement?

In our experience, the most common reaction to these questions, by a landslide, is that clients pause, sigh, and then say politely that they are not really sure what the treatment was, that the therapist was very nice and supportively listened, offered advice, and helped resolve life stressors, but that they became concerned because they did not feel as though they got much better. They then typically go on to explain that they want someone to help them make some changes in their life. They want a therapist to listen and be supportive, while also providing direct help in changing how they experience themselves and the world, how they relate to people, or how they cope with their emotional distress. In short, clients often want a therapist who is empathic, supportive, and compassionate, without being passive. They want a strong listener who understands the centrality of the therapeutic relationship and who can motivate, direct, and provide learning experiences in therapy sessions to directly change dysfunctional behavior and provide relief from emotional suffering. This is just the type of therapist who can attend to TIB thoughtfully with clients' values and goals in mind.

TIB can take many forms and be incredibly challenging. As clinicians, we need solutions for these challenges. However, what we need are solutions that are both conceptual and practical and that can be applied flexibly across diverse clients and diverse treatments. This book is for clinicians and those interested in learning how to address difficult behaviors that occur during mental health assessment and treatment. It is for students across the scope of mental and behavioral health training. Clinical psychologists, psychiatrists, clinical social workers, addiction counselors, nurse practitioners, licensed professional counselors, marriage and family therapists, licensed substance abuse specialists, and other clinicians all may find it helpful to learn ways to manage TIB.

DIALECTICAL BEHAVIOR THERAPY

Throughout this book, we emphasize how to conceptualize TIB using an approach from an evidence-based cognitive behavior therapy for BPD called *dialectical behavior therapy* (DBT). DBT was developed several decades ago by Dr. Marsha Linehan at the University of Washington. It was the first empirically supported behavioral treatment for BPD, and since the first randomized trial was published (Linehan, Armstrong, Suarez, Allmon, & Heard, 1991), DBT has been disseminated nationally and internationally as an intervention for BPD. Throughout this book we orient you to DBT principles and strategies, with the assumption that you are not already an intensively trained DBT clinician. For now, it is useful to highlight that in DBT, therapists are trained to expect client TIBs and are prepared with a conceptual framework and behavioral strategies so that, no matter which TIB occurs, the therapist is ready to respond effectively. Our experiences as DBT clinicians, researchers, and supervisors have led us to conclude that therapists who are not trained in or using DBT would also benefit from learning how to respond effectively to TIB. After all, TIB occurs for most, if not all, clients; individuals meeting criteria for BPD are not the only ones to get in their own way during treatment.

This book is for clinicians trained across diverse theoretical schools of psychotherapy. Psychodynamically trained therapists have various terms for processes that are germane to TIB: resistance, transference, countertransference, unconscious defenses, and the like. The process of transference is a core component of the therapeutic process for many clinicians and provides a different conceptual framework from what we outline. Client-centered approaches, embodying the stance that clients have the answers and all capabilities within them, may provide nurturance and support, open-ended statements and affirmations, reflections, paraphrasings, and summarizations during discourse with the client. A straightforward cognitive therapy response to TIB might be to examine the underlying cognitions, attitudes, rules, and beliefs related to the TIB. A behavioral treatment, functional analytic psychotherapy (Kohlenberg & Tsai, 1991), offers a detailed approach for the management of clinically relevant in-session behavior, which is similar in certain ways to what we outline when discussing how to manage TIB from a DBT perspective. And, as we detail in this book, in DBT, one member in the ever-growing family of cognitive behavior therapies, there are explicit strategies for managing TIB.

Although DBT is a contemporary cognitive behavior therapy, an aim of this book is to provide strategies that are principle-driven and practical, tools that nearly any clinician can use to help them competently manage TIB. We do not believe that DBT is the first or best model for conceptualizing or changing TIB. Those are empirical considerations best left to laboratories and randomized trials. We do not believe any one theory or brand of psychotherapy is the best way to manage TIB. However, we do think the strategies and techniques used in DBT to attend to TIB may be helpful to therapists beyond those already doing DBT.

In this volume we provide specific examples of tools and strategies used in DBT to manage TIB, with the goal of helping clinicians, especially those who are not trained in DBT already, to develop new ways to respond to difficult-to-manage TIB. Chapters 1 through 4 provide the basic framework needed to address any TIB, whereas Chapters 5 through 12 collectively address common client and therapist TIB in psychotherapy and ways to overcome specific and expected challenges when addressing TIB.

To be more specific, in Chapter 1, we set the context for the challenges clinicians face when addressing TIB by answering the question: Why do clients sometimes get in their own way in psychotherapy? In Chapter 2, we provide detailed descriptions of core DBT principles used to conceptualize and relate TIB to other problems being addressed in therapy. In Chapter 3, the therapist's boundaries and limits are discussed, with an emphasis on ways that clinicians can observe and work within their own personal limits when TIB occurs. Chapter 4 outlines primary tools and strategies from DBT that are used to manage TIB. In Chapters 5 (missing therapy visits), 6 (not completing therapy homework), and 7 (hostility or anger during psychotherapy), we delve into specific applications of DBT strategies and techniques for particular TIB. Chapter 8 provides detailed suggestions for ways clinicians can decide when and how to directly talk about TIB with clients. In Chapter 9, we discuss the common problem of client avoidance of unpleasant emotions, thoughts, and particular topics during psychotherapy. Chapter 10 is devoted to considering ways to conceptualize and respond to potentially sexually related behavior during psychotherapy. Chapter 11 addresses common TIB that occurs during the process of terminating psychotherapy. Finally, in Chapter 12, we discuss the critical role that therapist TIB can have on the psychotherapy process, and we offer solutions to manage these situations.

By using DBT-based strategies for managing TIB, we hope you will be able to improve your psychotherapy skills with some new tools for dealing with some of the more difficult moments clinicians face. As you read through the rest of this book, we recommend that you think about some of the more difficult clients you have treated, asking yourself whether there is anything different that could have been done in their care by changing how you addressed any TIB. By the end of this book you will not be a DBT therapist and you will not be an expert in treatment of BPD, but you will have learned some of the core ways in which we who practice DBT effectively handle TIB in our clients with BPD. If TIB can be addressed successfully with those who have BPD, we are confident these same strategies can be used with other clients. Before thinking the way you do psychotherapy is simply incongruent with behavioral therapies, cognitive behavioral therapies, or with DBT specifically, we encourage you to keep reading, to think about how you have dealt with common TIBs in the past, and to openly consider ways you might respond to them in the future.

No matter your theoretical orientation or training in psychotherapy, for this moment, think about your own experience with TIBs. Bring to mind a client you are currently treating or have recently treated. Identify the top three most frustrating moments during these therapy sessions. What did the client do or say just before you became frustrated? What happened when you were frustrated? What did you want to happen instead? What was the problem the client wanted help with, and how did that problem show up during psychotherapy? What TIBs were there, and how could you have been more effective dealing with them? As you think about this, consider a case when TIB was significant, impossible to ignore, yet difficult to overcome.

BETH: A CLIENT WHO GOT IN HER OWN WAY

Several years ago, I (MZR) was doing psychotherapy with a client who, sadly, got in her own way.[1] Beth was a woman in her late 30s presenting with obesity and binge eating, posttraumatic stress disorder (PTSD), and problems with substance use. She had been in treatment with me for several years, on and off, doing cognitive behavior interventions for her various problems. Beth was extremely bright and endearing, kind to a fault, both with her therapist and with others. In hindsight, when she eventually got in her own way during treatment, it should have been predictable and easy to see coming. But, as it often turns out, the luxury of hindsight was not there at the time, and it felt a bit surprising. Until she got in her own way one too many times, it seemed clear to me that she had been a treatment success.

Beth had been through 2 years of DBT, including individual sessions and group skills training. She did not like going to group, but week after week, month after month, she had kept on coming, dutifully learning the skills and improving. She was better at regulating her emotions and tolerating emotional distress; she had improved her ability to be nonjudgmental and experience unpleasant emotions mindfully and had mastered several interpersonal effectiveness skills. After she finished group skills training and most of her out-of-control behaviors (recurrent urges to self-harm, binge eating, impulsivity) were under control for a long period of time, we decided it was appropriate to do an evidence-based treatment for PTSD. This is a common next step after the first stage of DBT. She had held off on addressing her PTSD symptoms for several years, afraid to directly talk about when she had been drugged and raped in her teens. Prolonged exposure is a gold standard behavioral treatment for PTSD (Foa & Rothbaum, 1998). The randomized

---

[1]The key details in all case studies in this volume have been altered to protect clients' confidentiality. No real names are used, and in all instances the descriptions used are prototypes of experiences across multiple clients and/or details have been changes about specific cases such that the case described does not reflect or identify any one specific former client.

controlled trials suggested it should work well for many people. Having implemented this intervention many times before with multidiagnostic and difficult-to-treat clients, I felt confident in my ability to deliver the intervention. And Beth was now ready to do the work.

I followed the treatment manual shamelessly, opening it up during exposure sessions and using it frequently as a resource to structure the therapy sessions and psychotherapy homework. As a DBT therapist, the implementation of prolonged exposure meant another opportunity to model therapist imperfections as acceptable and ordinary. This demonstration of therapist fallibility happened here and there as treatment continued with as much fidelity as feasible, given usual life circumstances. Beth traveled and missed sessions. She overslept or had other appointments that kept her from regularly coming to our sessions. Therapists have lives too, so when family vacations or work meetings happened on our scheduled appointment days, more therapy sessions were missed. Still, by the end of several months of prolonged exposure, to her great surprise, the PTSD symptoms were nearly gone. Naturally, she still had some problems to resolve, but the nightmares were gone, the avoidance was minimal, she was less agitated, was sleeping better, and so on. After years of suffering, her diagnosis of PTSD was no longer appropriate.

First the focus had been on DBT skills, then on PTSD and prolonged exposure. She was improved, happier, and finding more satisfaction with work and dating. This was evidence that perhaps despite her core sense of self as broken and irreparable, as goods damaged by shattering sexual traumas, treatment was helping her to get better in many ways. We looked at changes in her self-reported PTSD symptoms over time on psychometrically validated PTSD symptom scales. We celebrated her victory overcoming the crippling shame that she had kept for so long. She no longer blamed herself. She no longer believed she had deserved to be taken advantage of by her perpetrators. Beth had been secretly drugged and sodomized and was still emotionally scarred, but she knew now that she was not at fault. These changes were profound and were the result of session after session, exposure after exposure, grinding away at the conditioned emotional responses of PTSD. New learning, extinguished emotional responses, and more flexibility in how she experienced her negative emotions and related to others all characterized her newly forming sense of self. It was, it seemed at the time, the treatment outcome we wanted. What began as a host of diverse psychiatric symptoms, life dysfunction, and psychological distress was now about as good an outcome as could be envisioned. It was time to either end our work together or identify newly attainable goals.

Even without any acutely debilitating problems, Beth decided to continue psychotherapy. She talked animatedly about how much therapy had helped her. She proclaimed to have been treated by the "best therapist" she had ever had. She seemed genuine, even heartfelt, without being inappropriate. Therapy had been a long slog for Beth; it was emotionally draining and challenging all along, and she recognized it. As can be guessed, however, her declaration about having the best therapist portended, as this statement often does, an unfortunate turn of events soon to come in her treatment.

As we rounded the corner into the next phase of treatment, Beth still struggled to regulate her emotions. Her affective lability was sharp and unpredictable. Her rumination was prodigious. In addition to the index trauma we had processed, Beth had been raped multiple times by other men. The process of exposure therapy revealed that she believed, in every cell of her being, that she was fundamentally unlovable. It did not matter that her PTSD symptoms were gone. She still needed help.

Beth was a storyteller, and the story her mind told her is one that many clients tell. Her psychological narrative was clear, crystallized as truth, and not something any therapy would easily change. Her mind was like an insufferable radio personality, hyperbolic self-loathing streaming for so long that she had become convinced that she was defective, biologically predetermined to fail, incapable and unworthy of being loved. Her mind had persuaded her to believe in a particular narrative: She was and would always be irreparably damaged biologically, and this would make her fundamentally undesirable interpersonally. Her mind was a used car salesman, and it had sold her a poisonous lemon.

Worse, Beth disclosed during one highly emotional session that she believed being drugged and raped many times by multiple men was, put simply, something she deserved. She experienced herself as a relational reject. Somehow she thought she was supposed to be treated poorly by others and fail in relationships. Success was anathema to her, always out of reach and ego-dystonic. Not surprisingly, her shame during treatment sessions was persistent. She would study the floor as she talked to me, her eyes averting mine; tears would flow regularly, and she would berate herself at every chance for not being a good client.

Beth was ashamed about her inability to be productive at work, ashamed that she could not reliably show up on time for her appointments, especially the ones on Fridays, or do the behavioral homework she had agreed in our sessions to do. She was ashamed about "wasting" time in therapy and about many things. Now, with the acute symptoms gone, it was time to help her learn to relate to people better. This meant that we would need to confront and change how she experienced herself, and her shame, in the context of meaningful relationships. In hindsight, it is embarrassingly easy to see how this would end.

We would have to treat the shame Beth was feeling in the therapy session. We would have to pay attention to her shame—the thoughts, physical sensations, action tendencies, and associated feeling states that she would feel whenever shame would show up in the therapy session. We would have to be intentional, deliberate, and collaborative. We would have to do this to help her develop insight and the resultant new patterns of relating to others without the emotion of shame being the cause or consequence of interactions. And we would have to change this long-standing pattern slowly, one context and experience at a time, starting with me in our sessions. Plans were made and we collaboratively predicted that she would invariably feel badly about herself at some point in each session, and in processing her feelings of shame she would likely feel uncomfortable. Being proactive about how to change her shame in sessions would provide a working framework to deal with what was already happening anyway. This seemed like a pretty good plan. We had been through so much together, and her chronic self-judgments and overlearned shame during our sessions surely could not stop us.

As you can probably guess, it did not go well. We identified and agreed on several treatment goals. All of them included using cognitive and behavioral skills to improve her interpersonal relationships. It is important to stop here and point out that this woman desperately wanted to feel less ashamed. She wished she could break free from the bind that shame had seemed to wind around her. Shame was both her noose and hangman, emotionally ambushing her on a daily basis. She had many moments during the day when she truly hated herself, and yet at the same time, Beth knew quite well that this was irrational. Like many clients, she had lots to love about herself. Smart, generous, and funny, with a wry British wit, she was easy to like. She had three siblings who were doctors, and elderly parents who had been wildly successful in the corporate world. This was part of the problem. Beth was born into a family full of apparent success. By Beth's way of seeing it, her parents and siblings had everything that she did not. They were successful, but she could never be. They had the good genes. She did not. They were the lucky ones. She drew the short straw.

At this point in our treatment Beth did not need any further psychoeducation. She was not experiencing "information deficit disorder," and no detailed explanations of this or that model of psychopathology would elevate her sense of self. She did not need to learn any more about how to challenge cognitive distortions. She did not need to keep rehearsing interpersonal effectiveness skills. She knew how to be assertive, knew how to look people in the eyes and ask for what she wanted. She was not aggressive and hostile, at least not in therapy, though she could be emotionally turbulent, prickly, or even surly. What Beth seemed to need was to learn through relational experiences that she was not a failure and that her shame responses in therapy were both expected and capable of being changed. Like a lot of clients, Beth needed to learn through her relationship with her therapist to feel less ashamed and more interpersonally confident. In realizing this, it became more important than ever before to consistently create and maintain a safe and trusting environment for her so that she could eventually come to experience herself as OK. But this is where she got in her own way.

Beth let her shame keep her from coming to treatment. She missed an appointment, oversleeping, as she explained. She was apologetic and promised not to do it again. The next week she cancelled the appointment, saying she had no money for the co-pay. The following week she described major life changes that had happened since the previous therapy session. It took most of the therapy session to discuss these new developments: a new boyfriend, new job, new friends, a fresh new outlook on herself. She smiled and said she felt the best she had felt in a long time. Picking up the conversational pace, she continued: PTSD symptoms were in remission, there had been no binge eating, and she was sleeping well and not feeling anxious anymore. This was all great news, except that the new boyfriend was 20 years older than her, a recovering drug addict who she impulsively fell for and, consistent with her core belief that she was unworthy and unlovable, who was awfully cruel to her. In addition, her close colleague at work had recently turned on her, berating and belittling Beth in front of coworkers at a holiday party. Beth declared that she was going to stand up to this aggression, not involve herself with this colleague any longer, and maybe even tell her off. She boldly asserted that she did not deserve to be emotionally abused. Those days were over. Her primary psychiatric symptoms were gone, she had a new boyfriend, and she was ready to stand up and defend herself. Things were looking good to Beth.

Except that there was still a problem. She disclosed anxiously at the end of the session that because she was doing so well now, she had decided not to return to the emotion regulation skills group after recently agreeing to do so. As she talked about her decision not to go the skills group and her unwillingness to comply with our agreement, she sharply looked away. She started to cry. She apologized shamefully, saying that she was a disappointment, a waste of time, and that other clients deserved this therapy hour more than she did. Shame squeezed her again, tears racing down her cheeks, but as soon as the emotional faucet had turned on, she turned it off. She wiped her tears, giggled, and said she knew she was being irrational. The session wound down, we scheduled for the next week, and parted. She did not come back to therapy for a long time. What had happened? Beth's shame was tied to escape behavior. When she felt intense shame, she prepared herself to exit the situation. She did not think she deserved the help. She chose not to comply with the therapy. She tried to avoid talking about this by detailing extensively all of the new and fabulous things in her life. But when she slipped into the shame spiral that last session, she was preparing to escape. The very problem she needed help for, the very problem we agreed to work on, had become the problem that interfered with her treatment. Her shameful sense of herself in relationships brought her to therapy. That same shame was there throughout treatment. We chipped away at it, but her fundamental sense of self had not changed enough. In the end, her shameful sense of herself in relationships had become the TIB that ended her treatment. It ended her treatment, and it helped to jump-start this book.

2

CORE DIALECTICAL BEHAVIOR THERAPY PRINCIPLES APPLIED TO THERAPY-INTERFERING BEHAVIOR

Psychological treatment is a complex endeavor, and it is easy to sidestep onto pathways that take both the therapist and the client in the wrong direction. This is probably true of any effort at changing long-standing patterns of behavior. Consider how difficult it is to start sleeping more consistently, working on stress reduction, eating more healthfully, and increasing exercise. Many of the changes we expect of our clients are even more challenging. We often ask depressed clients struggling to get out of their bed each morning to actively get out and see people. We encourage anxious clients paralyzed by avoidance to approach and engage the world around them. Clients who have good reasons based on their relationship histories not to trust others must learn to trust their therapist in order to trust others. Whatever the therapist's theoretical orientation, the work we do requires our clients to do extraordinarily difficult things. It is as though, at times, we are asking them to walk through a burning building to have a chance to experience the relief and freedom existing on

http://dx.doi.org/10.1037/14752-002
Managing Therapy-Interfering Behavior: Strategies From Dialectical Behavior Therapy, by A. L. Chapman and M. Z. Rosenthal

19

the other side. No matter the potential reward, we cannot expect our clients to walk in a steady and straight path through that building. It is far more normal for them to ambivalently approach, take paths that lead directly away, get lost, run too fast into the building, or freeze with fear or uncertainty. It is simply the norm for clients to do things throughout the therapeutic process that get in the way of the changes they are seeking.

Therapy is much like the practice of mindfulness (discussed further in this and other chapters). Mindfulness does not involve sustaining your attention completely on one thing in a fixed manner, but rather involves the act of guiding your attention back to that one thing over and over again whenever your attention strays (Kabat-Zinn, 1996; Linehan, 1993b). In therapy, clients' behavior will periodically stray off the path to what they hope will be a better life. Being in therapy often involves gently guiding oneself, with the therapist's assistance, back to that path.

In this chapter, we discuss some core principles to help guide therapists and clients as they navigate effective paths through therapy. To help guide dialectical behavior therapy (DBT) clinicians and non-DBT clinicians alike in these situations, we focus on four key principles: (a) conceptualizing therapy-interfering behavior (TIB) behaviorally, (b) applying dialectical principles to TIB, (c) emphasizing the role of emotions and emotion regulation in TIB, and (d) practicing mindfulness in response to TIB.

CONCEPTUALIZING THERAPY-INTERFERING BEHAVIOR BEHAVIORALLY

From a behavioral perspective, TIB is just like any other behavior. Behavior often occurs and persists because it works. What we mean by *works* is that behavior serves some important purpose or function in the context in which it occurs. Although space limitations will not permit us to provide a detailed discussion of behaviorism (we refer the reader to Farmer & Chapman, 2008, 2016, for a detailed examination of behavioral principles and how to incorporate these into treatment), technically, when a reinforcer follows a behavior, that behavior is more likely to occur under similar circumstances in the future. *Antecedents* for behavior, often referred to as *discriminative stimuli*, signal the availability of a reinforcer contingent on the occurrence of a particular action or set of actions, much like a green traffic light indicates that, if you keep driving (the behavior), you will end up closer to your destination (the reinforcer). Understanding the reinforcers for TIB helps the therapist determine exactly how the behavior works for the client. Perhaps the client who is yelling at the therapist has learned that yelling works in many ways—to blow off steam, get someone to comply with her or his wishes, eliminate demands or requests from someone else, or to mask or regulate other emotions that are difficult to tolerate. The client who repeatedly misses therapy sessions might have learned that activities occurring outside of the therapy room are more reinforcing (e.g., spending time with friends, exercising, going on the Internet, using alcohol or drugs) than are those that occur in therapy (e.g., confronting painful emotions, answering difficult questions).

Any behavior, therapy-interfering or not, is understandable in the context of the client's (or therapist's) learning history, current contexts and contingencies, and the therapeutic relationship. One important assumption along these lines is that everything is exactly as it should be, given the causes and effects operating in the client's (and therapist's) life (Linehan, 1993a). Even behaviors that appear outrageous, such as the client physically attacking or trying to initiate sexual contact with the therapist, ultimately are understandable in the context of the client's life, current skills, and the therapeutic environment. Indeed, TIBs often fall within functional classes of behavior (Farmer & Chapman, 2008, 2016) that were effective in previous contexts but do not serve a similarly useful function in the therapy context. Avoidance of topics associated with shame, for example, makes sense in the context of a history of severe abuse or trauma, when the client learned to hide vulnerabilities, emotions, or thoughts. In the current therapeutic context, however, hiding and avoiding discussions are generally ineffective.

Taking this perspective that all behavior is understandable can orient the therapist toward assessing and understanding, rather than simply managing, TIB. When TIB is particularly aversive, such as threats or yelling, it is easy for therapists to act as if the primary goal is simply to manage the behavior. This happens regularly with suicidal behavior. With extremely suicidal clients, it is hard to get out of the cycle of crisis management, and yet, crisis management itself does not alleviate or treat suicidality. It is critical to assess and understand the factors maintaining the client's suicidality (Linehan, 1993a). Similarly, the therapist who remembers that the most important goal in dealing with TIB is to understand it will be more likely to assess the behavior in a way that opens the door to effective intervention. Furthermore, an accurate assessment and understanding of the client's behavior will help the therapist to validate the client. Accurate validation, in turn, can help to strengthen the therapeutic relationship, help the client feel understood, model effective self-validation (Linehan, 1997), and realign the therapeutic dyad when challenges make working collaboratively difficult.

Another implication of a behavioral perspective is that TIBs are rarely solely due to either the client's or therapist's actions. Rather, TIBs are more likely to result from, and are often maintained by, transactions between the client and therapist. As with any relationship, therapy unfolds as a series of transactions between each party. What the therapist says or does influences what the client says or does, and vice versa. The therapy room is a complex system consisting of the physical environment; the therapist's and client's behaviors, thoughts, and emotions; and the therapist's and client's learning history, biological makeup, and so on. Therefore, from a behavioral perspective, solutions to TIB must involve changes in the therapeutic system and context, not just in the behavior of one of the individuals within this system. This systemic, contextual view of the therapy process is consistent with and complements the dialectical principles discussed in the next section.

APPLYING DIALECTICAL PRINCIPLES
TO THERAPY-INTERFERING BEHAVIOR

Marsha Linehan did not set out on a mission to make DBT a "dialectical" treatment per se. Rather, in her treatment development work with highly suicidal women, she first recognized that a purely change-oriented cognitive behavior therapy (CBT) approach was insufficient, led to clients feeling invalidated, and failed to address important factors underlying the clients' difficulties—lack of acceptance of themselves, their thoughts, emotions, and experiences. It then became clear that an approach purely focused on therapeutic validation and acceptance was likely to fail and to be nearly as invalidating as a purely change-based approach. Indeed, therapists working with highly suicidal or multiproblem, multidiagnostic clients often feel as if they can never get it quite right. The therapist moves in the direction of change, and the client feels misunderstood and needs more validation and acceptance, but then when the therapist moves toward acceptance, the client urgently wants things to change. We often observe this in our clinics. One of the most common complaints among clients who have had difficulty in their previous treatment was that the therapist spent most of the time engaging in reflective, empathetic listening, rather than offering suggestions, tools, or skills. These same clients who had trouble with a purely acceptance-oriented approach sometimes later say they want more acceptance and less change.

As an example, let us say a client shows up to treatment with her foot on fire. The therapist completely focused on acceptance might say, "Boy, that looks hot. I'll bet you're in a lot of pain. It's excruciatingly painful when your foot is on fire, and it makes a lot of sense that you're screaming and jumping up and down." A therapist focused on change from a purely cognitive perspective might encourage the client to evaluate her thoughts about the predicament. If the focus is on skills training, the therapist might suggest that the client should learn fire-avoidance skills or pain-tolerance skills. All of these responses are likely to be woefully inadequate and invalidating. The situation calls for a synthesis of acceptance (of the client's pain, and also in the sense of trusting the client's own experience) and change (helping the client put out the fire). In this case, helping the client to change can be the most validating, accepting, and compassionate thing a therapist can do (Linehan, 1993a).

Reality Consists of Polar Opposites

Dialectical theory involves a few key assumptions (see Linehan, 1993a). The first is the assumption that reality consists of polar opposites. There is tension between these opposites, primarily because each pole is incomplete on its own. In DBT, these opposites consist of acceptance and change (although, arguably, these constructs and the therapeutic actions stemming from them are not necessarily logical opposites), and the tension between these poles is considered the dialectic. With severely miserable clients, acceptance on its own is inadequate and incomplete, but the same is true of change. As with *thesis* and *antithesis*, each pole (acceptance or change) has elements that the other is missing; hence, the therapist's job is to strike the most effective balance or synthesis of acceptance and change. Even when an effective balance or synthesis occurs (which might be considered another thesis), there is always another antithesis around the corner. As a result, the therapist might use a particularly effective intervention or strategy at one time only to find that something different is required when a similar situation occurs again. It is also important to keep in mind that the optimal balance of acceptance and change is unlikely to involve 50% of each. With some clients, a heavy dose of acceptance, listening, and validation is needed before change can occur. In these cases, any movement toward change before the client has had an adequate opportunity to express her- or himself or feels fully understood is likely to fail. Other clients, however, may be willing or able to work on change immediately with minimal acceptance or validation. The therapist remains aware of this assumption that reality consists of opposites, and when she or he is encouraging change and hits a roadblock, the strategy is to switch gears and assess, validate, and accept. Alternatively, when assessment, validation, and acceptance fail to move therapy forward, the therapist may switch gears and focus on change strategies.

When we say acceptance or change, we are talking about strategies or interventions, skills, and therapeutic style. In terms of strategies or interventions, change-oriented approaches include many of the core interventions used in CBT, including cognitive restructuring, problem solving, contingency management, exposure therapy, and skills training, among others. Acceptance-oriented interventions tend to focus on understanding, accepting, and validating the client's experience, but also include strategies that appear change-oriented, such as cognitive interventions to counter self-invalidation or self-judgments. DBT includes a variety of skills to help clients accept themselves, their thoughts and emotions, events in their lives, and other people (namely, mindfulness, radical acceptance, empathy-building interpersonal skills, and mindful awareness and observation of emotions and other internal experiences). Change-oriented skills include those geared toward changing emotional experiences, solving problems, distracting and self-soothing to tolerate distress, and increasing assertiveness.

Balance can also occur in the therapist's communication style (Linehan, 1993a). The communication style may at times be acceptance-oriented (commonly referred to as *reciprocal*), consisting of the therapist conveying warmth, positive regard, responsivity to the client's experience and priorities, and validation. At other times, the therapeutic style may encourage change through irreverence in the therapist's demeanor or statements. *Irreverence* typically consists of the therapist making unexpected statements, commenting on implications of behavior that the client had not considered (e.g., for a client who says she wants to die, saying, "Be patient, we all die eventually—let's work on your life"), using humor, and using a matter-of-fact demeanor in the presence of seemingly outrageous or shocking events or behavior (Linehan, 1993a). Often, irreverence functions to help the client attend to and process her or his immediate experience or see things from a different viewpoint and keeps the client sufficiently "off balance" as to promote change (Lynch, Chapman, Rosenthal, Kuo, & Linehan, 2006). A detailed review of therapeutic style is beyond the scope of this volume, but we highlight case examples throughout the book in which the therapist balances reciprocal and irreverent communication styles.

Reality Is Constantly in a State of Change

A second important assumption is that reality is constantly changing. Perhaps especially when it comes to TIB, what works on one occasion might not work at another time or in a different context. One week, the client comes in and is working on activity scheduling for depression, has done her or his homework, and things are going quite well, and the next week, he or she comes in and says, "Activities? What do you mean? I can't do any of that stuff. I'm way too miserable to even talk or think about that." Because the optimal balance of acceptance and change may change across sessions, clients, contexts, and so on, the therapist must not only accept constant change but also always be asking her- or himself what might be missing or left out (Linehan, 1993a). Moreover, the therapist is also freed from having to be perfectly consistent in her or his manner or actions. The focus here shifts, therefore, to what is the most effective approach or style, right now, in the current situation.

When Polarization Occurs, It Is Effective to Work for Synthesis

Many of the implications of this dialectical view directly pertain to the ways in which the therapist addresses and manages TIB. A dialectical philosophy, for example, allows the therapist to give up "being right" (Lynch et al., 2006). When the therapist and client become polarized, the therapist ideally recognizes this and understands that there is validity to both the client's and the therapist's perspective. Moreover, to give up either side of the argument would result in a compromise that is unlikely to help the client move forward. Therefore, when the therapist puts dialectics into action, the goal is a *synthesis*, or bringing together of the client's and therapist's positions, rather than either side compromising or giving up.

For example, a client may say that she could not do the homework because she was too miserable all week to get out of bed. The therapist thinks that getting out of bed and slowly engaging in pleasurable and mastery-inducing activities is exactly what the client needs. Both positions are valid. Getting out of bed might feel to the client like climbing the steepest of mountains, and this may be exactly what the client needs to do to eventually set herself free from depression. The synthesis must involve the therapist recognizing the validity or truth in the client's position, while maintaining the conviction that activation is important homework.

Another common example pertains to nonsuicidal self-injury (NSSI). We know that continued engagement in NSSI results in several negative outcomes (interpersonally, emotionally, and physically; Esposito, Spirito, Boergers, & Donaldson, 2003; Favazza, 1998; Joiner et al., 2005; Leibenluft, Gardner, & Cowdry, 1987). It can be important, therefore, for clients to agree to at least work on reducing NSSI. From the client's perspective, however, NSSI works, often reducing emotional arousal quickly and reliably. As a result, the client may seem "resistant" and unwilling to give up or work on reducing this behavior. If, however, the therapist recognizes the wisdom in the client's perspective (i.e., "Why would I give up something that works so well without even knowing whether anything you have to offer will help or work nearly as well?"), the behavior seems less like resistance. Rather, the client's position is perfectly understandable and in some ways reasonable. A synthesis may involve the therapist helping to teach skills to replace the function that NSSI serves, while the client simultaneously works to reduce this behavior and to accept the loss of immediate relief or other such functions that may not be entirely replaceable by behavioral skills.

EMPHASIZE THE ROLE OF EMOTIONS AND EMOTION REGULATION IN THERAPY-INTERFERING BEHAVIOR

Another important principle is that many TIBs often occur in response to emotions or function to regulate emotions. As a result, it is helpful to have some familiarity with an emotion regulation framework for conceptualizing TIB. Within a DBT framework, *emotions* are "complex, brief, involuntary, patterned, full-system responses to internal and external stimuli" (Linehan, Bohus, & Lynch, 2007, p. 582). Similarly, Gross (1998) defined emotions as response tendencies including time-limited (e.g., briefer than "moods") changes in autonomic responses, expressive tendencies (e.g., facial expressions, voice tone, verbal communication, posture), desires (in DBT "action urges"; Linehan, 1993b), and actions, among other factors. These models of emotion often also include cognitive appraisals or interpretations of the situation, triggering or prompting events for emotions, and factors that increase vulnerability to emotions (such as recent stressors or difficulties with self-care related factors, such as sleep, eating, medication, drugs, alcohol, etc.). In short, emotions are full-system events, including contextual, cognitive, physiological, expressive, and action components.

Many of the difficulties that multiproblem clients with borderline personality disorder (BPD) face appear to be related to difficulties in the emotion regulation system. This focus on emotions and emotion regulation stems from the theory underlying the treatment. Although this theory, the *biosocial theory* (Crowell, Beauchaine, & Linehan, 2009; Linehan, 1993a), specifically focuses on BPD, those using elements of DBT may consider how a similar biosocial theory, focusing on emotion regulation, might apply to a variety of other clinical problems. According to this theory, BPD results from the transaction of an emotionally vulnerable temperament with an invalidating rearing environment. Individuals vulnerable to the development of BPD have a low threshold for emotional activation (emotional sensitivity), intense emotional reactions (emotional reactivity), and a delayed return to baseline emotional arousal. The invalidating environment consists of caregivers who (a) indiscriminately reject the child's communication of private experiences (thoughts, preferences, opinions, emotions) by criticizing, trivializing, or punishing the child; (b) oversimplify the ease of problem solving when the problem is experienced by the child as overwhelming and painful; and (c) intermittently reinforce the child's periodic excessive emotional expression (thus making such expression resistant to extinction; Linehan, 1993a).

The biosocial theory is a transactional model (Crowell et al., 2009; Fruzzetti, Shenk, & Hoffman, 2005; Linehan, 1993a) whereby the child's behavior and temperament transact with the invalidating environment. Children who are highly emotional require more skilled parenting and may set the occasion for invalidating responses on the part of parents who lack the skills to regulate their own emotions or who do not have the knowledge or skills to respond effectively. At the same time, invalidation increases emotional arousal and can directly lead to emotional dysregulation, both in the short and the long term. When the invalidating environment is characterized by abuse or trauma or when it fails to provide adequate support in the face of abuse from other sources, the environment may play an even stronger role in the development of BPD. Those with BPD specifically and emotion regulation problems more broadly often function much like a powerful car with a malfunctioning brake system: Their emotions are strong and often experienced as overwhelming and intolerable, and they lack the skills to regulate these emotions.

Problems with emotion regulation can result in a variety of TIBs that are functional in the short term and dysfunctional in the long term. Perhaps the most obvious example of TIB (discussed in detail in Chapter 7) related to emotion regulation includes angry or aggressive behavior. Angry behaviors during therapy sessions may elicit negative reinforcement in the form of emotional release, blowing off steam, or the withdrawal of demands on the part of the therapist (e.g., the therapist "backing off" and ceasing efforts geared toward problem solving). Any of these consequences would be expected to down-regulate undesired emotions and perhaps to up-regulate desired emotions. A client who has difficulty getting out of bed and therefore misses her session may be regulating her emotions by staying in bed. The client having difficulty with an emotionally evocative homework assignment may avoid uncomfortable emotions by avoiding the homework assignment and doing something else instead. Challenging behaviors occurring within the session, such as inattentiveness, dissociation, confusion, changing of the topic, and so forth, may also serve to up- or down-regulate emotions in a particular way. The therapist can effectively manage TIB by (a) understanding how these behaviors work for the client by influencing the emotion regulation system and (b) attending to the client's affect and helping the client label, describe, and regulate her or his emotions.

The therapist might also attend to her or his own emotions. For the therapist, it can be frustrating when clients consistently engage in TIB, particularly in combination with limited or slow progress. Effective management of TIB involves the therapist attending to her or his own emotional reactions to the client's behavior. Often, the first step in dealing with frustrating TIB is for the therapist to step back mentally and observe and describe her or his own emotional state. If a client has appeared late for the fourth session in a row, the therapist might take a moment to notice the sensations or feelings of frustration, label her or his emotions, notice any urges to engage in particular actions as well as any thoughts that are associated with the emotions, regulate these emotions in some way, and then determine an appropriate course of action. These are the same steps that we often teach our clients. Indeed, both therapists and clients can go astray if they lack a clear understanding of their emotions and do not take the time to check in on their emotional state.

MINDFULNESS-BASED PRINCIPLES

Mindfulness skills and principles also are extremely useful for therapists dealing with TIB. Mindful practice as a therapist can foster a sense of *spaciousness of mind*, or the willingness to accept and accommodate reality (including a broad array of client behaviors) as it is. Because one of the principles underlying mindfulness is that everything is exactly as it should be in this moment and could not be any different, the mindful therapist can step out of the struggle with reality. Instead of saying, "She shouldn't be doing this!" "Why is this happening?" or "This is inappropriate and needs to stop," the therapist learns to observe and notice the behavior as it is (as well as the consequences of the behavior for her- or himself, the client, and the therapeutic process) and to let go for that moment of any attachment to things being different than they are. Essentially, the therapist uses the principle and skill of *radical acceptance* to acknowledge reality as it is and to let go of the struggle to change or deny it (Linehan, 1993b, 2015). The idea is not to relinquish expectations for effective and collaborative behavior but to let go of attachment to those expectations. At the same time, the dialectical synthesis is that the therapist may be working hard to help the client change and reduce TIB.

Along with the focus on mindfulness and acceptance comes an emphasis on the therapist practicing *nonjudging*, one of the core mindfulness skills. Nonjudging involves the individual first becoming aware of when she or he is placing people, thoughts, emotions, situations, or actions into categories such as good, bad, right, wrong, should, should not, and so on. That said, therapists are not advised to give up their "judgment" when it comes to determining what is effective or ineffective for themselves or their clients. Discernment and the ability to distinguish between effective and ineffective behavior are critical for both therapist and client. Indeed, this is sometimes what the client is paying the therapist to do. Nonjudging also is not the same as labeling everything as *good* (that would be a judgment as well). Rather, therapists (and clients) are charged with becoming aware of and reducing their use of global determinations of good versus bad and instead sticking as close to the objective, concrete facts as possible. It can be effective for therapists to adopt this nonjudgmental stance toward even the most egregious behaviors, both in the way that they think about and talk with the client and in the ways in which they discuss client behavior with other therapists, consultants, trainees, or supervisors.

When we are teaching therapists to be nonjudgmental, we often say the same thing that we say to our clients: "Observing and describing the facts is the best antidote to judgmental thinking." Therapists can practice nonjudging by simply describing the behavior they are dealing with in the most precise, concrete, and behaviorally specific terms possible. If, for example, the therapist has the thought that the client is being purposely "resistant" to change, "derailing the therapeutic discussion," or trying to "manipulate" the therapist, she or he could practice nonjudging by stepping back and objectively describing the client's actual behavior. For example, to describe what she meant by "resistant to change," the therapist might state,

> When I suggested some ways for Joan to use skills to reduce her anxiety before looking for a job on the computer, Joan said that such skills won't work for her, and that she doesn't really think the skills are very helpful in general.

To describe what she meant by "derailing the therapeutic discussion," she might say,

> When I asked her whether she thought she could schedule herself to look for jobs for 20 minutes per day, she changed the topic and started asking me about my family and my sex life with my husband.

Unfortunately, nonjudging and sticking to the facts do not always come easily to therapists, because mental health professionals often are trained to be assumption-making, inference-making, analytical machines. We make meaning out of almost everything. The idea, then, is to become concrete. One of us was teaching this skill to a client, and he told the client that it helps to try to model one's behavior after someone one knows, perhaps someone who is annoyingly concrete and factual at times. He asked the client whether she could think of anyone like that, and she said, "Yes, definitely." He asked who that was, and she said, "You!" Making lemonade out of lemons, the therapist replied, "Well, then, I guess you're lucky to be working with me. You will learn how to describe effectively, and how to tolerate people you find annoying!"

MOVING FORWARD

We focused on four key principles in this chapter. As a starting point, conceptualizing TIB from a behavioral and functional perspective orients the therapist to the purpose or function of the client's behavior or how it works for the client. This is an essential first step in helping the client change TIB. Combining an emotion-regulation framework with behavioral principles helps orient the therapist to the potentially important role of emotions and emotion regulation in TIB. A behavioral conceptualization also helps the therapist to remember that TIB occurs within a therapeutic system whereby the therapist and client both shape each other's behavior. Using a dialectical viewpoint allows the therapist to observe, balance, and synthesize the many polarities that arise in the context of the therapeutic relationship. TIB is both perfectly understandable and must change. Acceptance- and change-oriented therapeutic styles, skills, and strategies complement and balance one another, and the effective management of TIB often involves the therapist finding the best balance of strategies for this particular client at this particular moment. Finally, the practice of mindfulness when addressing TIB can help the therapist to step back, observe, and target TIB nonjudgmentally and effectively. Mindfulness facilitates the kind of spaciousness of mind required to both accept and change challenging behaviors. With these principles in mind, in Chapter 3 we begin our discussion of how to address TIB by describing several core steps and strategies.

3

CORE DIALECTICAL BEHAVIOR THERAPY STRATEGIES FOR MANAGING THERAPY-INTERFERING BEHAVIOR

In this chapter, we provide a set of steps, tools, and strategies to manage therapy-interfering behavior (TIB). The principles discussed in Chapter 2 provide the framework with which to apply the strategies we present in this chapter. In future chapters, we discuss the specific application of many of the core strategies presented here to specific types of TIB. We have found that keeping the general principles in mind, in combination with having effective tools at the ready, has made us much more confident when confronted with unexpected or potentially overwhelming TIB.

HIGHLIGHTING AND ASSESSING THE PROBLEM

Among the first steps in the management of TIBs are highlighting and assessment. Imagine you and your client are walking down a hallway together, talking casually about the downpour that has just started. In this hallway,

http://dx.doi.org/10.1037/14752-003
Managing Therapy-Interfering Behavior: Strategies From Dialectical Behavior Therapy, by A. L. Chapman and M. Z. Rosenthal

there are several rooms with doors closed. Some you notice, others you do not—after all, you are busy walking and talking. But along the way to your destination, an open door catches your attention. *Highlighting* can be thought of as remarking out loud that the door is ajar, and *assessment* is like walking through the door and exploring the room together. Highlighting TIB opens up the topic for discussion, and subsequently, the therapist and client engage in collaborative assessment to better understand what is driving the TIB. This assessment often follows the framework of a functional analysis of behavior. We discuss these strategies next.

Highlighting Therapy-Interfering Behavior

As an example of highlighting, when a client has periodically missed therapy sessions, the therapist might state, "I've noticed that you have missed about one of every three of our last several sessions. I think we should talk about this." For a client who is not speaking or providing enough detail in response to the therapist's questions, the therapist highlighting the problem might say, "I'm not sure whether you've noticed this, but when I ask you questions, you often say 'I don't know' or provide fairly brief answers without much detail. Would you be willing to talk about this for a few minutes?" Although the therapist may have hypotheses, assumptions, or interpretations regarding the client's behavior, we recommend that she or he temporarily keep these off the table in favor of collaborative and unbiased exploration of the issue. The therapist may certainly raise hypotheses, but doing so prematurely can narrow the focus, and important facts or details may be left out.

Effective highlighting also includes a clear rationale for why it is important to discuss the specific TIB in question. One way to do this is for the therapist to highlight contingencies, such as the negative effect of the TIB on the therapist, the therapeutic processes, or the client's ability to reach important goals. In the case of the client missing sessions, for example, the therapist might add the following:

> This work requires a lot of consistency. To really benefit, you have to attend sessions and do your practice homework. I'm concerned that your missing at least a third of our sessions is going to make it harder for you to reach your goal of reducing your fear of men and working on your posttraumatic stress symptoms.

As discussed in Chapter 2, the therapist using a dialectical philosophy may sometimes balance her or his style of highlighting. Highlighting can occur in a direct, straightforward, reciprocal manner, or an irreverent manner. With a client working on reducing her drinking, for example, if she were to show up having drunk a bottle or two of wine the previous night, the therapist could highlight this in a reciprocal (e.g., "I see you had a couple of bottles of wine last night. Do you think we should put this on the agenda today?") or an irreverent manner (e.g., "Well, I see you're back on the bottle!"). In terms of highlighting, irreverence can be helpful to increase awareness, attention, and engagement in the psychotherapy session process. Perhaps the client has gotten stuck in a rigid behavioral pattern or way of thinking. In this case, the therapist commenting in an unexpected manner on the behavior might help the client to switch gears and consider a different perspective or better understand the problems with her or his thinking or behavior. For a client who has missed a therapy session, irreverent highlighting might involve the therapist saying, "It's very difficult to do therapy with someone who is not here." When a client is texting during a group session, the therapist using irreverence might say, "You wouldn't by any chance be doing two things at once now, would you?" (We are indebted to Dr. Marsha Linehan for some of these irreverent lines and examples.) As discussed in Chapter 2, irreverence can sometimes highlight the importance of change in a salient and vivid manner.

Assessing and Understanding the Problem

Another important step is to work with the client to collaboratively assess factors that may have contributed to the TIB. One strategy for doing this is to conduct a functional analysis of the events surrounding the target behavior (Farmer & Chapman, 2016; Linehan, 1993a). Sometimes referred to as a *chain analysis*, a functional analysis involves the assessment of factors surrounding a single instance or occurrence of the target behavior. Instead of assessing lateness in general, for example, the therapist and client reconstruct events leading to lateness on a particular day, for a particular session.

Ideally, a functional analysis gathers specific information about the events preceding and following a target behavior. The therapist is attuned to small details and inquires about thoughts, emotions, and actions occurring throughout the chain of events. Attempts to gather all possible information about events surrounding the behavior, however, are likely to result in excessively lengthy functional analyses, leaving little room for problem solving. The challenge, therefore, is to gather enough information to highlight fruitful directions for intervention.

It has sometimes been suggested that functional analyses constitute an aversive contingency for the client's behavior, because the client might experience the functional analysis as unpleasant. Although it can be difficult and upsetting for clients to talk in excessive detail about their problem behaviors, it is important for the therapist to avoid making the functional analysis an unpleasant or punishing undertaking (Rizvi & Ritschel, 2014). Instead, we recommend that the therapist approach this task with the spirit of exploration and curiosity, and that she or he convey this spirit to the client, as in the following example:

> We have a wonderful opportunity here to really understand what makes it hard for you to fulfill obligations like showing up on time for therapy or being organized at work. Imagine how different your life would be if we could really understand and get to the bottom of this problem and start chipping away at it.

Any behavior (not just TIB) can be the target of a functional analysis, and this assessment strategy can help the client and therapist to understand important, broader patterns of behavior. A functional analysis can, for example, be used to understand TIB occurring outside of session (e.g., lack of homework completion) or within sessions (e.g., angry outbursts, lack of talking), or other behaviors related to TIB (e.g., alcohol or drug use). Often, understanding one problem behavior can help highlight broader patterns to address in therapy. "Marita," for example, frequently talked over the therapist or changed the topic. The therapist discussed how this behavior might interfere with therapy, and after a functional analysis, it became clear that the primary function of these behaviors was to avoid uncomfortable emotions (particularly sadness). This was part of a broader pattern of emotional avoidance that contributed not only to other TIBs (avoidance of homework) but also to the very problems for which Marita had presented for therapy (depression, social isolation).

In conducting a functional analysis, it can be effective to attend to several key anchor points in the chain of events surrounding a target behavior. Some of these anchor points include (a) vulnerability factors, (b) prompting events, (c) the specific TIB, and (d) events or consequences occurring after the TIB (Farmer & Chapman, 2016; Linehan, 1993a). *Vulnerability factors* are those that might have made the TIB more likely, such as poor self-care or recent stressful events. The *prompting event* is the triggering event and establishing operations that set the occasion for the TIB. Finally, the consequences following the TIB could include potential reinforcers for the behavior, as well as any aversive consequences. Such consequences might be immediate (occurring right after the behavior) or delayed, internal (changes in thoughts, emotions, urges, etc.) or external (changes in the environment or in others' behaviors). The following is an exchange between a client and her therapist about the client's tendency to switch topics when they discuss important problems. Subsequently, we highlight some of the anchor points in this chain.

Therapist: Marita, I've been thinking a lot about our last session, and I think there's something important for us to talk about.

Client: OK, what's that?

Therapist: Well, I've noticed that, often, when we start to talk about some of the problems you've wanted to work on, you tend to change the topic. When I steer things back, you sometimes appear frustrated and sort of shut down by not talking or asking me why we're talking about this. Have you noticed this?

Client: Maybe, I guess. I just sometimes think there are better things to talk about than my problems getting out of the house.

Therapist: OK, well, that may be true. We can see. That has been our goal, though, and I remember you saying that it's really important to you. I'm afraid that if we keep starting to talk about it and then stopping, it's going to be hard for you to make progress. For that reason, I'd like to talk a little more about what's happening. Would you be willing to do that?

Client: Sure, we can do that.

Therapist: OK, well, you probably remember how we do this—with a functional analysis, right?

Client: We've done that before for homework stuff, right?

Therapist: Yeah, we have. It's sort of like talking the problem to death. If we put our heads together and understand what happens in those moments when you seem to be changing the topic and so on, we might find a way around it. I don't know this for sure, but if this is another example of you avoiding things, and we figure out what to do about it, we could learn something that might help you in other important ways too.

Client: OK, that sounds fine.

Therapist: Let's start with last week. We were talking about you taking small steps to get out of bed and into the kitchen to make yourself a cup of coffee, and you started talking about your opinions about that controversial topic in the media. Do you remember that?

Client: Yeah, well, I've had problems with drugs like that mayor, and I know he shouldn't be doing those things and looks like a total fool, but they always are so judgmental about drug users.

Therapist: Marita, I'm afraid this might be another example of you taking an exit away from our conversation. Let's get back to what we were talking about. Sounds like you remember. So, what were you thinking and feeling just before you started talking about this topic?

Client: I don't know. I guess I was starting to feel anxious. I mean, it's really hard for me to get myself going, and I know I have to. It's just so overwhelming. I don't remember exactly what I was thinking, but maybe that this is really hard.

Therapist: Very nice—good that you noticed all that. So, you may have been feeling anxious and overwhelmed about all that's involved in getting yourself going, and thinking this is hard. What else did you notice? Any physical sensations? Any other emotions or thoughts?

Client: I guess I was feeling sort of a clenching or sinking feeling in my gut. Like, I felt like I needed to get out or something. Stop talking about it. I felt really tense. I remember thinking that I just can't do this.

Therapist: OK, this is really good. I think we're starting to get to the bottom of what's happening here. It sounds like you felt like you hit the wall, were overwhelmed and just wanted to escape and stop dealing with it. I get that—what we're working on is so hard, like climbing a mountain. I can see why you'd want to just turn around and go back sometimes. How did you get to talking about that mayor who used drugs?

Client: I had an image of being in bed watching the news, and that's what was on that morning, and I just wanted to talk about it.

Therapist: OK, then, when you started talking about the mayor, what happened?

Client: I guess we both sort of got into a conversation about it, and I don't know . . .

Therapist: True, somehow, that topic was so tempting that I temporarily forgot and may have let you avoid things! I'll work on that. So, one thing we know is that you temporarily no longer had to talk about getting up and around in the morning. Did you feel any different?

Client: I don't think I felt tense anymore, or not as much, but I was, like, angry about the news thing.

Therapist: What about when I asked you again about getting out of bed and what we could do about that—what did you feel and what was going through your mind then?

Client: It's hard to remember all of this, but I think I was frustrated that you were bringing it up again. I mean, you know how hard it is for me. Like, why is she putting me through this?

Therapist: Right, I'm encouraging you to address something that's really painful and hard, and you don't want to feel that way. I can see how frustration might have come up. Was that the first reaction, or were there other feelings, too?

Client: I don't think it was first. I think I felt that sinking, clenching, tense feeling before I got annoyed with you.

Therapist: OK, maybe the tension and anxiety came first, then. Let's see if there was anything specific about what we were talking about that really brought up those feelings. Was it that we were talking about your getting going in the morning in general, or was it something specific that I asked you or said?

Client: It's hard to know, but I think it was when you asked what I think I could do to make it easier not to just press the snooze button and stay in bed.

Therapist: Interesting. Do you think you would have felt the same way and wanted to escape if I hadn't asked you to come up with a solution for that?

Client: I don't think so. It's just that when I start to think about what I can do, it feels like it's too much, too much work to think about it. I also was thinking it's never going to change.

Therapist: I thought it might have something to do with your having to solve a problem. It's sort of like you start thinking and then it all becomes too hard and overwhelming, and you think it's hopeless. Is that right?

Client: Yeah, that fits pretty well.

Therapist: That's the best news I've heard today.

Client: What?

Therapist: Well, we know that's exactly what happens to you when you try to get out of bed in the morning, go take a shower, get dressed, and so on. You hit the wall, feel really tense, start to get overwhelmed, think it's never going to change, and say, "Forget it!" or other more choice words, and then just go back to bed, stay in bed, or distract yourself by playing on your iPad. Does this sound familiar?

Client: Yeah, that's about the gist of it. I don't know how to get out of that whole thing.

Therapist: We have an opportunity now to take a really important step. If the very same thing is happening in here, then, we can work in it whenever it pops up in our work. And if we work on it in here and you get a lot of practice, I think you might start noticing things getting easier at home too.

Client: I'm glad you think it can change. That makes one of us.

Therapist: Ha, well, I'll wear you down eventually, don't worry about that. OK, here's what we've got so far. You and I were talking about ways for you to take small steps to get out of bed, get into the kitchen, and make your coffee, and you started to feel really tense and overwhelmed and just wanted out. You were thinking this is all too much for you, and that you're not able to go on or keep working on this. Then you were reminded of the mayor and his drug using, started talking about it, and I let up on the getting out of bed thing, and you felt a little better. And, of course, you felt tense and irritated when I got back to it again. Does that seem right?

Client: Yeah, that's about it.

Therapist: OK, so what does this tell us about your changing the topic and getting annoyed with me during our sessions?

Client: I'm avoiding again?

Therapist: I think so. I think that something's in it for you to change the topic. You get to stop talking about something that you're overwhelmed with and feeling tense about, you feel better, and you don't have to deal with it. I also think that when you get frustrated with me, and you express that, I might be backing off sometimes, which is probably how your frustration is working for you. Remember what we discussed about positive and negative reinforcement?

This example illustrates some key features of a functional analysis as well as how the therapist and client might use this strategy to refine their conceptualization of the problem behavior. The therapist first highlighted the problem of the client avoiding and switching topics during the last session (and during other sessions), then enlisted the client's involvement in a discussion of this, provided brief orientation to the functional analysis, and then began the chain. The therapist was behaviorally specific about the actions in which the client engaged and did not include assumptions, inferences, or judgments at this stage. The therapist then explained why the problem behavior was a problem in view of the client's therapy goals. Although the prompting event appeared at first to be simply the discussion of how to get going in the morning, the therapist discovered that the specific prompting event was the therapist asking for the client to engage in problem solving in session. The therapist realized this by asking the client what it was about the discussion that may have triggered her emotional response and by engaging in hypothesis testing (where the therapist asked what might have happened had she not prompted the client to come up with a solution), involving changing the variables and examining whether the outcomes would be similar or different (Linehan, 1993a). This strategy of *hypothesis testing* can highlight the specific aspects of the situation to which the client is responding. In addition, the therapist assessed the consequences following the behavior, including a lowering of tension, anxiety, and irritation, and the withdrawal of demands by the therapist.

ADDRESSING THERAPY-INTERFERING BEHAVIOR

Functional analyses and other assessment strategies aim to clarify factors influencing TIB and highlight effective directions for intervention. Although many factors can influence TIB, organizing them according to the following categories can help highlight the way to effective intervention: (a) motivational deficits, (b) skill deficits, (c) environmental contingencies, (d) avoidance coping, (e) problematic thinking patterns, and (f) problematic environments and life stressors. Many of the interventions described next have been detailed in other texts (e.g., Farmer & Chapman, 2008, 2016; Linehan, 1993a) as methods for helping clients achieve their therapeutic goals.

Addressing Motivational Deficits Related to Therapy-Interfering Behavior

One problem driving TIB is difficulty becoming motivated or sustaining motivation to make important changes in therapy. Often, motivational deficits appear to be the culprit when TIB or other problem behaviors persist despite several efforts to assess and solve the problem, when the client seems particularly reluctant or uninterested in changing, or when there seems to be a mismatch between the therapist's focus on change and the client's readiness to change (e.g., the therapist is talking about skills to help the client cut down on drinking, and the client has yet to seriously consider reducing alcohol consumption).

From a behavioral perspective, motivation is not a force within the client that must both spring and propel her or him toward change. Rather, motivation or commitment to change is evident when the client speaks about change (*change talk*; Miller & Rollnick, 2012), takes action steps, and exhibits a sustained commitment to change (Farmer & Chapman, 2016). Motivation is regarded as distinctly different from how much a person "wants" to change. An important assumption here is that clients both want to change and have to become more motivated to change (Linehan, 1993a).

Several factors influence whether a client engages in change-oriented talk or behavior. Therapy can go astray when the therapist does not recognize these factors. For example, it is common for therapists to assume that clients are being "resistant" and are unmotivated (Freeman & McCloskey, 2003) when, for example, they do not complete their homework or make slower progress than desired or expected. Motivation, however, may not be the primary force driving these TIBs. A client who does not have the skills necessary to complete a behavioral assignment to make small talk at a party, for example, might seem unmotivated, but in reality, she or he needs more than motivational enhancement to ensure that this assignment will go well. People may "lack" motivation for many reasons, including skill deficits, lack of awareness of TIB, problematic thinking patterns or beliefs, lack of understanding of or adequate orientation to treatment, a lack of clarity around values (or a disconnect between values and actions), among other factors.

Let us say that "Alan" agreed to embark on a 6-month course of cognitive behavior therapy (CBT) for depression, and yet, he shows up for only one of every two scheduled appointments. The therapist has conducted a functional analysis each time Alan has missed an appointment and has put considerable effort toward problem solving (e.g., having him set his alarm earlier, put the alarm clock across the room, schedule reminders into his smartphone, ask someone else to pick him up and drive him to therapy). Each week, something seems to impede Alan's attendance. The therapist decides to assess how committed he is to attending therapy and working on the goals they have set, and then, they both realize that Alan's commitment has waned. As it turns out, the immediate, powerful reinforcement value (e.g., positive reinforcement in the form of comfort, negative reinforcement in the form of avoidance of anxiety, effort) of remaining at home or in bed often outweighs the longer term reinforcement of therapy attendance (positive reinforcement in terms of expanding his social network and increases in positive and mastery experiences, negative reinforcement in terms of reductions in shame and negative self-talk). The problem was not Alan's lack of "wanting" to help himself; he desperately wanted to improve his life. Rather, the balance of potential reinforcers and punishers did not support social engagement.

In the following section, we comment on a few of the core strategies used in dialectical behavior therapy (DBT) and other approaches (see Linehan, 1993a; Miller & Rollnick, 2012) to help build motivation. Most of these strategies hinge on the therapist's understanding of the client's goals and values. Knowing what is important to the client, the therapist can help gear interventions toward aims that are naturally motivating to the client and can clarify how the reduction of TIB can help the client achieve those aims. A therapist might help a client who has difficulty with an assignment to schedule pleasant and mastery-inducing activities by revisiting why this is such an important assignment, in view of the client's therapy goals (e.g., reducing depression, developing new relationships, doing well at school).

Other strategies also help to elicit change-oriented talk and highlight the link between the client changing TIB and reaching important goals. The following are some examples of these strategies:

- considering the pros and cons of changing versus not changing her or his behavior;
- highlighting the client's apparent ambivalence about change;
- arguing against change to elicit counterarguments from the client (the devil's advocate strategy; Linehan, 1993a); and
- throwing the ball into the client's court by saying that the client has the freedom to choose not to change, but if she or he wants a better life, the only choice is to change (freedom to choose and absence of alternatives; Linehan, 1993a).

For a client whose TIB involves arriving late for therapy, the therapist might state the following.

Therapist: OK, we've talked about this quite a bit, haven't we? We've only really had 25-minute sessions because of your arriving late. I know it's really hard to get here on time, and there are many things in the way. I suspect one thing in the way, though, is that you haven't really jumped into therapy in a committed way with both feet. Does that sound about right?

Client: Yeah, I mean, I guess I want help but sort of don't want it, and I'm having a hard time caring that I'm not getting there on time and getting the full therapy.

Therapist: Right, when you're feeling as depressed as you are, a lot of things seem pointless, and it's hard to muster the desire or to care about doing things. Here's the thing, though: Therapy is totally voluntary. You can keep arriving late and missing sessions. You can choose not to work on this, and we can just try to get as much done as we can in the little time we have. My fear, though, is that the only way for you to get your life on track and really get closer to what you want (a job, closer relationships with friends, more happiness each day) is for us to find a way around the barriers to your coming in.

Addressing Skill Deficits

When skill deficits contribute to TIB, effective interventions involve improving the client's skills and capabilities in certain areas. The therapist might determine whether a skill deficit is present by the therapist having the client try out certain behaviors in session by, for example, having the client demonstrate interpersonal skills in a role-play scenario, prompting the client to label or describe emotional states (when emotion regulation or recognition deficits are suspected), eliciting solutions to problems (when problem solving deficits are suspected), and so on. Other approaches might include inquiring about the client's use of skills in different situations, soliciting feedback that the client has received from others on interpersonal behavior, and closely observing the client's behavior.

Assessing and clarifying the specific skill deficits contributing to TIB can highlight directions for effective intervention. Several types of skill deficits may contribute to TIB, such as problems with self-management or organization, emotion regulation or anger management skills, communication skills, and so on. As an example of poor anger management skills contributing to TIB, one of our supervisees was recently seeing a client who said, "I hope you have a thick skin." He then leveled several criticisms of the therapist's approach and past actions in a hostile voice tone and began to yell. The team had previously discontinued this client's attendance in a DBT skills training group (in favor of individual skills training) because his hostile and aggressive statements were distressing to other group members. He had had three chances to effectively navigate group before this occurred. After a fair amount of assessment, it was clear that several factors were at play, including (a) the client often avoided bringing up things that bothered him until he got to the boiling point and was enraged, (b) he lacked the skills to communicate his strong preferences in an appropriately assertive (but nonaggressive) manner, and (c) he had difficulty recognizing the signs that his anger was building. Once the therapist and client identified these targets, they worked to build his skills in communication, emotion recognition, and anger management. Although the changes were not immediate, over time he learned to manage his anger and express his wishes effectively.

Another common skill deficit that can interfere with therapy involves difficulty understanding and labeling emotions. When, for example, "Kate's" therapist asked her how she was feeling or to mindfully observe her emotions, Kate often said she was not feeling anything, did not know what she was feeling, or criticized the therapist for suggesting something that will "never work." The therapist concluded that Kate was avoiding her emotions, was not motivated to remain in contact with them, and was unwilling to collaboratively work on therapy goals (one of which was to better understand and manage emotions). After further assessment, however, it was clear that Kate was a high-functioning individual with autism who simply lacked the skills to connect her physical sensations with specific emotional states and, as a result, had little awareness of her emotional experience. Once the therapist figured this out, therapy focused on gradually helping Kate learn to identify and describe emotions.

In DBT, the primary method to address skill deficits is a skills training group. This group typically occurs once weekly for approximately two hours. Skills training can also occur in an ad hoc, as-needed manner in individual treatment when the therapist observes that the client's deficits in particular areas of skill may be influencing TIB. The following is a brief summary of each set of DBT skills (see Linehan, 1993b, 2015, for a comprehensive manual on these skills).

- *Mindfulness skills* involve strategies for clients to attend to their experience of the present moment, including nonjudgmentally observing and describing their experiences in the here and now, actively participating in activities in the present, focusing on one thing at a time ("one-mindfully") and on effective behavior ("effectively").
- *Emotion regulation skills* involve strategies for the client to learn to understand and label emotions, modify factors increasing vulnerability to negative emotions, change prompting or triggering events for emotions, change behavior in a way that regulates emotions ("opposite action" or acting opposite to the behavioral urge associated with the emotion), and to mindfully observe and accept emotions.
- *Distress tolerance skills* involve distraction, self-soothing, and other strategies to help the client ride out painful emotions and avoid exacerbating challenging situations or crises. Distress tolerance also includes skills to help clients become motivated to be skillful (by entertaining the pros and cons of tolerating distress or using skills vs. more self-destructive behaviors) and to accept reality as it is.
- *Interpersonal effectiveness skills* involve helping the client learn to maintain focus on important goals in interpersonal situations, communicate wishes and desires effectively, maintain self-respect, and build or enhance relationships.

Although a detailed description of DBT skills and skills training methods is beyond the scope of this chapter, we describe some principles for therapists to keep in mind. When using skills training strategies, it can be helpful to consider the client's current stage or phase of learning with respect to the particular skill set. Three common stages in learning new skills are skill acquisition, strengthening, and generalization (see Farmer & Chapman, 2008, 2016; Linehan, 1993b, 2015).

In the *skill acquisition phase*, a client is beginning to learn what the skills are and when and why they should be used. The focus is on providing information about the skills, why and when to use them, demonstrating and modeling effective skill use, and providing opportunities for preliminary practice. The emphasis also is on the behavioral principle of *shaping*, whereby the therapist provides reinforcement and encouragement for successive approximations to the desired result (Miltenberger, 2011). When the therapist coaches the client and provides feedback, the strongest emphasis is on what the client is doing right, rather than what she or he could improve.

During the *skill strengthening phase*, the focus is on the client developing competency and refining her or his use of the skills. Much like learning any other skill, such as martial arts, it is first important for the client to understand and attempt the skills (e.g., how to perform a correct side kick) and then to practice regularly to refine the skill (e.g., practicing to build the proper hip muscles, ensure that the leg, foot, and torso are in the correct position). During this phase, the therapist provides opportunities to practice the skill during sessions and homework assignments for regular practice outside of session.

Subsequently, during the *skill generalization phase*, the therapist encourages the client to use the new skill regularly in a variety of contexts to transfer the skill from therapy to various relevant situations in the client's daily life. The emphasis here is on ways to adapt the skills for use in a variety of situations and on the client using the skills when needed. Regardless of whether a therapist is practicing DBT, CBT, or another form of therapy, keeping these three phases of skill learning in mind can facilitate interventions to improve clients' skills and reduce TIB.

Managing Contingencies Effectively

When a functional analysis reveals that contingencies operating within or outside the therapy relationship are influencing TIBs, contingency management can be an effective intervention. To effectively manage contingencies, the therapist must have a clear understanding of the function of the TIB, paying particular attention to potential reinforcers and punishers for TIB.

Sometimes the contingencies are operating in exactly the opposite direction of what would be desirable: Adaptive or desired behavior is being punished or extinguished, and undesired behavior is being reinforced. A client with anger management problems, for example, may experience more immediate and powerful reinforcers for angry outbursts (e.g., feeling relieved or in control, the therapist or other people acquiescing or readily complying with requests) than for more skillful communication. Therapy attendance may be less immediately reinforcing (and may in some cases be punishing) than activities in which the client engages when she or he is not in session (e.g., spending time with friends, using drugs or alcohol, watching television, staying in bed). When it comes to behavioral activation assignments to treat depression, the immediate consequences of sitting down and reviewing actions, thoughts, feelings, and behaviors on a particular day (e.g., the work involved in self-monitoring assignments, intense anxiety or shame, avoidance of fatigue) might be sufficiently aversive as to outweigh the longer term reinforcers.

One of us saw a client who called repeatedly in a crisis and, after a few minutes, appeared to calm down considerably, thanked the therapist, and ended the call. The calls continued to increase in frequency, to the point that the therapist was becoming overwhelmed. When discussing this with the client, it became clear that the immediate reinforcers involved in the phone calls (the immediate help and support provided, advice on problem solving, and reassurance) were much more powerful and reliably available than were the reinforcers for the use of behavioral coping skills on her own. Indeed, from what we know about the behavioral principle of *matching*, people will match their behavior to the availability, magnitude, and immediacy of reinforcers (Herrnstein, 1961; Hopko, Lejuez, Ruggiero, & Eifert, 2003). It is not surprising, then, that clients have such a hard time sticking with the tasks needed to make therapy work.

Specify Behaviors to Increase and Decrease

One of the first steps in contingency management is to clearly specify the behaviors to decrease and increase. Consider a client who has missed four out of eight sessions. The client's attendance rate might seem to be the most obvious behavior to increase, but focusing only on the client's attendance rate will likely have limited effects. For the client's attendance to increase, she or he also has to increase other behaviors that make attendance more likely, such as using a calendar or alarm, arranging her or his schedule to fit in the therapy session, managing emotional reactions or anxious anticipation of therapy, and so on. To determine which behaviors to decrease, the therapist should assess what the client is doing instead of coming to therapy, such as using drugs or alcohol, exercising, reading, gaming or going on the Internet, or watching television. For attendance to occur, these behaviors must decrease or occur at different times. As with changing other forms of behavior, changes in TIB are much more likely to occur when the therapist and client are aware of which actions the client has to increase and decrease (Farmer & Chapman, 2016).

Attend to Contingencies in the Therapy Relationship

When addressing TIB, it is helpful for the therapist to attend to contingencies operating in the therapeutic relationship. It can be easy for therapists to inadvertently reinforce TIB and for clients to reinforce their therapist's TIB. A colleague saw a client ("Ed") who was intensely afraid of experiencing or expressing sadness, either inside or outside therapy sessions. Whenever the therapist brought up topics associated with sadness, such as the client's conflictual relationship with his father, lack of a job, or difficulty maintaining friendships, Ed often changed the topic, said "I don't know" to most of the therapist's questions, appeared visibly angry, criticized the therapist for asking too many questions or for how she asked such questions (e.g., "Why did you say it that way? Any reasonable therapist would have asked that a totally different way!"), or changed the topic entirely. Once in a while, the therapist found herself veering off course, going wherever the client led her, because it was a lot easier to do that than to keep moving forward and face the client's anger and frustration. The client's TIB, perhaps initially learned in other contexts, may have been maintained by the therapist's TIB (negatively reinforced by avoidance of sadness and further discussion or questions from the therapist), and the therapist's TIB was negatively reinforced by avoidance of discomfort and potential conflict. If so, an open discussion about this can be effective, as shown in the following example.

> We have an important problem to discuss. I really think that we need to continue to work on exposure for your social anxiety, and we've had our sessions set up to do this. But, I've noticed that when you tell me how scared you are to come into therapy and do exposure, I often back off and say you don't need to do it this week, or it's up to you, and you can decide. It's true that it's up to you, but I think I'm doing you a disservice by letting you totally off the hook when you're anxious. I think it's because I don't like to see you in discomfort, so what's in it for me is that I feel better when I say we don't have to do exposure, because you seem to feel better. But, this just perpetuates the problem you're here for in the first place—avoiding things you're anxious about!

Addressing Fear, Escape, and Emotional Avoidance

Exposure, mindfulness, and acceptance-based strategies can be helpful when fear, anxiety, escape, or avoidance influence TIB (Farmer & Chapman, 2016). Exposure interventions might aim to help the client develop new associations with the feared situation and to enhance inhibitory learning (Craske et al., 2008). The client is exposed to the feared situation repeatedly and encouraged not to escape from or avoid this situation (either physically or mentally). Exposure strategies have been detailed extensively elsewhere (Abramowitz, Deacon, & Whiteside, 2011), and we demonstrate these approaches in other chapters in this book.

Other interventions and skills addressing fear, escape, and emotional avoidance include mindfulness, distress tolerance, and acceptance strategies. When TIB is related to difficulty tolerating emotions, the therapist might coach the client on how to tolerate and experience emotional distress without engaging in escape or avoidance behavior. When a client is having difficulty tolerating the behaviors of other group members in a group therapy session, for example, the therapist might help her or him to mindfully observe and experience the emotions that arise without leaving the room or engaging in judgmental or critical behavior. Other strategies might involve the temporary, effective use of distraction skills, such as drawing or engaging in mental distraction skills (e.g., counting backward by sevens, counting the ceiling tiles, diverting attention to other group members). Clients who have difficulty experiencing particular emotions and who engage in avoidance-related TIBs (e.g., switching the topic, becoming angry with the therapist for asking questions) may benefit from the skill of *mindfulness of current emotion*, whereby the client mindfully experiences relevant emotions without engaging in escape strategies (Linehan, 1993a, 2015). These are just a few examples of contexts in which building emotional tolerance and acceptance can help reduce TIB. Mindfulness and acceptance strategies are detailed extensively elsewhere (e.g., Baer, 2006; Linehan, 1993b, 2015), and throughout this volume we periodically discuss their use with various forms of TIB.

Problematic Thinking Patterns

Marita came to group the other week and said,

I didn't do my homework at all. I don't see how filling out a couple of forms is going to help me, as I can work all of this out in my head anyway. I haven't looked at the skills binder for 8 weeks, and I don't think I'm getting anything out of group, nor am I going to get anything out of it. I'm thinking of quitting.

When asked about homework involving the cognitive skill of "checking the facts" (Linehan, 2015), Marita said that she does not have to practice this, because her thoughts are logical and accurate. She said all of this rather loudly in front of the other group members. The group members and leaders were, by now, somewhat used to Marita's somewhat charmingly blunt way of describing her experiences, but it was clear that something had to be done to address her thoughts about group.

There are many possible avenues for intervention with Marita, but a good place to start was her style of thinking, specifically her thoughts that she is not benefitting and will not benefit, and so forth. For example, it could be helpful to confront and highlight the problems in the logic of her thinking, such as her saying she is not benefitting from a group that she is not really doing (half the time her mind is elsewhere, and she does not review the skills or do the homework) or by remarking irreverently that the therapist is honored to meet someone, for the first time, whose thoughts are 100% accurate. Behavioral experiments to test out these thoughts by having her change her behavior and see whether she starts to notice benefits also would be helpful. In fact, after the therapist highlighted the problems with her thinking and suggested that she test the idea that she will not find group to be helpful (by doing her homework and paying attention during group), she returned the next week and had done most of her homework. She actively participated, providing helpful suggestions to other clients. The problems are not likely solved for good, but strategies targeting Marita's thinking patterns provided a good start.

Problematic thought content or style may influence TIB in several ways. The client may, for example, have low *self-efficacy beliefs* about her or his ability to do what it takes to benefit from therapy. Some clients, for example, may not believe they are able to organize themselves to attend therapy regularly, learn new skills, or change some of the patterns that get in the way of their developing a life worth living. The client may also have low *outcome expectancies* or hopeless thoughts about the prospect that therapy might actually help. Indeed, the therapist may also experience such thinking patterns, experiencing *impostor syndrome*, thinking that she or he is ineffective or unable to help the client or having overly ambitious or overly meager expectations for the client's progress. In addition, another thinking pattern that might influence TIB is judgmental thinking on the part of the therapist or the client. In these cases, cognitive interventions may help the client or therapist become more aware of her or his thinking patterns, generate more adaptive thinking, and provide a springboard for behavior change (see Beck, 2011; Farmer & Chapman, 2008, 2016; Leahy, 2003, for several helpful cognitive interventions).

Therapists also may have problematic cognitions related to TIB. When confronted with Marita's behavior, therapists may assume that she is being "resistant" and unwilling to change (Freeman & McCloskey, 2003). Jumping to conclusions about client behaviors or making assumptions such as these can erode empathy and often result in TIB on the part of the therapist. The therapist may, for example, become unduly frustrated with the client, be less willing to help the client, or may overlook important influences on the client's actions.

We suggest that therapists consider using some of the same strategies to address their own thoughts as they would use to help clients address their thoughts. One place to start is for the therapist to check her or his assumptions against some of the core assumptions of DBT (detailed in Linehan, 1993a). As an example, if the therapist is assuming that the client does not want to change or is being purposely "resistant," she or he might try to remember the assumption that clients are doing the best they can, that they want to change, and at the same time, have to become more motivated and skillful (Linehan, 1993a). Extreme assumptions on the part of the therapist often represent a failure in dialectical thinking—a failure to look at both sides of the coin or to realize that both sides are the same coin. Clients both want to change and have to become even more motivated to change. Clients are both doing the best they can and have to do better.

Recently, in one of our clinics, a former client asked to return to therapy. She had seen a couple of therapists already and, in both cases, became obsessed with the idea of having a posttherapy friendship (it was explained that this would not be possible), to the point that she did not focus on much else, and despite the therapists' best efforts, treatment devolved to the point where the client terminated, feeling angry and hurt, harshly criticizing the therapist and clinic. During treatment, this client called the therapist daily in crisis, texted multiple times per day, and engaged in several other behaviors (e.g., stating that this treatment was "crap" and useless) that contributed to thera- peutic burnout. Several months later, the client left a voice message for the therapist saying, "You were right," and thanking her for all her help. Then, more recently, she asked to return to treatment. When discussing this with the therapist, the supervisor recommended that she discuss some of the problems that got in the way of treatment last time and emphasized that these must be protectively solved for treatment to work this time—a reasonable plan. Then, both the therapist and the supervisor realized they were only looking at one side of the issue—the client's "bad" behavior during the last round of therapy. They had overlooked the fact that, during much of treatment, the client made considerable progress, was often delightful, and had worked hard to improve her life. The therapist and supervisor, and to some extent the rest of the team, had gotten polarized, stuck on the idea that this client had engaged in "bad" behavior that had to be fixed for her to return to treatment. It was important for the therapist, supervisor, and team to think through what was being left out—a key dialectical thinking strategy.

In addition to the standard cognitive and behavioral interventions used to address problematic thinking (see Beck, 2011; Farmer & Chapman, 2008, 2016; Leahy, 2003), another approach is for the therapist and client to prac- tice the mindfulness skill of nonjudgmentally describing the facts. Often, when clients express judgments ("My boyfriend is a total jerk," "I'm com- pletely inept," "I don't have what it takes to change or to do this treatment") or make assumptions or inferences ("You didn't reply to my email the same day because you don't care about me," "You think I'm a bad person"), the therapist might prompt them to describe the facts without adding assumptions, inter- pretations, or judgments. This is a central practice in mindfulness—observing and experiencing reality and then describing what was observed or experi- enced. Simply describing the facts without adding anything also is similar to what Suzuki, in his book *Zen Mind, Beginner's Mind* (1970), called "leaving no trace." The idea is to avoid adding anything to the reality at hand. Facts are facts, and thoughts are thoughts. Thoughts, although sometimes accurate, are never facts. Take the following example.

Client: I was just lazy, and that's why I didn't do my homework.

Therapist: OK, "lazy" is a judgment. It's hard to call yourself that without judging yourself. I'd like you to practice describing the facts.

Client: The fact is that I was too lazy to do my homework.

Therapist: All right, the fact is that you didn't do your homework, but what do you mean by "lazy"?

Client: I don't know, I guess I was feeling tired and not really wanting to do anything. I kept remembering about the homework and then just doing something else like playing on my phone or watching TV.

Therapist: Nicely done. Did you notice that you just described the facts? Knowing this stuff, that you were tired, feeling unmotivated, and that you decided to do something other than your homework, is a lot more helpful than just calling yourself lazy, don't you think?

Client: I guess, but isn't it the same thing?

Therapist: No, now we have something to work with. If you're just fundamentally lazy, then we're done; I don't have a treatment to make you a better or less lazy person. But I can come up with a treatment that will help you get going when you really don't want to. We have skills for that, and they work really well.

Problematic Environments and Life Stressors

Barriers to effective engagement in therapy also can include problematic environments or acute or chronic stressors. "Sam" was going through an acrimonious divorce, had little money, and was trying to retain custody of his child. He could barely afford treatment and sometimes did not show up because he was unable to pay for parking. He had difficulties arranging childcare, was addressing the recurrence of cancer, and was barely keeping his head above water at work. Not surprisingly, Sam sometimes missed sessions and struggled to keep up with his skills training homework. "Winifred," who was trying to stay off drugs, was living from week to week in women's shelters in an area of town rife with drug-using residents. Previously a sex worker, she was trying to move away from this occupation but kept returning to it when she ran out of cash. Winifred made a diligent effort to attend therapy group and work on her skills, but huge environmental barriers had to be solved before she could really jump into treatment with both feet.

The lives of clients with borderline personality disorder often are characterized by what Linehan (1993a) referred to as "unrelenting crisis." At times, it seems as if one horrendous event after another keeps happening to the clients we see. Therapy becomes much like a professor trying to teach a class while her students keep lighting the desks on fire. For therapy to proceed effectively, these crises and problems have to be solved. On a less dramatic scale, stress at home or work, financial or occupational problems, or a lack of social contact or support also can interfere with the client's quality of life and ability to engage in treatment. Therefore, the therapist and client may have to work together to find solutions to problems in everyday living.

Therapists also may experience problems in living that interfere with therapy. Such problems may include relationship difficulties, emotional or psychological problems or disorders, inadequate self-care or social support, work in a stressful or difficult environment, tension between coworkers, staff, or administration, and so on. It is imperative that therapists monitor the effect of life challenges and stressors on their professional work. When such factors contribute to therapist TIBs or portend professional burnout, the therapist must take steps to address these problems. Some helpful first steps might involve connecting with a supportive personal and professional network, seeking consultation, and possibly seeking therapy. The DBT consultation team functions much like "therapy for the therapist," in that the focus each week is on how the therapist is doing in her or his work with clients. The team monitors and addresses factors such as therapeutic burnout, motivational issues, skills that have to be improved, and compassion fatigue, among others. The team also helps the therapist to solve problems contributing to potential TIBs. In one consultation team, the therapist noticed that her work was suffering because of an overwhelming amount of work as well as obligations in her personal life. She could barely find the time to buy groceries, let alone field several calls per week from her suicidal clients, prepare effectively for sessions, and manage emotions and worry arising in the context of her work. After some problem solving, the team pitched in and helped the therapist by having someone buy her groceries every other week and by putting into place a temporary rotating phone schedule, whereby other team members took the therapist's calls every other weekend. After a few weeks, she had the breathing room to come up with more long-term solutions and felt more capable of doing effective therapy.

Here we discuss a general framework and set of steps for problem solving to reduce stressors and environmental barriers to treatment. Other volumes have included discussion of these basic steps (e.g., Farmer & Chapman, 2016; Linehan, 2015; Nezu, Maguth Nezu, & D'Zurilla, 2013). One way to organize problem-solving steps is to follow the six steps summarized by the acronym SOLVES (taken from Farmer & Chapman, 2016). The following is an example of the use of problem solving to address therapy attendance problems of a client named "Rodrigo."

- S = Specify the problem. Rodrigo periodically arrives late for therapy and has missed three of the last 10 sessions. His boss often asks him to stay late at work during certain times of the year (e.g., holiday sales), and as a result, he is sometimes unable to make it for the 5 p.m. group sessions or for his individual therapy appointments. Rodrigo really wants to be in therapy and is frustrated and having hopeless thoughts about the situation (e.g., "I can't do anything about this. I'm at the mercy of my boss. I really need help, but maybe I shouldn't be in therapy").
- O = Outline your goals. Rodrigo wants to come to therapy to address his anger and alcohol problems. He has lost relationships because of these issues and is afraid that, unless he gets his anger under control, he will lose his current girlfriend or erupt at work and get fired. His goal is to learn to manage anger, reduce his alcohol use (he binge drinks three to four times per week), and to attend his weekly therapy sessions. Longer term goals are to advance in his job, continue his long-term relationship, and develop closer connections with friends.
- L = List the alternatives. This is often the phase of problem solving whereby brainstorming occurs. Rodrigo and his therapist set a timer for 5 minutes and wrote out as many possible solutions as they could conceive, without immediately evaluating any of the solutions. The idea was that anything goes, so solutions such as quitting his job, quitting therapy, arriving drunk at work in order to get fired, and so on, were perfectly allowable during this brainstorming phase.
- V = View the likely consequences and select a promising alternative. Rodrigo and his therapist selected a couple of the most promising solutions to evaluate: (a) asking the treatment team whether he could switch to another group occurring later in the evening and (b) asking his boss whether he could only stay late on days other than Monday (when therapy occurs). As they reviewed the pros and cons of these solutions, it became clear that the primary cons to solution (a) are that the other therapy groups have wait lists, he would have to wait several weeks to get into one of these groups, and that he likes and would miss his group. The primary cons of (b) were that Rodrigo would be anxious about asking this of his boss and would have to come

up with an explanation for his unavailability on Monday evenings (he did not wish to reveal his mental health problems).
Ultimately, they decided that Rodrigo would first ask his boss
whether he could be exempt from late hours on Monday due
to prior commitments (which he would describe as a "class")
and that if this does not work, he would go on the wait list for
another group. They also decided that in the meantime, Rodrigo
would do extra therapy homework on evenings on which he has
missed all or a portion of group.

- E = Establish and implement a plan. Rodrigo and his therapist
worked out the details of the plan and also addressed potential obstacles to the plan by troubleshooting. Troubleshooting
always is an important step in problem solving, because a perfectly reasonable plan can go awry for many reasons, such as
the client forgetting to do it, the client losing her or his nerve
or motivation, the environment reacting in unexpected ways
(e.g., the boss getting upset when Rodrigo asked for extra time),
and so on. Often, we have found that one of the primary reasons
solutions did not work as planned was that the plan did not take
into account these potential obstacles.

- S = Survey the outcomes. During this phase, the client and
therapist attend to the actual outcomes of the solutions implemented. After putting this plan into action, Rodrigo's boss agreed
to allow him to avoid staying late on Mondays, unless another
staff member was unexpectedly ill, in which case Rodrigo agreed
to miss his "class" and put into action the plan of doing extra
therapy homework after he got home.

Although this does not fit neatly into the SOLVES acronym, another
important step in problem solving is to elicit a commitment from the client to
actually implement the solutions devised. Eliciting a commitment might be
as simple as asking the client whether she or he agrees with it and is willing to
put the plan into action, or it could involve commitment strategies (outlined
in Linehan, 1993a, and discussed periodically throughout this book) or motivational interviewing strategies (Miller & Rollnick, 2012).

MOVING FORWARD

In this chapter, we reviewed a set of strategies that a therapist can use
to address nearly any TIB. Often, the first step is to recognize TIB, considering the effect of this behavior on therapy and the therapy relationship.

Next, highlighting the TIB and providing a good rationale for discussing it can set the stage for effective work. One of the most important steps is to assess, often using a functional analysis, the factors contributing to the TIB and then to select appropriate interventions. Such interventions could include any of the core DBT or CBT strategies discussed in this chapter or other effective therapeutic interventions. Throughout this process it can be effective for therapists to balance acceptance and change-oriented strategies and styles and to ensure a clear commitment from the client to try out new skills or solutions. In addition, troubleshooting the factors that could interfere with effective solutions can make the overall plan more airtight and realistic.

4

SETTING THE STAGE: ORIENTING AND OBSERVING LIMITS

So far, we have reviewed ways of thinking about the role of therapy-interfering behavior (TIB) and how and why clients or therapists might get in their own way (Chapter 1), key principles to keep in mind (Chapter 2), and core strategies (Chapter 3). In this chapter, we discuss and demonstrate ways to address TIB from the beginning portions of therapy. Addressing TIB starts at the beginning of therapy, and it is helpful to start with a clear game plan. As such, in the beginning phases of treatment, the therapist orients the client to her or his approach to therapy and to TIB, laying the groundwork for any ongoing work. In this chapter, we review ways to orient the client to TIB at the beginning of treatment and show how orientation continues throughout therapy.

It is also helpful to begin with a clear idea of how the therapist would address client behavior that stretches her or his own personal or professional limits. Indeed, some of the factors that interfere most with therapy involve

http://dx.doi.org/10.1037/14572-004
Managing Therapy-Interfering Behavior: Strategies From Dialectical Behavior Therapy, by A. L. Chapman and M. Z. Rosenthal

demands that the therapist is unable or unwilling to meet, or behaviors that stress the therapeutic relationship, contribute to therapeutic burnout, or reduce the therapist's motivation to treat the client. In dialectical behavior therapy (DBT), the therapist monitors and observes her or his limits throughout treatment, and when these limits are stretched, the therapist addresses this directly with the client. In this chapter, we describe and illustrate how a therapist might use a DBT framework to effectively address and observe therapeutic limits.

ORIENTING TO THERAPY-INTERFERING BEHAVIOR

Orientation provides the client with a road map for therapy, making the therapeutic journey smoother and more efficient. Orientation might involve explaining the rationale for and type of therapy provided, as well as related expectations and roles of the therapist and client. Discussions of the general therapeutic structure and rituals, any relevant rules, the therapist's limits, and so on, can help clarify what to do (and sometimes what not to do) and when to do it. Such orientation also can help lay the groundwork for clients and therapists to effectively manage future bumps in the road. In DBT skills training groups, for example, we have found that orientation of the clients to the expectations and norms of the group (e.g., completing weekly homework, arriving on time, practicing being nonjudgmental of him- or herself and other group members; Linehan, 1993b, 2015) can facilitate a smooth and effective group process.

Orientation also facilitates the socialization of the client to the therapeutic process. Being in relationships with different people is sometimes like visiting different countries: It is easier to navigate those relationships if we are familiar with the preferences, values, and expectations of our relationship partners. Similarly, different therapeutic relationships may involve different expectations, norms, preferences, and procedures. It can be tempting to orient in a perfunctory manner or to launch into treatment quickly because it may seem like all the preamble is a waste of time. This would be a lot like going to a new country with no map and no plan—it might be exciting for an experienced traveler but can be disorienting for a client. Thorough orientation may slow things down in the beginning, but this investment of time will pay off as therapy progresses.

Some clients' previous experiences with medical or health professionals may not have involved discussions of whether they are actively engaging in treatment (e.g., doing their homework, showing up on time) or heart-to-heart talks about the relationship between the client and provider. Indeed, these types of discussions may be particularly foreign for clients who have only ever had brief appointments with their physician or psychiatrist. Other clients may have seen therapists or counselors who do not explicitly address TIB. Some providers may assume that if the client is not attending sessions or completing homework, it simply is not the best time in the client's life for treatment, or she or he is unmotivated and unlikely to benefit from treatment. In contrast, we recommend the viewpoint that noncompliance is an opportunity to help the client overcome important obstacles and learn something new that may generalize to other areas of her or his life. Similarly, TIB affecting the therapeutic relationship presents an opportunity to learn to repair and strengthen relationships. Therefore, we recommend addressing TIB directly and collaboratively; hence, it is important for the client to know this ahead of time, so that she or he knows how and why therapy may, at times, focus on TIB.

Orientation to TIB at the beginning of therapy addresses several topics. Such orientation should include (a) a clear definition and explanation of TIB; (b) clarification that the client or the therapist may engage in TIB; and (c) framing of TIB as an accepted, natural part of therapy and as an opportunity. We should note that the following orientation may appear too comprehensive and detailed for some clients. For clients who typically show up to therapy, are polite and easy to work with, and tend to do their homework, these orienting conversations may be considerably briefer than those for clients for whom TIB is likely to play a significant role in therapy.

Clearly Define and Explain Therapy-Interfering Behavior

Clearly defining TIB will help ensure that the therapist and client have the same understanding and recognize TIB when it occurs. Generally, it is helpful to convey that TIB is any action or set of actions on the part of the client or therapist that interfere with therapeutic progress or make it difficult for the therapist and client to work effectively together. Not only are factors that limit therapeutic progress (e.g., lateness, absences, and lack of homework completion) important to pay attention to but the therapeutic relationship also requires attention. The client or therapist may both be "working the program," by doing all the things they are supposed to do (e.g., homework, showing up on time), but if the client is also engaging in behaviors that may contribute to therapeutic burnout (e.g., repeatedly calling in a crisis at 3 a.m.), therapy may be ineffective. Therapists who are consumed with worry or burned out by too much contact, who feel devalued or denigrated, or who face harsh criticism or yelling on a regular basis may find it challenging to maintain their motivation and skill. As a result, the therapy may suffer, and the client will make limited progress. It is important to remember that talking openly about TIBs as they affect the therapist is not equivalent to oversharing, inappropriate self-disclosure, or countertransference. Therapy is a relationship, so it is reasonable to expect that the client's behavior will affect the therapist, and opportunities for growth can arise from discussions of how the client is affecting the therapist. The following is an example of how a therapist might begin this orientation to TIB, including a discussion of how we define TIB.

Therapist: Now that we've finished our assessment and have had a chance to discuss your goals and put together a road map for our work, I'd like to talk with you about something else that's really important.

Client: Oh, OK, what is that?

Therapist: Well, we need to talk about some of the obstacles that might get in your way in therapy. Sometimes, we call these obstacles *therapy-interfering behaviors*. Therapy-interfering behaviors are things that you or I might do that could make it hard for you to benefit from therapy. Can you think of anything you might do, or might not do, that might make it hard for you to get the most out of therapy?

Client: Hmm, you mentioned that there will be homework, and I should say that I really hate the word *homework*. It sounds awful and brings up memories of school. I don't know if I'm going to be able to do homework every single week. I mean, I can barely get myself together to make breakfast in the morning, and even coming up here took a lot of effort.

Therapist: Right, homework is a perfect example. Not doing your homework would definitely interfere with therapy. This is because I'm not expecting that you'll be magically cured by spending an hour a week talking with me in this office. Changing your life is going to require some work during the rest of your week, while you're living your life, wouldn't you agree?

Client: Yes, of course. I mean my life kinda sucks right now, and I know it is going to be a lot of work to change things. Sometimes I can't imagine being able to do it.

Therapist: Right, it would be hard to imagine right now, sort of like climbing a huge mountain. Well, let's say you're having a hard time completing your homework, and yet, we both know that whatever homework you have will probably help you, at least over the long run. Then, we'd put our heads together, try to figure out what's getting in the way, and do some problem solving.

Client: That sounds OK.

Therapist: OK, good, well, homework is one example. Another example might be your not showing up for therapy. It's pretty hard to do therapy with someone who isn't here! Or, maybe, with how depressed you are, you might start to feel like this is all too much, and you might have the desire to quit at times. If any of this is happening, we'll work together to find a way around it. How does that sound?

Client: OK, I'd be willing to do that.

Therapist: OK, so the next thing that might get in the way of therapy might be things that you or I am doing that make it hard for us to work together. This is the idea that for this to really work out for you, our working relationship has to be strong. If we're not working well together, therapy probably won't work for you. Does that make sense?

Client: Yeah, but my other therapists never really talked about that. They just seemed to get fed up with me and told me right now probably wasn't the time for me to be in therapy.

Therapist: Oh, I'm sorry to hear that. What happened?

Client: Well, I wasn't doing what they were asking me to do, and I had a hard time showing up and was late a lot. I guess I also can be a little difficult when I get angry, too.

Therapist: Difficult how?

Client: Well, I have a problem with yelling. I don't mean to, but I just can't seem to stop myself.

Therapist: That's good to know. I can handle a little yelling, but maybe we could both agree to keep it to a minimum, huh?

Client: Yeah, that would be good!

Therapist: Would you say, then, that we should add anger management to our goals?

Client: Yes, definitely. While we're at it, maybe we can get people to stop pissing me off so much.

Therapist: Ha, I'm good, but I'm not that good! OK, listen, if any of this is happening with us, I will bring it up, and we'll talk about it. If you're doing things that make it hard for me to work with you, I'm going to be up front about it, and we'll deal with it directly, ideally even before it really becomes a problem. In fact, I don't really see it as a problem so much as an opportunity for us to work on things that may get in your way in other relationships or other areas of your life. What do you think about that?

Client:	That sounds good, I really don't want to be doing things that bother you and not even know it.
Therapist:	Right, well, neither do I! Now, let's spend some time talking about what didn't work out so well with your previous therapy so we can try to prevent those things from happening with us.

In this example, the therapist set the stage by clearly defining and conveying the importance of addressing TIB. The therapist also began to do some troubleshooting by asking the client directly about possible TIBs, and in this case, lack of homework compliance emerged as a potential issue. The therapist conveyed that TIB may involve actions that make it hard for therapy to progress or that strain the therapeutic relationship. In this case, the client indicated that she or he was not used to discussing these issues and that previous therapists had taken a different approach to TIB. With such clients, it is especially important to clarify how TIB will be addressed, and in this case, the therapist described a collaborative, problem-solving oriented approach. When the client brought up the yelling, the therapist suggested this as a treatment goal and reaffirmed that the approach to therapy challenges would be collaborative problem solving.

Explain that Therapy-Interfering Behavior Can Be a Two-Way Street

The client is not the only one who may engage in TIB. Therapists sometimes get in the way of effective therapy in several ways, such as by showing up late, being inattentive to the client or her or his needs, avoiding discussions of (or confrontation about) certain topics out of concern about hurting the client's feelings (or "fragilizing" the client), missing appointments, ineffectively managing frustration or irritation, making ineffective treatment decisions, conveying dismissiveness or failing to convey the importance of issues that are important to the client, not following the treatment manual, following the manual too closely without regard to the client's uniqueness or to the detriment of the relationship, and so on (we discuss these in more detail in Chapter 11). The therapist may not convey all these ways in which she or he may go astray (or the client may simply leave), but some concrete examples can help make this important point. As shown in the following example, it can be helpful to let the client know that the therapist also will examine and address her or his own TIB.

Therapist:	Right, well, the second part of this is that you have to tell me if I'm doing anything that makes it hard for you to work with me. Would you be willing to do that?
Client:	Yeah, well . . .
Therapist:	Hmm, somehow I don't feel convinced.

Client:	It sounds like a good idea, but I think I'd have a hard time doing that. I mean, you're the doctor, right? Why should I tell you how to do your job?
Therapist:	So, am I to take it that you've never been annoyed or dissatisfied by anything your other doctors or therapists have done?
Client:	Um, no, certainly not, of course I have. I just haven't ever talked with them about it.
Therapist:	Here's your chance! At some point, I can pretty much guarantee that we will have a session you might not find tremendously helpful. At other times, I might be missing the point or not really understanding where you are coming from, so my suggestions might not make sense or might seem off the mark. There may be times when I encourage you to change aspects of your life (like the fact that you spend most of the day in your room) that you aren't ready or able to change. It's possible as well that you might feel hurt in response to something I've said. If any of this happens, it's important for you to know that you can bring it up with me. I'll be open to your comments and feedback and willing to work with you to improve things.
Client:	OK, as long as I know you'll take me seriously. I mean, sometimes people just seem to disregard what I say.
Therapist:	Oh, then what happens?
Client:	I usually feel hurt and unimportant, and then I kind of pull back or get really angry.
Therapist:	It is really hard when people come across like they aren't taking you seriously. I hope that if I do that, you'll let me know. Can we agree that you'll do that?
Client:	OK, yes, I'll do that.
Therapist:	If, in your experience, you've been dismissed or disregarded, it might seem pointless to even talk about stuff that's bothering you. So, we have to work to change your experience, so you learn that when you bring up important things about how we're working together, I will actually take it seriously. And, the best way to do that is to get started now and get you some practice with this. Here's what I'd like you to do: I'd like you to give me some feedback about something you have liked about the way we've worked together so far and also something you have found less helpful. Then you can really see how these conversations will go. Are you willing to do that?

In this example, the therapist conveyed that if he or she engages in TIB, the client is welcome to bring it up. The therapist provided the client with "permission" to give feedback and share reactions to the therapist's actions, thereby helping to establish a relationship characterized by openness. The therapist also nondefensively stated that TIB might occur despite his or her best intentions, and if that happens, he or she would appreciate and welcome feedback. Particularly for clients who are sensitive to criticism, this open, nondefensive stance on the part of the therapist can help to model a new, more effective way to respond to critical feedback. In addition, the therapist did some troubleshooting by helping the client anticipate factors that would reduce her or his willingness or ability to comment on reactions to the therapist's actions. When the client expressed concerns about being dismissed (because of past experience), the therapist validated those concerns and conveyed hope that things will be different in this relationship.

Having identified a possible barrier to the client discussing TIB in the future, the therapist could go in several directions. He or she could, for example, address the client's belief, hope that she or he will bring up concerns despite the belief, further explore the belief and where it came from, or have the client practice the type of behavior she or he is hoping to observe later on. In this example, the therapist chose the latter approach. This intervention is also a behavioral experiment that will facilitate the client's practice in providing feedback. Ideally, the client will also experience (rather than just be convinced cognitively or intellectually) positive consequences from doing so (her needs and wishes being taken seriously), increasing the chances that the client will provide feedback again in the future. Clients who are reluctant to engage in heart-to-heart discussions of TIB, either on their own or the therapist's part, may have similar difficulty with open communication in other relationships. As such, the therapist may generalize patterns within the therapeutic relationship to experiences in the client's daily life by assessing whether this pattern occurs with others. If so, the therapist has the opportunity to help the client generalize to other relationships what she or he is learning (this is often one goal of treatments that use the therapeutic relationship as a vehicle for change, such as functional analytic psychotherapy, Kohlenberg & Tsai, 1991; transference-focused psychotherapy, Yeomans, Levy, & Caligor, 2013; mentalization-based treatment, Bateman & Fonagy, 2013).

Convey Acceptance of Therapy-Interfering Behavior and Make Lemonade Out of Lemons

During orientation, we also suggest that the therapist convey acceptance of TIB as an inevitable part of therapy and an important opportunity. He or she might also suggest that that treatment does not involve avoiding mistakes at all costs but, rather, learning from the inevitable bumps in the road. TIB is an opportunity to learn something new. This framing of a problem as an opportunity is akin to the dialectical strategy in DBT called *making lemonade out of lemons* (see Linehan, 1993a). For example, a client who yells at the therapist might expect the therapist to argue back, validate the client's distress and back down, or other characteristic responses to expressed anger. Making lemonade out of lemons, the therapist might instead state, "OK, I can see you're really angry with me, and to be honest, I'm glad this is coming up right now. This is a perfect opportunity for us to work together on the very problem that brought you to therapy in the first place." Often an unexpected response, framing problems as opportunities can reorient clients who are stuck to ways to solve or accept their problem. Conveying acceptance of TIB as a natural part of therapy, an important part of the learning process, and an opportunity also can help the client feel more comfortable with discussions of TIB. In addition, this stance also runs counter to the self-deprecatory thinking with which clients often struggle (e.g., "I'm a failure because I'm not getting better as quickly as I had hoped, I have a hard time doing my homework, show up late, am burning out my therapist, just like I burn out everyone else").

The following is a brief example of how this might be addressed in a therapy group:

> This is not a no-mistakes-allowed kind of group. We know that at times, it may be really hard to do your homework or show up on time, and sometimes you might find your motivation flagging and simply decide not to do what you know you should be doing. All of that is to be expected, and when these things happen, we see that as an opportunity to simply help you get back on track. We'll help you think through solutions and find ways for you to continue to get as much out of therapy as possible.

Continue Orienting Throughout Therapy

Ideally, orientation regarding TIB and other treatment targets continues beyond the beginning of therapy and occurs in small doses throughout treatment. Such orientation might involve conveying the rationale for the therapist and client focusing on and solving TIB related problems, orientation to exactly how they will work together on TIB, and orientation to how and why the client may implement some of the solutions discussed. The following is an example of how this "mini-orienting" might work in the case of a client who was chronically late for therapy.

Therapist: Sandy, I'm glad to see you, and I'm noticing that you're about 20 minutes late, so this means we're going to have to have a shorter session. I know that's not ideal, as you really need help with your depression and with what's happening with your boyfriend. [*The client's boyfriend had been diagnosed with schizophrenia.*] As I recall, you were late the last two sessions as well, so I really think we're going to have to spend a chunk of our time putting our heads together to figure out what's happening and how to get you here on time.

Client: I know I need to work on it, but I'm not sure what to do. I can't keep coming all this way and paying all this money for such short sessions. I just don't know what's the matter with me.

Therapist: I know, it can be really demoralizing when you just can't seem to get yourself to do something you know that you need to do. Although I wouldn't want you to continue to be late so often, I'm actually glad it has come to this.

Client: What do you mean?

Therapist: Well, I think that this is a wake-up call—an opportunity for us to work on something that causes you a lot of stress in other areas of life. Haven't you told me that you've lost jobs because you weren't getting your paperwork done, had a hard time following the procedures, and showed up late too often?

Client: Yeah, that's true. I'm not sure why I'm so disorganized.

Therapist: Well, for whatever reason, doing things you're supposed to do, getting organized, and playing by the rules so to speak—these things are not exactly your strong suit. But, we'll figure this out, and if we can crack this pattern, I think you'll notice that you will be even more able to get close to the life you want, with a job, being able to support yourself, and so on.

Client: That sounds good. I really don't want this to keep happening. I'm getting fed up with myself. So, what are we going to do?

Therapist: Let's start by reviewing what happened today. Remember when we talked earlier about how we'll work together to do something called a functional analysis if you're doing things that are really getting in your way?

In this example, the client has engaged in TIB by arriving late. The therapist highlighted the behavior, clarified the problems associated with lateness (by clarifying the contingency or the relationship of lateness to the amount of session time available), and oriented the client to the task at hand: understanding how the client has ended up being late. In addition to the mini-orienting to the task of assessing the problem and the importance of and rationale for talking about it, the therapist also framed this event as an opportunity (making lemonade out of lemons) and generalized beyond this instance to highlight a broader pattern of behavior. As discussed in Chapter 3, there are many strategies for the management of TIB, and in this case, the therapist started off by using *contingency management*—only allowing the client the remaining session time. We further discuss this and other strategies pertaining to lateness in Chapter 5.

OBSERVING PERSONAL AND THERAPEUTIC LIMITS

Throughout treatment, it can be helpful (and sometimes essential) for the therapist to remain aware of her or his own personal and therapeutic limits. Limits have to do with what the therapist is capable of or willing to do or to tolerate. Therapists may have limits regarding a variety of different aspects of therapy or client behavior. Some common examples include the following:

- requests or demands on the part of the client, such as for a certain amount or type (e.g., text message, telephone, e-mail) of between-session contact; extra work on the part of the therapist outside of sessions (e.g., requests to read e-mails, books, journals; to write letters);
- questions regarding personal information, such as age, living situation, romantic history, sexual preferences, and so forth;
- challenging in-session behavior, such as yelling, verbal aggression, lack of talking, interrupting, complaining, threats, and so forth;
- unrelenting suicidal or other crises;
- issues with hygiene; and/or
- extreme differences in personal values or worldviews (e.g., working with a client who expresses strong prejudiced or racist views).

A therapist who is failing to monitor and observe limits is engaging in TIB. This is because, over time, when limits are stretched, the cumulative effects can include burnout, a reduction in effectiveness or skill, reduced willingness to help the client, and the experience of contact with the client as aversive. Therefore, in DBT, therapists attend to and monitor these limits, and when the client pushes these limits, the therapist discusses this with her or him.

Observing limits involves the therapist monitoring whether the demands of the client exceed the therapist's willingness or capabilities and whether the therapist is willing to tolerate certain client behaviors in the short or long run. This process, therefore, is similar to how we might observe limits in our daily lives. If you have an arrangement with your partner that you will wash the dishes every evening while she or he tackles the laundry and vacuuming, you would be observing limits if you were to say, "I notice the laundry has been piling up, and I don't have any shirts to wear. I'm disappointed about this, and to be honest, I'm a little less willing to hold up my end of the bargain with the dishes." Although the therapist–client relationship is a professional one, it is also a relationship between people, each with their own preferences, limits, and abilities. Observing limits, therefore, can be just as (if not sometimes more) important in therapy as it is in relationships with friends, family members, and loved ones.

Particularly in longer term treatment, therapists who assume that their relationships with clients are dramatically and qualitatively different from other relationships run the risk of being blindsided by erosion of the therapeutic relationship. Decades of research has suggested that the ratio of positive to negative interactions, over the long run, is a strong predictor of relationship satisfaction and stability among couples (Gottman, Driver, & Tabares, 2002). Although the therapeutic relationship involves very different social roles for each participant, there is no reason to believe that this general rule (that the ratio of positive to negative interactions may influence relationship quality) would not hold true in therapy as well. Over time, therefore, a therapist "putting up with" extremely negative or challenging behavior that pushes her or his limits will likely find that the therapeutic relationship weakens.

Whether the therapist's limits are being stretched sometimes has to do with the duration of the client's behavior. Some therapists, for example, may be able to tolerate short-term suicidal crises that come to a resolution, but if the client experiences and communicates repeated, ongoing crises, the related demands (in terms of time, regulation or tolerance of his or her own distress, worry, or concern) can exceed the therapist's limits. Occasional hostile criticism, yelling, or even verbal aggression may be tolerable over the short term, but over the long term, such experiences may lead to burnout and erode the quality of the therapeutic relationship. The same is true of limited therapeutic progress, which can be a major source of stress among therapists. With certain types of client populations, such as multidiagnostic, complex clients, acceptance of the reality of slow and episodic progress can help to prevent burnout (Linehan, 1993a); however, when treating a client showing a lack of progress for several months or longer, the therapist may be uncomfortable continuing with treatment unless changes are made and progress increases. Therefore, it is important for therapists to approach limits with both a short-term (e.g., "How does this affect me and our treatment now?") and a longer term (e.g., "Might this behavior, if it were to continue, contribute to burnout?" "Would I be able to tolerate this for the next 10 sessions?") perspective.

"Alfonse," age 32, had difficulty with transitions in relationships, was sensitive to rejection, and had difficulty tolerating feelings of loneliness. He was highly educated in his particular field but had been unemployed and struggling with depression and symptoms of borderline personality disorder for many years. His new therapist, a predoctoral intern, had just begun with a caseload of a few clients, including Alfonse, who had transferred from other interns completing their training. Alfonse had a particularly close relationship with his previous therapist, who was often readily and quickly available by phone or e-mail between sessions. This type of arrangement, of course, is common in DBT, with the hope that telephone skills coaching between sessions will help the client generalize to daily life what she or he is learning in therapy. Thus, when the client called a couple of times in the first week for assistance with sadness and other strong emotions regarding his other therapist's departure, this budding therapist was happy to help and get his feet wet with phone coaching. The next week, however, Alfonse called every day, and the following week, he called every day of the week and several times throughout the weekend, often in an intense crisis. The therapist began to feel overwhelmed and stressed and began to have an aversive reaction to the sound of his pager (strong emotional tension and the thought, "Not again!"). He knew that if this were to continue, he would be heading for burnout in the near future. He had gotten to the point (past the point, in fact) where he had to observe his own limits.

When the therapist told Alfonse that he wished to discuss how the phone calls had been going, Alfonse became visibly tense and anxious and said, "I've been through this before, and I really hate talking about the phone calls. Fine, I'll cut down on them! You don't have to say anything." The therapist did some assessment of how Alfonse reacted to these discussions (with shame and embarrassment) and then conveyed that although he knew that these discussions were hard, he would be doing Alfonse a disservice and treating him as fragile if he were to simply drop the subject. How would Alfonse ever learn to take this kind of feedback, learn from it, and use it to strengthen relationships if he avoided the discussion? The therapist then communicated that daily calls were too much for him, in that he was feeling more stressed and less able to strike the kind of work–life balance that allowed him to do his best work. He told Alfonse that although other therapists may have different limits than his, he was learning that he could tolerate about three to four calls per week and that he would be more willing to be available if some of the calls occurred before the crisis hit or if they involved positive updates on progress. Alfonse agreed to decrease the calls to three per week and to work on preventing or calling in advance of crises. After some future discussion, it turned out that, in past treatment, discussions of phone calls and therapist limits had largely involved the therapist communicating that Alfonse was "too dependent," had "poor boundaries," and that by remaining available, the therapist would be colluding with Alfonse in maintaining his own pathology. No wonder he felt ashamed when the topic was addressed.

At times, therapy-interfering attitudes or behavior on the part of the client can make it difficult for therapists to observe limits. One of our student clinicians, for example, was seeing a client struggling with chronic dysthymia, a lack of social support, difficulty maintaining a job, and a chronic pain condition. He desperately wanted emotional support, someone to talk to, and to feel less alone in life, but he also had a history of difficulty in close relationships and stated that he often burned out relationships: "Once they really get to know what it's like to be in a relationship with me, they just burn out and leave." During a recent session, the student oriented the client to her limits around between-session phone contact, and she mentioned that she strongly prefers to receive a phone call rather than a text message or e-mail if the client wishes to speak with her between sessions. Two days later, she received an urgent text message from the client. Trying her best to manage contingencies effectively while understanding that she just recently oriented him to her limits, she texted back and asked him to call her if he needed help. During the next session, she reiterated that she preferred not to text and likely would not respond to text messages but was happy to receive a phone call. Three days later she got two urgent text messages from the client. She did not reply to the texts, but then over the weekend, received an e-mail stating that the client was quitting therapy. She managed to convince the client to come in for a session to discuss his decision, and when she did so, he said that he thought her limits around texting were unreasonable and that she should be available in whichever way he found most convenient, because she was the professional and he was the client.

The key to success in this situation was to maintain a dialectical stance whereby the therapist searched for the kernel of truth in the client's position, while not giving up her position and effectively orienting the client to her limits. As one might imagine, it took some work on the part of the therapist to both find and validate the kernel of truth in what the client was saying ("It makes perfect sense to me that you might think that, as you are paying me to help you, and it probably doesn't seem like much skin off my back to respond to a couple of simple text messages from time to time"). The therapist also explored how the client felt when he did not receive a response (hurt, rejected, sad, angry) and validated those feelings as well. She also oriented the client to the fact that, in any therapeutic relationship, the therapist's needs (however few) must be respected and taken seriously for treatment to work best for the client. Although the therapist does not require excessive care and feeding, she does require some. Moreover, this event opened up a discussion of how this problem occurred for the client in other relationships and how the client might work on better balancing his needs with those of people with whom he was close. They also began to work on his intense emotional reactions and tendency to try to escape (e.g., quit therapy, end relationships) when he felt his needs were not being met.

Being Dialectical About Limits: Limits Are Idiographic, Relational, and Contextual

Within a dialectical framework, limits are a unique, idiographic characteristic of the therapist. Different therapists may have vastly different limits. Some therapists are quite comfortable treating angry clients and have no difficulty with their clients yelling at them, whereas other therapists might be unable to function effectively under these conditions. Yelling or verbal aggression, for these therapists, may be a deal breaker. Some therapists are willing to be available for client calls in the middle of the night or during vacations, whereas other therapists prefer to protect their personal time and limit the amount of work they do during off hours or days. Certain therapists have a tremendous capacity to accept and work with clients with dramatically different views or value systems (e.g., clients who express prejudice regarding race or sexual orientation), clients who engage in often-maligned behavior (e.g., those who have sexually offended against children or who have committed homicide), or those who engage in behavior that falls far outside accepted social norms (e.g., sexual activity with animals). Other therapists, in contrast, may realize that they are less effective with people who engage in certain behaviors or who have certain characteristics or views and, therefore, may have tighter limits. Indeed, during the DBT consultation team meetings, the team leader begins the meeting by reading an agreement that orients the team to the philosophy of treatment. One such agreement is the following: "We agree to observe our own limits. As therapists and group members, we agree to not judge or criticize other members for having different limits from our own" (e.g., too broad, too narrow, "just right"; Linehan, 2008, p. 427).

On the other side of the dialectic, therapists sometimes have limits that are too narrow to facilitate effective work with particular clients. As an example, one aspect of DBT is the availability of the clinician for telephone contact (or e-mail, text-message, or other communication forms) between sessions to help the client generalize skills to the natural environment. Telephone consultation is a core aspect of DBT (Linehan, 1993a) and a component of standard care for suicidal clients (e.g., see Bongar & Sullivan, 2013). This aspect of treatment, however, sometimes strikes fear into the hearts of the clinicians we train. Some clinicians desire to do DBT but believe that availability between sessions would go beyond their personal limits. Others are willing to be available only during regular working hours. We have not yet come across a clinician who has shaped her or his client to only have crises during regular working hours. Therefore, on the basis of what we know so far about the efficacy of DBT and the standard of care for highly suicidal clients, such limits may be too narrow to effectively work with this population. Other examples of ineffectively narrow limits might be clinicians doing anger management treatment who cannot tolerate the client's angry behavior, clinicians working with adolescents who are unwilling to have sessions or consult with the parents, and so on.

Because therapeutic limits are idiosyncratic, it is important for therapists to take responsibility for their limits. When these limits are stretched, therapists can use the same interpersonal skills often taught to clients, describing the behavior and the therapist's related thoughts and emotional reactions nonjudgmentally using "I" statements. The therapist might, for example, state that when the client describes members of a particular race in derogatory terms, she or he feels uncomfortable and has a hard time remaining unbiased. Recall that TIB is defined functionally by its effect on the therapy or the therapeutic relationship. When observing limits, therefore, the therapist emphasizes the effect of the client's behavior on her or his own ability to help. This model of limits is more of a relationship-oriented model than a pathology-oriented model. This means that the therapist typically would not normally suggest that the client's behavior is problematic in its own right (i.e., that it is pathological or would be a problem in any context) or that it represents an underlying pathology. The limit-pushing behavior is problematic in the context of the specific therapeutic-client relationship. Regarding limits around between-session contact, for example, other providers or support persons (e.g., friends, loved ones) may have dramatically different limits. Therefore, the fact that the therapist feels burned out does not mean that the client is excessively dependent or needy.

In the case of Alfonse, the therapist acknowledged that the problem was the negative effect of the calls on his free time and work–life balance. In contrast, a pathology-oriented model might necessitate that the therapist communicate that Alfonse was being too dependent and had to learn how to get his needs met on his own. This may be the case, but "too dependent" depends greatly on the nature of the relationships and people with whom Alfonse is involved. For some therapists and others in Alfonse's life, daily calls may be perfectly acceptable and, therefore, would not be considered signs of his being too dependent. Indeed, to our knowledge, there is no master playbook that specifies reasonable "boundaries" and rules regarding social behavior within or outside therapeutic relationships. This is not to say that the therapist may not discuss Alfonse's approach to relationships and support seeking. Indeed, this could be an important discussion, and it would be reasonable for the therapist to assess whether Alfonse has ever experienced these types of challenges with other therapists, friends, or loved ones. In addition, the therapist being honest, frank, and clear about his reactions to Alfonse's behavior, in the context of a warm and supportive therapeutic relationship, may facilitate learning that generalizes to other such relationships.

Another characteristic of limits in DBT is that they may change in response to changes in context. The therapist's life situation, for example, may change, making it harder for her or him to be as available as before. We both have children, for example, and when our first children were born, we each experienced many months of the usual newborn sleep deprivation. The loss of sleep was worse for our wives, to be sure, but it did affect us too. Prior to having kids, we were willingly available for middle-of-the-night calls from DBT clients, but in those sleepless and stressful months, we each narrowed our limits regarding when we could receive phone calls. Limits also may change in accordance with changes in the therapeutic relationship. A therapist might, for example, be more willing to be available to provide extra time or help or to tolerate the client yelling at him or her if the relationship is strong and mutually rewarding. A natural contingency for a client consistently treating a therapist in a hostile or disrespectful way might be to reduce the flexibility of limits regarding contact out of the psychotherapy session.

Observing Versus Setting Limits

Observing limits differs from setting limits. *Setting limits* involves the therapist providing a rule that she or he expects the client to follow, whereas *observing limits* involves the therapist monitoring the effect of the client's behavior and discussing this when needed. Observing limits requires the therapist to mindfully observe the client's actions and her or his reactions. Setting limits involves conveying rules, such as the therapist communicating when she or he is available for telephone calls (e.g., 9 a.m.–8 p.m., Monday–Friday), rules regarding lateness (e.g., the therapist will wait 15 minutes and then consider the session cancelled), and therapy attendance, among others. When the therapist orients the client to any existing limits during the beginning phases of treatment, the client will know what to do and what to avoid to effectively navigate the therapeutic relationship. Effective management of TIB often involves a combination of observing and setting limits. The following is an example of how a therapist might communicate limits regarding between-session contact.

> *Therapist:* OK, so we've talked about the fact that I'm available by phone between sessions to help you. Do you remember what the point of these phone calls is?
>
> *Client:* I'm not sure. Was it in case of emergency or if I need help with my emotions?

Therapist: Exactly, yes, you can call me if there's an emergency, although I'd prefer it if you could get to me even well before an emergency strikes. In any case, the main point is to help you take what you're learning in therapy and use it in your daily life when needed. You're going to be learning a lot about different ways to manage your emotions, change your thinking, and deal more effectively with other people. It's one thing to talk about that stuff in here, but it can be a whole different story when you try it out in your everyday life. So, I'd like to be able to help you with that.

Client: That sounds good. I know I'm going to need a lot of help! Other people have often told me that I'm a little too needy, but I really feel alone, and I have a hard time with that.

Therapist: Oh, well, you can rest assured that I'm not going to call you "needy." But, if I find that you're calling me more than I can handle, I'll definitely let you know, and we'll try to find a way for you to get the help you need while keeping me sane! Does that sound reasonable?

Client: Yes, I'm glad to hear you'll let me know. I know you're busy, and I don't really want to bother you or be a burden.

Therapist: If it really bothered me, I wouldn't invite you to call in the first place. I'm actually looking forward to having a chance to help you with things that are happening in the middle of the action of your daily life.

Client: When would I be able to call you?

Therapist: Right, good question. Let me tell you now about how available I'm likely to be. Generally, I don't actually answer my phone. I'd ask that you leave a voice message with just a little information on what kind of help you need, and then I'll get back to you. I can't promise to always get back to you right away, as I might be in a meeting, traveling, giving a full-day presentation, or so on. So, I'll do my best to get back to you at least by the time I go to bed that evening. Sometimes it will be a lot sooner than that. The deal, though, is that you have to wait until you hear from me and avoid doing anything harmful to yourself. Can you agree to that?

Client: That might be hard, especially if I have to wait a long time. But I get where you're coming from, and I'll do my best.

Therapist: Regarding times, you can call me whenever you want, but I'm much more likely to call you back if you call sometime between 6 a.m. and 10 p.m., when I go to bed. You can call me in the middle of the night if you need to, but you might not get me (my phone might be off), and if you do, I might not be as helpful if I'm groggy. But, if you do call and I can't answer, I'll do my best to call you first thing in the morning. I know it might be hard to wait, and sometimes my being less available at night might also be difficult for you. So, let's talk about how to manage that.

In this example, the therapist is setting rather than observing limits, but in a manner that allows for some flexibility. For example, the client can call the therapist in the middle of the night if she or he wishes, but effective help may not always be forthcoming. This is an example of the therapist specifically describing behavior (calling in the middle of the night) and its likely consequences (groggy or unavailable therapist), thereby clarifying the contingency and allowing the client freedom to choose what to do. The client may then call and discover the consequences. Emphasizing the value of learning from experience, rather than setting up conditions for rule-governed behavior, is likely to result in more flexible and sustainable behavior change (see Hayes, Brownstein, Zettle, Rosenfarb, & Korn, 1986). In addition, the therapist acknowledged that these limits may present some challenges for the client and discussed how they might manage that. The therapist also oriented the client throughout this excerpt to the rationale for the telephone calls (generalization of treatment gains) and conveyed enthusiasm and interest in helping the client.

Limits Are Changeable and May Be Stretched When Needed

Therapists sometimes need to be willing to stretch their limits. Clients may need extra sessions for a specified period to help them get through a difficult time, or they might need more phone support than usual or for the therapist to assist them with other aspects of their care, such as coordination of care with other treatment providers, consulting with attending psychiatrists to ensure coordination of treatment, and so on. When these demands are both necessary and stretch the therapist's limits, it is helpful for the therapist to orient the client to the temporary nature and rational for these extended limits. Orienting the client to the time-limited nature of the therapist stretching limits can help to prevent reinforcing repeated crises or other such dysfunctional behavior.

At one of our clinics, a client was being seen in a DBT skills group while concurrently seeing an individual psychologist in the community. Anecdotally, we have found that although this arrangement (where a client is receiving DBT in a "group-only" fashion) can be effective, greater efforts are sometimes required in terms of case management to help sustain the client's involvement in treatment and to maximize success. This particular client,

"Sally," contacted the therapist to say that she was judging herself harshly for her strong emotional reactions during group, was thinking of quitting therapy, and had been hospitalized for depression. The therapist, being extremely busy (and trying desperately to find the time to write this book), would not usually do this on a weekly basis with a group client that he is not seeing individually, but decided that stretching his limits would help prevent the client from dropping out and could enhance her progress. As a result, he had regular contact with her during her hospital stay, helped her to get a pass to attend the DBT skills group each week, coordinated care with her individual psychologist, and picked her up and dropped her off from the hospital (she was certified, and the hospital was across the street) during group evenings. During one session, the client bolted from the clinic immediately after group and was later found on a bridge and taken back to the hospital. The therapist remained willing to stretch limits and accommodate the client during her hospital stay, but he did require her to come up with a plan to prevent this from happening again. The client expressed gratitude for this support, remained in group, and began to show signs of improvement in her involvement in group.

MOVING FORWARD

Strategies to manage TIB often start at the beginning of therapy with orientation and observing limits. Effective orientation involves the therapist clearly defining TIB, discussing how both parties might engage in behavior that interferes with therapy, and framing TIB as an expected part of therapy and an important opportunity to learn new things (i.e., making lemonade out of lemons). Orientation to the collaborative problem-solving approach to TIB is also helpful. Orientation also occurs throughout treatment and can set the frame for future in-session opportunities to change clinically relevant behavior. In addition, observing limits involves the therapist mindfully observing whether the client's demands or behavior go beyond what he or she is willing or able to tolerate. It is important to recognize that limits are idiographic, contextual, and changeable—a product of the therapist and the therapeutic relationship—rather than general, rigid rules or social guidelines. It can also be effective for the therapist to stretch her or his limits temporarily, with adequate orientation and clear goals. Occurring throughout therapy, orientation and observing limits help to provide a clear road map or framework for therapy and the therapeutic relationship and guide the client back on track when treatment begins to go awry. Therefore, these strategies are not only essential at the beginning of therapy but also help to keep therapy on course over the longer run.

5

ENHANCING THERAPY ATTENDANCE

Despite current advances in communication technologies and tele-health, it remains difficult to have a therapy session with someone who is not there. The focus of this chapter is on therapy attendance. Problems with attendance, including absences, treatment refusal, lateness, and premature termination or dropout, are ubiquitous across therapy settings and particularly common among the types of multidiagnostic clients we often see in dialectical behavior therapy (DBT). Only if therapists manage this set of therapy-interfering behaviors (TIBs) effectively will they have the opportunity to use some of the other strategies we review throughout the rest of this volume.

Lateness and therapy absences affect both the "dose" and consistency of therapy and are thereby likely to interfere with progress. Clients who do not attend treatment may fail to receive the help they need and may use even more resource-intensive services in the future (e.g., inpatient or hospital treatment). Attendance problems may be a sign of waning motivation for treatment, poor

http://dx.doi.org/10.1037/14752-005
Managing Therapy-Interfering Behavior: Strategies From Dialectical Behavior Therapy, by A. L. Chapman and M. Z. Rosenthal

self-management skills, difficulties in the therapeutic relationship, avoidance of challenging topics or interventions (e.g., exposure therapy), or a lack of fit between the therapeutic work and the client's goals. From the therapist's perspective, lateness and absences may pose inconveniences in terms of scheduling or may have financial consequences if the therapist, for example, is unable to bill clients for missed sessions. Therapists also might work extra hours between sessions to reel wayward clients back in, and sometimes this work persists beyond the therapist's limits. In addition, therapists can become demoralized or discouraged when client absences seem to pose a roadblock to recovery (Sledge, Moras, Hartley, & Levine, 1990). Next, we describe, discuss, and illustrate some of the strategies we most commonly use, consistent with the principles and core strategies discussed in Chapters 2 and 3.

KEY PRINCIPLES

Therapists should keep a few important principles in mind when addressing problems with attendance or lateness. First, directly discussing and targeting lateness and absence is the most efficient route to behavior change. Therapists sometimes approach issues of attendance with the attitude that if clients miss or do not arrive on time for sessions, they may not be ready for therapy, or with the notion that the client's intrinsic motivation will eventually blossom (or not) without intervention. This may be the case for some clients, but in the case of multiproblem clients with chaotic, crisis-ridden lives, or those who desperately need help (i.e., are suicidal), the therapist may have to take extra measures to help the client to follow through. In DBT, therefore, we have by necessity spent a lot of time in our teams and with our colleagues and trainees discussing ways to maximize attendance, prevent dropout, and manage problems such as tardiness. Also, problems with attendance also may reflect broader difficulties with self-management, self-regulation, and organizational skills. Therefore, directly addressing attendance might help clients learn to tackle these other problems.

Second, as discussed further later, problems with therapy attendance often relate to an imbalance in contingencies. One helpful assumption to make is that the client wants to change her or his life and wants help but that, somehow, attending therapy is less reinforcing than are alternative activities occurring outside of therapy. Behavior change is hard. We are often asking our clients to do some of the hardest work they will ever do, such as facing extremely painful emotions, learning and practicing new skills, changing ingrained thinking patterns and habits, and so on. Rather than assuming that the client is unmotivated, "self-sabotaging," or "resistant," we find it helpful to assume that the client is doing the best she or he can do at the moment and wants help to develop a better life. At the same time, the client has to become even more motivated and more skillful (Linehan, 1993a). That is where we come in as therapists.

Third, as discussed in Chapter 2, a dialectical stance can be helpful in the therapist's attempts to address attendance problems. From a dialectical perspective, the therapist must at once be fully attached to the client attending therapy and improving her or his life and willing to let go of this attachment when needed. Therapists who remain stuck at one pole ("The client must come in for therapy") risk becoming rigidly focused on getting the client to come in, missing out on understanding why the client is having difficulties with attendance, and pushing the client out of therapy. The therapist must be fully committed to treatment with the client and willing to accept and let go when needed. The therapist does not, however, let go of concern for the client's well-being.

A dialectical stance also reminds the therapist, when therapist and client are polarized (e.g., the therapist pushes for attendance, while the client digs in her heels and says it's too hard to come to therapy), to attend to the wisdom or grain of truth in the client's perspective and to work for synthesis. Consider a client, for example, who says that therapy is not helping and hence he is thinking of quitting. The therapist might be thinking, "Of course therapy isn't working. He doesn't do his homework, shows up late, and isn't really doing therapy." The therapist and client become polarized, with the therapist encouraging the client to work harder and get something out of treatment, and the client saying it is not working. Remembering to search for the grain of truth in the client's position, the therapist might step back and try to see the situation from the client's perspective. How does it make sense that the client is experiencing therapy as ineffective? Why might he or she not want to come in for treatment? Once the therapist does this, she or he may be able to effectively validate the client's position and then work for a synthesis (e.g., the client has to work harder to get something out of therapy, and the therapist has to find ways to make the treatment more effective or relevant). In addition, a dialectical stance also reminds the therapist to (a) effectively balance validation with attempts to solve attendance problems, (b) balance the use of change- or acceptance-oriented behavioral skills, and (c) balance therapeutic styles and strategies. Some of these are discussed further next.

EVIDENCE TO GUIDE INTERVENTIONS TO ENHANCE ATTENDANCE

Over the past 3 decades, numerous studies have examined predictors of therapy attendance and interventions to enhance it and prevent premature termination. The research has focused largely on treatment refusal and premature termination; common outcomes examined include number of sessions attended, attendance at the first therapy session, and early attrition (e.g., after the first session). Several interventions have been examined, including thorough orientation and socialization to the therapeutic process, motivational enhancement, the provision of choice regarding therapists and appointment times, imaginal rehearsal of session attendance, case management and telephone reminders of appointments, and therapist feedback on client progress, among others (Oldham, Kellett, Miles, & Sheeran, 2012).

How well do all of these interventions work, and what works best? A recent meta-analysis examined the effectiveness of interventions to promote attendance and reduce premature termination and treatment refusal. The review focused on 31 studies involving randomization of clients to an active intervention versus a control intervention and the use of objective measures of attendance (Oldham et al., 2012). Findings indicated that Cohen's d effect sizes for interventions to enhance attendance ranged from very small (0.05) to large (1.53). The interventions with the largest effect sizes involved providing clients with choice regarding therapists and appointment days and times at the beginning of treatment. Other interventions associated with larger effects included motivational interviewing, orientation and providing information about treatment, appointment reminders, and case management (Oldham et al., 2012). Many of these strategies are consistent with the approach and interventions we discuss in this chapter.

ORIENTATION AS A PREVENTIVE STRATEGY

Drawing from research described earlier, we begin by discussing the application of orienting strategies to therapy attendance. From the first contact with a potential treatment provider or her/his staff members, clients are exposed to both formal and informal orientation. In many clinics, clients first call the receptionist to inquire about services, and she or he provides information on fees, session cancellation policies, types of treatment available, available clinicians, appointment times, and procedures for initial assessments. Orientation to these types of details can provide clients with enough information to make an informed decision about whether to schedule a first session and what to expect about their experience in the clinic.

Where possible, it can be helpful in the orientation phase to provide flexibility and choices (Oldham et al., 2012). Accordingly, where possible, it can be helpful to provide clients with the opportunity to express preferences regarding the type (e.g., master's level, student, counselor, psychologist), gender, or schedule of their potential clinician. We recognize that choice may not always be possible in many treatment settings, but therapists might consider ways to provide some degree of freedom and choice regarding the specifics of therapy (e.g., appointment times, start dates, the opportunity to have a brief informational interview session prior to formal assessment or treatment).

Aside from administrative orientation and the provision of choice, another important aspect of orientation in this area is psychoeducation regarding the importance of session attendance. For clients who respond well to research data, psychoeducation might involve a snapshot of what we know from the psychotherapy research. Generally, the research on session frequency and attendance in psychotherapy has suggested that outcomes tend to follow a pattern of diminishing returns over time across many forms of therapy (Harnett, O'Donovan, & Lambert, 2010; Howard, Moras, Brill, Martinovich, & Lutz, 1996; Stulz, Lutz, Leach, Lucock, & Barkham, 2007). In DBT, some evidence has suggested that clients make the most significant treatment gains in the first 6 months (Linehan et al., 2006; McMain et al., 2009). Nearly all of the randomized trials on DBT, for example, have focused on weekly outpatient individual therapy sessions (1 hour) as well as weekly group skills training (approximately 2 hours; Stoffers et al., 2012). Therapists can, therefore, emphasize that regular, consistent therapy attendance starting from the very beginning is likely to produce benefits in a quicker and more efficient manner than if the client sporadically comes to treatment. In addition, we recommend presenting this information in a way that resonates with the client (e.g., avoiding jargon) and frames regular therapy attendance as an important step in achieving important goals.

A strong therapeutic alliance can facilitate session attendance, particularly at the beginning of treatment. If the client is avoiding therapy because of problems in the therapeutic relationship, the client's "solution" may become the problem, particularly at the beginning of therapy. Some research, for example, has suggested that the therapeutic alliance is particularly important for therapeutic change in the first few sessions. Moreover, there is evidence for a negative association of therapeutic alliance and session-by-session outcome as measured by regular symptom assessment (Kolden et al., 2006). It is quite possible that, initially, during what some refer to as the "remoralization" phase of therapy (Howard et al., 1996), a strong therapeutic bond can boost therapy effects and allow for deeper discussions of more painful and emotionally evocative issues in subsequent sessions. Previously avoided emotions or thoughts are now at the forefront, particularly in the context of a strong therapeutic alliance. Clients who attend sporadically from the very beginning miss the opportunity to develop a strong therapeutic alliance and experience the types of initial improvements that can fuel continued attendance. Difficulties in attendance or a poor therapist–client match can stifle the development of a relationship in which it is safe to face difficult problems. Early in therapy, some of the options for addressing this problem may be to (a) discuss and assess the client's concerns about therapeutic fit; (b) identify factors that both the therapist and client may need to work on, accept, or change; and (c) provide options for and consider referral or transfer to another therapist.

HIGHLIGHTING AND ASSESSING ATTENDANCE PROBLEMS

The strategies presented here in regard to therapy attendance follow the same steps and procedures outlined in Chapter 3. Throughout therapy, when clients are absent or late for therapy, the therapist must first recognize and define these events as instances of TIB. Common strategies to target therapy attendance include highlighting the problem and understanding its essence. In this section, we focus on strategies the therapist can use to recognize and define attendance problems as TIB, highlight and assess problems, and consider how a dialectical framework can help to balance strategies and therapeutic style.

Defining the Behavior as Therapy-Interfering

As discussed in Chapter 3, highlighting is often among the first sets of strategies the therapist might use to target any TIB. Before highlighting the problem, however, the therapist must first define the behavior as therapy-interfering. Recall that we are defining TIB by its effects on the therapy or therapeutic relationship, not on the basis of reasons for or causes of the TIB. Therefore, in terms of how we define TIB, it does not matter why a client missed therapy. In terms of how we address TIB, however, the causes and reasons might matter tremendously.

Let us say that Barbara, who struggles with drug and alcohol problems, has missed three sessions over a 6-week period. The first time, she was hungover, her alarm went off, and she went back to sleep and missed her session. The next week, she stopped off at her drug dealer's place on the way to therapy, got high, and forgot about her session. The following week, Barbara could not find child care for her daughter and called to cancel at the last minute.

In which of these situations would Barbara's behavior be considered TIB? Most people would probably agree that the first two alcohol- or drug-related scenarios constitute TIB. But what about the third one? If we define TIB by the reasons for or causes of the behavior, we might be less inclined to call the third scenario TIB; Barbara clearly tried to find child care and was unable to arrange it. So why would we expect her to come to therapy? However, if we define her absence in the third scenario by its effect on her ability to benefit from therapy, this is also an instance of TIB. If the therapist were to ignore the third scenario and avoid addressing it, how are we to know that Barbara would not continue to encounter these child care problems? Moreover, perhaps this is a broader problem that impedes work or social functioning, and she would benefit from some help with this.

The principle we are outlining here is to prioritize, target, and discuss TIB regardless of its presumed cause. This is not to say that the therapist would use the exact same words or approach across these three situations. If a client missed therapy because her mother passed away, the therapist may take a different approach than if she missed it because of a hangover.

Highlighting and Discussing the Problem

One of the most common errors we have observed among junior and experienced clinicians alike is inconsistency in bringing up therapy lateness or attendance. The client shows up after missing three sessions in a row, and the therapist proceeds with the session without mentioning it, or perhaps the client shows up 30 minutes late, and the therapist extends the session by 30 minutes. Or perhaps the client has had a pattern of sporadic attendance for weeks, and the therapist has yet to discuss how and why this is a problem. When a client is late or does not attend, and the therapist fails to highlight or discuss this, the therapist is not conveying the importance of session attendance. In addition, the therapist and client miss out on opportunities to discuss and solve problems with lateness or attendance.

One exception to this general rule is when discussions of attendance, lateness, or desires to quit become operantly maintained. For example, such discussions may function to avoid difficult or challenging interventions, such as exposure therapy or confronting, facing, or discussing problems about which the individual feels ashamed. In these cases, the therapist may engage in more minimal highlighting, quickly help the client solve the problem in order to prevent its occurrence in the future, and then discuss avoided topics.

Another important principle to remember here is the dialectical balancing of styles and strategies. As discussed in Chapter 2, in terms of styles, the therapist seeks an effective balance of irreverence versus reciprocity. In an example of *irreverence*, one of our clients once explained that she had missed a recent group session because she was afraid of being in groups. The therapist replied, "Hmm, do you think you'll become less afraid of groups if you don't show up?" Recently, another client said that she and her friend were considering signing up for an online weight and exercise program, but she was not sure she would do it, because she did not think it would work as well online as in person. The therapist stated, "The only thing we know for sure is that the program won't work if you don't do it." The same could be said for therapy. Sometimes irreverence involves stating the blunt facts of the matter. For a client who did not attend therapy because she was not sure it would work, a therapist might say, "We don't know if it will work if you do show up, but we know that it won't work if you don't show up."

Reciprocal highlighting often is preceded by validating, understanding statements; it involves less confrontation, is more warm and supportive, and may be more consistent with normative expectations regarding therapist behavior. In the previous scenario regarding group, the therapist might say,

> I know it's extremely hard to get yourself to go to group when you're so scared about how it might be. Of course, I also think that group is a critically important part of your therapy. Let's talk more about this.

There is a time to be irreverent and a time to be reciprocal, and the therapist's job is to explore when and how it may be effective to use these different styles. The following are some examples of how a therapist might make therapy attendance a priority and highlight the problem with sensitivity to different client situations. Some of these examples blend irreverence, validation, and reciprocity, whereas others stand more on one side (reciprocal, as with the first two examples) than the other (irreverent, as with the last three).

> "I notice that you have missed the last few sessions in a row, and I'm getting concerned that you're really missing out on the therapy that you need. I also know that the last two times had to do with alcohol. We've got to get a handle on this, as I know alcohol-related stuff has gotten in the way of work as well. If we can stop it from getting in the way of therapy, maybe we can help you with work and other areas, too. So, I think it's really important that we spend some time talking about what happened last week."

> "I was so sorry to hear that your mother has been ill, and I totally understand why you had to miss our meeting last week. I know from my own experience that when a loved one is seriously ill, your life can really be turned on its head, and I imagine you're dealing with a ton of worry, anxiety, and sadness. Let's figure out how you can make sure you get the support you need during this time. We might also need to put our heads together to find a way that you don't miss out on therapy in the midst of all this. This may be the time when you need it most!"

> "I know you've been doing really well these days, getting out more and seeing friends, and I understand you were out for dinner when you missed our session last week. Here's the thing—while I think it's so fabulous that you're getting a lot of momentum and not letting your anxiety stop you from seeing people, I also think we have some important work to do. I feel the urge to let it go, because ironically, your progress is getting in the way of your attendance! But, I also know that you still have a lot of goals to work on, and we won't be able to work on them together if you're not here."

"I missed you last week during our regular session. I was sitting here noticing that I really can't do much to help you when you're not here. It's sort of like trying to teach swimming lessons to someone who won't jump in the water."

"I notice that you're about 20 minutes late, so we're really going to have to work hard over the next 30 minutes. Let's start by figuring out how you ended up being late this week. You know, I must say that it's very hard to do therapy with a client who isn't here. What happened last week?"

Assessing and Understanding the Essence of the Problem

When it comes to attendance and lateness, as with other TIBs that make therapy impossible to proceed, it is important to consistently assess the key factors contributing to the problem. As discussed in Chapter 3, one helpful assessment strategy is *functional analysis*. Although a functional analysis does not have to occur following every instance of lateness or therapy absence, it is important to set the norm that these problems will be examined in detail, particularly in the beginning of treatment. It is often clinically wiser to begin "tight" (consistently conducting functional analyses and targeting problems with session attendance) and then to "loosen up" if needed (after several functional analyses, the problem is clear, and the therapist no longer does them each time the client is late), rather than the other way around. Therefore, we might generally conduct functional analyses consistently for a period, and then if the same patterns seem to emerge (e.g., "OK, this sounds like another one of those times when you were exhausted and sad and thought it was hopeless to come in, and it was easier [i.e., more reinforcing] to stay home than to go against your hopeless thinking. Is that right?"), jump more quickly into problem solving. The following example shows the level of detail and information a therapist might aim to gather in a functional analysis for a client in individual therapy who has missed sessions.

Stephen's alarm went off at 6 a.m. following a broken sleep. The night before, he had gone against his commitment to himself and drank a bottle and a half of wine, had a poor sleep (woke up several times), and shortly after he woke up, he felt ashamed and disappointed in himself and began to think that he could not seem to control his drinking. He thought, "I'm just back to square one again. There's really no point in trying. I don't know why I keep letting this happen!" He turned off his alarm, put his head under the covers, and stayed in bed until noon. When he got up, he felt tired, agitated, and anxious and was afraid of going to therapy and discussing his perceived "failure." He had lunch and then surfed the Internet for a couple of hours. Initially, when he began on the computer, he did not feel as disappointed or ashamed and had stopped ruminating. Eventually, the thoughts and feelings began to creep in again, along with strong thoughts of hopelessness ("There's no point in trying to quit over and over again. It's useless"). He then began to find websites that include wine ratings and varieties. He felt interested and excited while perusing these sites, had memories of wines he had tried in the past, and soon began to have the urge to drink. Stephen tried several times to do some other activity and even thought of some of his DBT distress tolerance skills. He went out for a drive, but he just happened to drive on the road that goes past his local wine store. He thought, "I shouldn't be doing this. Go home now, get ready, and go to see Dr. Smith." He thought of the pros and cons of drinking and of missing his session, but he had a hard time coming up with many cons for either. He also felt strong urges to drink (4/5), felt excited, and was beginning to plan his afternoon of wine. He ended up buying two bottles of red wine, went home, and over the next couple of hours drank them both. Stephen had a brief thought that he was missing his session but quickly focused on the movie he was watching. His urges to drink then decreased to near zero, and he stopped thinking about how things were hopeless or that he was a failure. An hour or so after he finished the wine, he called his therapist and left a message in a slurred voice that he was not going to be able to come in at that time or probably ever.

One of the major advantages of a functional analysis is that when the therapist and client collect this level of detail, several hypotheses emerge regarding the factors influencing the client's TIB. It is helpful to frame these hypotheses in terms of behavioral principles, focusing on antecedents, behaviors, and consequences, as well as the client's emotional responses and thinking patterns. In Stephen's case, for example, one hypothesis is that the essence of the problem contributing to him not going to therapy (and statements about quitting) concerns shame and hopelessness. Stephen felt demoralized and had hopeless thinking following his previous night's drinking, as well as thoughts consistent with the *abstinence violation effect* (Marlatt & Gordon, 1985), whereby he believed he had "ruined" his abstinence and, therefore, there was no point in trying to get back on track. His response to the hopeless thoughts and shame was to avoid them (staying in bed, going on the Internet), resulting in possible negative reinforcement in the form of reductions in negative emotions and thoughts and possibly avoidance of activities that might remind him of his therapy session (about which he felt anxious). His Internet browsing of wine sites resulted in possible positive reinforcement in the form of excitement and interest and negative reinforcement in terms of further avoidance of hopelessness, anxiety, and shame. These all are hypotheses, and for the consequences to constitute positive or negative reinforcement, there would have to be evidence of an effect on the client's behavior over time.

In a dialectical fashion, although assessment is geared toward highlighting avenues for change, precise assessment of the essence of the problems contributing to TIB also facilitates acceptance and validation. In the case of Stephen, the essence of the problems appeared to be (a) strong shame reactions to perceived failures and (b) the fact that hopeless thoughts were functioning to shut down his behavior and help him avoid taking the steps to help himself. The shame and derogatory thoughts about failure may also serve a similar function in that if he thinks of himself as a failure, it may be easier to jettison (at least temporarily) his goal of abstinence. Further assessment would seek to clarify this. The therapist's task is to use assessment to understand the essence of the problem and then to validate the valid and avoid validating the invalid. The therapist in this situation could validate many aspects of Stephen's experiences, including how painful it is to experience such strong shame, how demoralizing it can be when he has been working so hard on his recovery to end up lapsing anyway, and how difficult it might be to come in and "face the music," so to speak, by talking about his lapse. The therapist also might convey an understanding that it is much easier to stay home than to come in and work on his drinking problem. Notice that the therapist would not validate the thoughts of failure, normalize the experience of shame in reaction to the lapse (because shame would not be justified; he would not be rejected by his therapist just because of a lapse, and lapses are a normal part of recovery), or convey that his strategy of perusing wine sites was wise.

> *Therapist:* OK, so I think we're getting to the crux of the problem here, don't you?
>
> *Client:* Yeah, I think so. I don't know, I just can't seem to stay off the wine. I've done everything else, the marijuana, the hard liquor, but I don't know if I'll ever be able to stop with the wine.
>
> *Therapist:* It's true, we don't know that, and the uncertainty is hard to take sometimes. We do know that you've made progress with tremendously hard things, like the drugs and the hard liquor. I don't have any reason to think that you can't keep marching forward in your recovery. One thing I know for absolute certain, however, is that, if you don't come in, I can't help you with the drinking.
>
> *Client:* Yeah, I guess that's true.
>
> *Therapist:* So, here's the thing. I get how hard and painful it must have been to feel so ashamed of yourself. Shame is a very difficult emotion to feel, and when you're ashamed, the natural tendency is to hunker down, hide, avoid people, and think a lot of negative things about yourself. I'm sure that was totally miserable.

Client: It really was. I mean it still sort of is. I still feel it now but not as bad.

Therapist: Well, we're going to work on that, because I think you'd be better off without the shame. For one thing, it's part of the whole cycle that gets you back into drinking and avoiding therapy. For another thing, a more effective emotion there would be a little disappointment, maybe. What do you think?

Client: I thought that before about the drinking but not the therapy. I guess that makes sense. I really didn't want to have to come in and talk about it.

Therapist: OK, who says you'd have to come in and talk about it? Maybe we would have talked about it, but were you thinking it was going to be a big thing, or I'd be disappointed in you or something? You know how I feel about lapses, right?

Client: You've told me, I know. A lapse is a bump in the road, but I'm still on the road. It's happened before, and it wasn't such a big thing. We just came up with a plan for next time, and it wasn't as bad as I thought it would be.

Therapist: Exactly, so we've got to get your brain to learn that the shame is not justified, and the only way to do that is for you to come in and learn it through your experience. But I also wonder whether you sort of knew that, but maybe let the shame shut you down anyway? Not on purpose, mind you—more like your brain was going to steer you to that wine store no matter what?

Client: Maybe. I mean I really do know that there's no good reason to feel ashamed or embarrassed, and our sessions really do help.

Therapist: Shame and hopeless thinking sometimes serve a similar purpose. You probably wouldn't have them if they didn't serve some purpose. And that purpose can be to make it easier to stop trying, stop taking risks, stop working, and to go with what you feel like doing. Depressed people experience this a lot: It's really hard to get out of bed already, they're tired, sad, can't think clearly, and then they have hopeless thoughts, like it's not worth getting out of bed or there's no point. Then they turn over and go back to sleep. The hopeless thoughts and the shame can help you in this way, but only in the short term.

Client: That makes sense. I know it's not on purpose, but I guess I do sort of shut down. I feel deflated and not like doing anything, and so I just give up. Maybe it is a bit easier to give up.

> *Therapist:* Of course it is! It's a lot easier. You're doing really hard work here. So, we've got to find ways to get you to stop listening to shame and hopeless thoughts and to do the opposite of shutting down.

In group settings, where it is critical to establish firm norms for group behavior, attendance, lateness, and homework compliance, consistent functional analyses can help to convey the importance of such norms and assist clients in staying on track. If the therapist does not address the behavior, members of the group might either become resentful or start going astray themselves. The therapist attending to these problems in group also provides an opportunity for other group members to reflect on and bring up instances of these issues in their own lives. When a client is having problems with lateness, missed homework, or attendance, we often ask other clients whether they have had similar challenges and how they might have solved or worked on these problems. We have observed that this strategy minimizes shame and embarrassment and can prompt other group members to provide support, validation, encouragement, and help to one another with problem solving. Excessive time spent managing TIB in group, however, can result in the rest of the group losing interest, becoming frustrated, or believing (sometimes correctly) it is a waste of time. Therefore, in groups, we recommend that therapists consistently highlight these behaviors but keep the functional analyses brief and efficient and quickly have the client commit to some new behavior over the next week (e.g., setting an alarm and putting it across the room so she or he cannot easily turn it off).

STRATEGIES TO SOLVE ATTENDANCE PROBLEMS

Once the problem is clarified, the therapist and client can work to solve it collaboratively, with an eye toward finding ways to balance problem solving and validation (as discussed in Chapters 2 and 3). Among the first sets of strategies to emphasize is the effective management of therapeutic contingencies regarding lateness and absences. Having appropriate contingencies in place or, at minimum, monitoring and keeping contingencies in mind can help to set an effective therapeutic frame supporting attendance. Following a clear assessment, the therapist also may target the primary factors impeding attendance, such as motivation and commitment, fears or overwhelming emotions, and skill deficits, among other potential factors. Regardless of the strategies used, troubleshooting to prevent further attendance problems can be an essential final step. We further elaborate on these strategies next.

Establishing and Maintaining Useful Contingencies

One set of strategies in DBT, behavior therapy, and cognitive behavior therapy (CBT) more generally to enhance attendance and client retention, involves *contingency management*. The primary aim of contingency management is to find a way to provide differential reinforcement of behaviors that enhance therapy attendance. Other behaviors that detract from therapy attendance may be reduced through extinction and possibly aversive contingencies (although see the later discussion, cautions, and suggestions about the use of aversive procedures). Contingency management sometimes involves direct-acting contingencies (Farmer & Chapman, 2008, 2016) or consequences following desired or undesired behavior, the specification and putting into place of certain "rules" to promote therapy persistence and attendance, or the therapist clarifying contingencies related to session attendance. Contingency management also might involve modifying consequences for session attendance, having the client use her or his own contingency management, such as stimulus control (e.g., reminders), or other such strategies.

Clarifying Contingencies

Clarifying and bringing contingencies to the client's awareness will help her or him better understand the effects and consequences associated with therapy attendance. The therapist might, for example, remind the client of the positive, longer term consequences of session attendance, linking attendance to goals that are important to the client. The following is an example of how a therapist might clarify contingencies with a client who struggles with debilitating anxiety about group therapy sessions:

> I know it is tremendously hard for you to get yourself here. It's a long commute, you feel anxiety and dread about seeing the other clients in the group, and you sometimes leave exhausted. The thing is that these negatives are short-term. In the long run, if you really learn these emotion regulation skills that we're teaching in group, you will be better able to accept and understand your emotions. I'm confident that you'll start to feel a lot more able to cope with overwhelming stress. You will also be able to manage your anxiety better, so that you can start to build relationships, and I know that's one of your most important goals.

As shown in this example, it can be helpful to highlight and validate the fact that there are sometimes negative shorter term consequences to therapy attendance. This point often resonates with clients' direct experiences: Coming to therapy may be like climbing a mountain every week. The short-term consequences, including physical exertion, burning legs, pain, and so forth, can be powerful. It can be easy to allow the dread of the climb to dictate one's behavior. Therefore, when highlighting contingencies, it is important to show how those repeated trips up the mountain will eventually get the client to where she or he wants to go. A quote by Suzuki (1970) regarding the practice of mindfulness captures this point quite well:

> Even though you try very hard, the progress you make is always little by little. It is not like going out in a shower in which you know when you get wet. In a fog, you do not know you are getting wet, but as you keep walking, you get wet little by little. If your mind has ideas of progress, you may say, "Oh, this pace is terrible!" But, actually, it is not. When you get wet in a fog, it is very difficult to dry yourself. So there is no need to worry about progress. It is like studying a foreign language; you cannot do it all of a sudden, but by repeating it over and over you will master it. (p. 46)

If there are shorter term positive consequences to attending therapy, the therapist might clarify those as well. For example, the client might find 1 hour per week to be an important time to focus on her- or himself, to be able to talk about things that she or he does not bring up with other people, to feel understood, or to feel like progress is being made. Clients might sometimes forget that they leave therapy sessions feeling much better than when they came in. We often hear this from our group clients in particular, who have often said, "I really didn't want to come in today, but I'm so glad I did. I feel so much better and less anxious than I did when I came in, and I really got a lot out of today." Sometimes it can be empowering for clients to remember that each session is one more step on the road to recovery or that by coming to therapy they are taking good care of themselves. When clients lose sight of these consequences, the therapist can help clarify and bring them back to the forefront.

Clearly Specifying Behaviors to Increase and Decrease

Contingency management works best when the therapist specifies which behavior is being reinforced or, in rarer cases, punished—the behaviors to increase and decrease (as discussed in Chapter 3). When it comes to session attendance, the behaviors to increase would include the client attending all scheduled therapy sessions, or some proportion thereof (e.g., 75%)—ideally arriving on time. Other behaviors to increase might include the client scheduling the session in a calendar, leaving home on time, regulating emotions interfering with attendance (e.g., anxiety), and so forth. The behaviors to decrease would include actions that do not support attendance, such as other activities scheduled during therapy sessions, remaining in bed all day, turning off the alarm, leaving too late to arrive on time, making mood-dependent decisions not to attend therapy, and so on. The therapist's first challenge is to clearly specify the behaviors to increase and decrease and then to be alert to their occurrence so that differential reinforcement may be applied for those behaviors to be increased and extinction or aversive consequences used for the behaviors to be decreased. We strongly recommend that therapists engage clients as active participants while specifying behaviors to be increased and decreased. If the client is aware of behaviors to be increased, in particular, as well as the consequences of these, she or he is more likely to make positive behavioral changes.

Consequences for Lateness or Absence

One way to manage contingencies is to apply consistent consequences for nonattendance or lateness. For example, when clients show up late, they have access to the remaining session time, but the therapist will not extend the session. If a client shows up 30 minutes late for a 50-minute session, she or he will have a 20-minute session. Although this consequence sounds like punishment (specifically, *negative punishment*, whereby something is withdrawn in an effort to reduce behavior), we believe this strategy is best considered an example of differential reinforcement (see Farmer & Chapman, 2008, 2016) of incompatible behavior. Arriving on time is incompatible with being late, and the client receives a full 50-minute session contingent on her or his on-time arrival. For clients who are paying a full rate for each session, another consequence is that they may end up paying for a full session and only receiving a smaller portion thereof. If the client, however, is motivated to avoid therapy, the withdrawal of the normal amount of session time may negatively reinforce lateness. We encourage therapists to attend to these details and monitor the effect of their contingencies on client behavior. One of our students, for example, was seeing a client who arrived late for every session (and had been doing so for 5 years previously with other therapists in the same clinic). For a few months, the student consistently conducted a functional analysis whenever this occurred and maintained the contingency of allowing only the remaining session time, but the client's behavior did not change. This case raises a few possible hypotheses:

- The withdrawal of session time negatively reinforces lateness.
- The client may lack the self-organization or management skills to arrive on time for appointments; thus, contingencies will not make a difference until the client has such skills.
- There may be contingencies for lateness that overpower the withdrawal of session time. Discussions of lateness, functional analyses, and so forth, may be positively (e.g., through focused attention and concern from the therapist) or negatively (e.g., through avoidance of discussions of other topics) reinforcing.

Once these hypotheses are identified, the therapist might conduct experiments to determine what is happening. One approach would be to provide the same amount of session time regardless of when the client arrives, to eliminate or reduce discussions of lateness, and/or to provide skills training to enhance self-management. It is important to monitor the effects of these alternative strategies on lateness, to do this collaboratively with the client, and to help enhance the client's awareness of these possible contingencies.

Another consistent consequence of lateness or absence might be a functional analysis focused on better understanding the client's difficulty with consistent and timely attendance. Clients often do not come to therapy with therapy attendance or decreasing tardiness as their main treatment goals. If a functional analysis is a consistent consequence of lateness or absence, the client has more session time to discuss desired topics (e.g., relationships, mental health problems) when she or he arrives on time or is attending consistently. As such, the consistent use of a functional analysis will not only help illuminate the factors contributing to problems with attendance but will also serve as contingency management. Specifically, this type of system has elements of both differential reinforcement for alternative behaviors (the client receives more time discussing desired topics when she or he is on time or attending consistently) and negative punishment (withdrawal of session time that could be used to discuss matters that are of higher priority to the client). However, the goal is to increase the reinforcement value of session attendance, rather than to make attendance aversive. One way to get around this possible barrier is to start with a discussion of the TIB and then discuss issues that are important to the client.

As an example of several of these principles in action, one of our students was working with "Jennifer," a client who traveled for over 3 hours to her therapy session. Her commute involved a half-hour drive, a 2-hour ferry ride, and another 45-minute drive. She met the therapist for individual therapy and then went to another location for her DBT skills group before staying the night at a relative's home and then returning home the next day. Jennifer was strongly devoted to her own recovery and was collaborative, tenacious, and diligent with therapy homework. She had tremendous difficulty, however, with the self-management activities needed to get herself to therapy on time. She frequently forgot the ferry schedule, did not check for traffic updates, left her home an hour too late, or had difficulty getting out of bed in time. As a result, this client frequently showed up 30 to 40 minutes late for her 50-minute session. Many therapists in this situation would go out of their way to provide extra time for the client (e.g., by extending the session time). After all, she was diligently traveling so far to get the help she needed. And this is what the therapist did at the beginning, while also consistently conducting functional analyses on the lateness, identifying and addressing skill deficits in self-management, and using shaping principles to improve the client's skills.

After several sessions, however, the behavior did not change, and even when Jennifer had put all of her new self-management tools into place, she still arrived late. Even when she did take the correct ferry and arrived in the city on time, she often visited friends, only to find that she had left it too late to get to therapy on time. The ferry schedule was such that had she left immediately for her session, she would have arrived an hour or two early. This was part of the problem. The immediate reinforcement of time spent with her friends was much more powerful than were the consequences for arriving early to therapy. When she arrived early, she was stuck in an unfamiliar city and had no idea how to spend her time while awaiting her session. Moreover, when she arrived late, she still received the same amount of therapy, and the only consequence was that she and the therapist would spend a portion of the session on the functional analysis. From this analysis, it became clear that time spent discussing lateness functioned to allow the client to avoid discussing more distressing issues, such as a tumultuous and abusive relationship with her partner.

Clearly, the therapeutic dyad had to change these contingencies. The first step was to rearrange the schedule of sessions so that the client could not receive the same amount of therapy if she arrived late. The sessions were scheduled for later in the afternoon, giving Jennifer enough time to get to her group session, but only if therapy ended on time. Jennifer also took a later ferry, whereby she had time to get to the office with less of a wait for her appointment, and she and the therapist worked together to find options for activities during that hour, such as activities that she enjoyed, as well as ones that she may not have enjoyed (e.g., her therapy homework). At first, Jennifer continued to arrive late, often receiving about a 20-minute session. The therapy discussions focused on topics that she had been avoiding, rather than continued functional analyses on lateness. Over several weeks, Jennifer began to arrive closer to being on time, and eventually, she was consistently early for her sessions. After Jennifer graduated from her skills group, had extricated herself from the abusive relationship, got a job that she enjoyed, and began to make important progress in several other areas, she decided that the regular commute was too much. Treatment faded to regular phone sessions and to helping Jennifer to connect with resources in her community. A couple of years later, the supervisor heard that Jennifer had taken a lead role in advocacy and peer support for people with mental health difficulties similar to hers.

Avoid Overusing or Emphasizing Aversive Contingencies

One common problem in the use of contingency management for attendance is the overuse of aversive contingencies, punishment, or response cost procedures. We often consult with other providers about their DBT programs, and these programs sometimes adopt rules involving punishment for lack of session attendance, without regard to the individual situation and experiences of each client. An example might be that clients missing a group session must complete a functional analysis worksheet and meet with the individual therapist before they can return to group. One problem with this arrangement is that the client, who already has trouble getting her- or himself to group, must often miss further groups while waiting to meet with the individual therapist. For clients who find group stressful, the more immediate and powerful reinforcers for lack of follow-through with these procedures (e.g., avoiding work, stress or shame related to lack of attendance, avoiding group) are likely much more powerful than the presumed positive reinforcer of their returning to group.

It can be problematic for many reasons to bring session attendance primarily under aversive control. The therapist must ask her- or himself what behavior is actually being punished. When a client misses a session and then loses something (e.g., negative punishment) or receives a negative consequence (positive punishment), is that punishment directly affecting the behavior of missing sessions? Possibly not, for a few reasons. First, missing sessions is an absence of behavior, not the presence of an undesired behavior. Behavior that supports session attendance (e.g., effective self-management and organization, use of skills such as opposite action or distress tolerance) must be increased, and punishment does not increase behavior, it only suppresses or reduces behavior. Second, if a client missed therapy the previous week and the negative consequence for that behavior does not occur until the following session, the punishment may be too delayed to have an effect on session attendance. Indeed, in the worst-case scenario, the punishment might reduce the future likelihood of attendance or result in the client's avoidance of sessions (to avoid the negative consequence) following an absence the previous week.

Rather than formally instituting aversive consequences, we recommend that therapists consistently highlight and discuss the client's problems with attendance. Simply confronting a client regarding a problem behavior can serve as an aversive consequence (Linehan, 1993a), which when combined with collaborative problem solving and support, can help to reduce the likelihood of attendance problems. The focus of contingency management ideally is on ways to make attendance (and attendance on time) reinforcing and on collaborating with the client on ways to increase behaviors that support attendance and timeliness.

Commitment Strategies

If the client is having difficulty with motivation to attend therapy, the therapist might use commitment and motivational enhancement strategies to highlight and amplify ambivalence, help enhance the client's awareness of important reasons to attend therapy, and elicit change-oriented talk and action. Many strategies can be helpful here, such as guiding the client to think through the pros and cons of attending therapy versus avoiding therapy, discussing the benefits of therapy and linking attendance to goals that are important to the client (i.e., "selling commitment"; Linehan, 1993a), reminding the client of her or his previous strong commitment to therapy, and so on. Another strategy, in Stephen's case, discussed earlier, might be the *devil's advocate strategy*, in which the therapist argues for the opposite behavior (against commitment to behavior change or against therapy attendance) by saying the following, for example:

> If I were in your shoes, it would be a lot easier to stay home, drink, and avoid therapy. You feel a lot better, at least in the short run, when you don't have to deal with the discomfort, shame, or embarrassment of coming in after you have slipped up. We're also doing some pretty hard and upsetting work these days and facing problems you've generally avoided. So, I'd be wondering what on earth is in it for me to keep coming in.

Often, the devil's advocate strategy elicits change-oriented talk (i.e., statements opposing the argument put forth by the therapist) on the part of the client (e.g., "Well, I know it's easier in the short run, but I had important reasons to come to therapy in the first place, and I know it will help me long term"). This, however, is not always the case. The client might actually agree with the therapist. It is fine if this happens. In these cases, the therapist should remember the dialectical principle of allowing natural change and also let go of attachment to a particular strategy or outcome. Once the therapist remembers this, she or he is freed up to move with the client, to try other strategies, or to go even further with the strategy she or he is already trying (e.g., devil's advocate), such as by saying, "Right, well, you could just dive right back into living life the way you did before, drinking most of the day and avoiding all of this work and discomfort." Another alternative is for the therapist to switch strategies to the pros and cons approach by saying, "Well, it's true—why don't we talk more about some of the pros and cons of staying the same." Alternatively, the strategy of *freedom to choose, and absence of alternatives* can be helpful here, whereby the therapist states that the client is free to choose to avoid working on reducing the drinking, but if she or he wants to have a better life and reach important goals, there is really no alternative but to work on the drinking.

Exposure and Opposite Action

When the client's emotions interfere with attendance, the therapist might address this through exposure or opposite-action (Linehan, 1993b) strategies. If shame drives attendance problems, the therapist might help the client learn to first identify and experience shame and then to determine what to do about it. Stephen, for example, may need to learn how to tolerate and experience shame without acting on it, which is much like what we ask people to do in the course of exposure therapy. Other strategies include opposite action for shame (see Rizvi & Linehan, 2005). In this case, the therapist would help the client first determine whether shame is justified or unjustified. Shame is justified when the client will be rejected if her or his behavior was to become public, and in this case, the therapist is not going to reject Stephen. When emotions such as shame are unjustified, the next step is to determine what the emotion makes the person feel like doing (the "action urge" associated with the emotion; Linehan, 1993b) and then for the client to do the opposite. In the case of Stephen, the action urge may be to avoid therapy, avoid discussing his drinking, stay home, look down and avoid eye contact, and essentially hide (hiding being a common action associated with shame; Lewis, 2010). The opposite action might be to come to therapy, sit up straight, make eye contact, and directly state to the therapist that he had a lapse in his drinking. The idea is that, over time, as the client learns that the dreaded event (humiliation, embarrassment, rejection) does not occur, the shame may decrease.

Many clients are afraid of attending group therapy sessions. In these cases, it can be helpful for the individual therapist to work with the client on such fear for a period before the client begins group. The therapist might, for example, assess the factors contributing to the fear, try to understand the threatening event(s) of which the client is afraid, and guide the client through exercises akin to exposure therapy or opposite action. One of our clients was afraid of attending group, and her fear was that she would say something strange or be inarticulate and that others would look at her with contempt or that she would be criticized or humiliated. The therapist guided her through a few imaginal exposure scenarios, starting with her simply attending group and everything going well. They increased the intensity of the fear-eliciting stimuli over time by the client imagining some people looking away or appearing confused when she was speaking and eventually getting to the point at which the client was imagining saying odd things or fumbling over her words and seeing negative reactions by others in the room. Although these feared events may never actually have happened, the client learned that she could survive group even if they were to happen. In vivo exposure also involved the client going into the room where group was held and doing a mock group with a couple of therapists. After a few sessions, the client's anxiety about group had diminished but was still significant; the main differences were her increased willingness to tolerate the anxiety and her commitment to attending group.

Improving Skills to Enhance Attendance

Other solutions to attendance problems might involve the building of skills, beginning with a consideration of which types of tasks or skills the client may need to attend therapy. For example, the client may have to be able to remember appointments, organize her or his time effectively, know how to use public transit, manage anxiety or distress related to therapy, or develop cognitive or emotion regulation skills to overcome barriers to treatment. Therapists might help clients who lack organizational skills and have difficulty with self-management by teaching practical strategies to increase organization and consistency. Some examples of these might be the client learning to set alarms on her or his smartphone, establishing a regular daily routine or rhythm, temporarily enlisting help in the form of reminders from a friend or loved one, using a calendar and organizing appointments in advance, and so on. Often, these organizational deficits are not specific to therapy, and changes in this domain may help improve the client's social and occupational functioning elsewhere as well. If a client feels anxious about attending therapy, the therapist may emphasize anxiety management strategies, such as diaphragmatic breathing or progressive muscle relaxation, or strategies to counter worrying thoughts as a way to facilitate therapy attendance (the use of exposure interventions to address these issues is discussed further next).

Solving Problems and Removing Barriers to Attendance

Other practical matters, such as finances, commuting, workload, and other factors, also can often interfere with therapy. When this is the case, the therapist and client may use standard problem-solving strategies, outlined in Chapter 3 (Linehan, 2015; Nezu, Maguth Nezu, & D'Zurilla, 2013). Some solutions may include referral to a less expensive provider, temporarily discontinuing therapy until the client's life allows for more room and time for treatment (although this would usually be a last resort), discussing strategies for the client to use to fit therapy into a busy life, or changing the mode (e.g., telephone, Skype) of treatment provision for clients for whom commuting is an issue. Generally, solutions that encourage the client to continue to attend treatment while solving these other problems or reducing their impact are most favorable.

One issue that sometimes arises in our discussions is whether to reduce session frequency for clients who have difficulty affording therapy. Sometimes this problem can be solved by helping the client learn to better manage finances, determining how the client might attain money for treatment, and so forth. At other times the problem is not that the client is unable to afford therapy but that he or she is using money that could be used for therapy for other things.

One of our clients, for example, was moderately suicidal, had serious difficulties with emotion regulation and interpersonal chaos, and periodically self-harmed and used drugs. We were concerned that she would not benefit fully from treatment if she remained only in individual therapy, but she said that she could not afford group treatment on top of individual therapy. The wait lists in town for publicly funded group DBT skills training were over 12 months, so this was not an ideal option. The therapist asked the client how much she was spending on drugs each week, and it turned out that she was spending twice the amount that it would cost for her to attend group, in part because she was buying drugs for her boyfriend. Fortunately, she agreed to reserve money for group each week, reduced her spending on drugs, and began attending group.

Sometimes the solution to financial barriers is to change the duration or frequency of sessions. Fortunately, there is some research to guide decision making in this area. Some research on therapy dose and response has shown that more frequent sessions may result in steeper growth curves, representing more rapid improvement (Reese, Toland, & Hopkins, 2011). The findings suggest that it is more effective, for example, for clients to attend eight sessions in 8 weeks versus eight sessions in 16 weeks. In addition, findings have suggested that the frequency of session attendance was associated positively with improvement rates even after controlling for total number of sessions. There has been some research on a model called the *good-enough-level model* (Barkham et al., 1996), which suggested two different trajectories of change: (a) early rapid responders, who improve to a "good enough" level and then discontinue therapy; and (b) later responders, for whom greater session number and frequency predict better outcomes. In addition, generally, improvement in psychotherapy seems to follow a negatively accelerated pattern of change, irrespective of the duration of treatment (Stulz et al., 2007). Therefore, overall, the findings have suggested that, as treatment proceeds, improvements are less rapid and it may be more effective to have a larger number of sessions in a shorter period than a smaller number of sessions spread over a longer period.

As an example of this, a client with severe sleep problems and depression recently said that she determined she could not afford to attend therapy weekly for a full course of treatment and wanted to attend biweekly or every 3 weeks. The therapist informed the client that weekly therapy over a shorter duration, perhaps with more limited goals, may be more effective than longer therapy occurring biweekly. More time-limited goals consistent with short-term therapy were set to (a) get the client a full sleep clinic assessment to determine whether she was appropriate for an evidence-based treatment for insomnia (e.g., CBT–insomnia; Malaffo & Espie, 2007; Perlis, Junquist, Smith, & Posner, 2005), (b) if so, to begin treatment of sleep problems, which is typically brief (4–8 weeks), and (c) to start with six or seven sessions of behavioral activation and activity scheduling for depression.

MOVING FORWARD

We presented in this chapter strategies to enhance therapy attendance that follow the same basic principles, steps, and procedures outlined in Chapters 2 and 3. It is helpful for the therapist to remember key principles such as (a) that directly targeting TIB is consistent with DBT's behavioral approach, (b) that clients want to improve their lives, but many factors can make it difficult to sustain attendance, and (c) that maintaining a dialectical stance will help therapists maintain a commitment to the client's well being, let go and accept difficulties with attendance, and search for understanding and a synthesis of the client's and therapist's perspective when polarization regarding attendance issues occurs. At the beginning of therapy, the focus is on clear orientation and socialization of the client to treatment. Throughout therapy, when clients are absent or late for therapy, the therapist must first recognize these events as instances of TIB. Common strategies to target therapy attendance include highlighting the problem, assessing and understanding the essence of the problem, the effective management of contingencies, problem solving, commitment and motivational strategies, and troubleshooting to prevent future occurrences of lateness or absence.

6

ENHANCING PSYCHOTHERAPY HOMEWORK COMPLIANCE

Now we turn to another common therapy-interfering problem in psychotherapy: clients not completing psychotherapy homework. Homework noncompliance is not specific to any diagnosis. Children and adults struggling with difficulties described in the *Diagnostic and Statistical Manual of Mental Disorders* (5th ed.; American Psychiatric Association, 2013) or receiving any psychotherapy (and, for that matter, pharmacotherapy as well) in any treatment setting (e.g., outpatient, intensive outpatient, inpatient) all can have difficulties being compliant with treatment recommendations. Indeed, noncompliance with psychotherapy homework may be one of the most common therapy-interfering behaviors (TIBs) clinicians encounter. If a group of clinicians were asked to raise their hands if they had a client in the past week who did not do what he or she agreed to do as therapy homework between sessions, many arms would go up. The clinicians would nod and sigh and, finally, tell stories about how hard it is to help clients make important changes in

http://dx.doi.org/10.1037/14752-006
Managing Therapy-Interfering Behavior: Strategies From Dialectical Behavior Therapy, by A. L. Chapman and M. Z. Rosenthal

their lives. As frustrating as it can be when clients do not complete psychotherapy homework, throughout this chapter we normalize and try to make sense of this kind of TIB. And as with other chapters in this book, we outline approaches from dialectical behavior therapy (DBT) that can be used to help with this specific kind of TIB.

We are not interested in leading the reader through a comprehensive journey accounting for all factors underlying psychotherapy homework noncompliance; that trail is long and well-trodden. Indeed, barriers and solutions to homework compliance have been written about extensively in many clinician-friendly books (e.g., Tompkins, 2004). Many of the barriers to homework compliance in psychotherapy are similar across treatment approaches (e.g., client centered, cognitive behavior, eclectic, psychodynamic). For example, in a psychodynamically oriented therapy, clients being asked to notice patterns of emotional reactions to people who remind them of their mother or father may "forget" to do this homework. In a solution-focused therapy, clients being asked to change how they interact with a coworker could return to therapy the next week with reasons why they did not "have a chance" to do this homework. And in cognitive behavioral therapies, clients being asked to complete a thought record or behavioral activities worksheet might "lose" their homework. Clients offer many different explanations for not following through with psychotherapy homework. No matter the reason given, we will address some common barriers to homework completion that we have heard over the years. If you are reading this as a clinician, we think you can be assured that the reasons your clients have TIB related to psychotherapy homework are likely the same ones we see with our clients. Of course, even though the problems may be similar, the solutions clinicians use may not be.

Clinicians can conceptualize homework noncompliance as TIB. Most therapists and clinicians try the usual solutions to helps clients make changes in their lives by doing their psychotherapy homework. Think about what you usually do. Maybe you have tried to make the homework simple at first, use reminders of homework at home and work, be sure the homework is important to the client, be sure they know how to do the homework, and so on. These and other solutions are tried and true. We use them with our clients, whether in DBT or any other cognitive behavior therapy. They certainly can work. In fact, some of the DBT-based solutions we describe are variants of standard ways a clinician generally trained in cognitive behavior therapies might respond to homework noncompliance. However, some of the solutions are arguably unique to DBT. We have done our best to make this worth your time to read, so whenever a more general approach is described at first, we specify how it might be applied uniquely in DBT.

As one example, it is important to select attainable homework assignments that are within the client's values, consistent with immediate goals, understandable, and able to be monitored. These are common considerations many others have discussed in detail to enhance homework completion (for a meta-analysis reviewing studies on this topic, see Kazantzis, Deane, & Ronan, 2000). However, the techniques and strategies in DBT allow therapists from other training backgrounds to handle homework noncompletion from a new angle and with a fresh approach. Importantly, we hope to help therapists find new ways to talk about homework noncompliance in a way that motivates clients to stay in treatment and does not lead to clinicians burning out. We are simply so enthusiastic about how DBT helps this kind of TIB that we hope by the end of this chapter clinicians will see new paths forward managing this common psychotherapy problem.

To understand how we respond to homework noncompliance in DBT it may be instructive to consider what problems we are treating. Because DBT is a treatment for borderline personality disorder (BPD), and BPD occurs in the context of many co-occurring problems, we end up treating a lot of the same problems in DBT that non–DBT therapists treat. Our clients have problems with self-injurious behavior, impulsivity, hostility, and other BPD diagnostic criterion behaviors, but they also are often depressed, anxious, use substances, binge or purge, have complicated and extensive histories of abuse and neglect, and have turbulent relationships with family and friends. They can be homeless, between jobs, and on medical or psychiatric disability. They may or may not take their medications consistently. Their commitment to treatment waxes and wanes, and sometimes, especially for those using substances, they seem to go missing for weeks at a time, not showing up to treatment appointments. In short, this is a difficult-to-treat population.

With so many diverse problems that need to be addressed and with the problems being severe and recurrent, one could take the stance that it is too much to ask these clients to do psychotherapy homework, that psychotherapy homework would just be one more thing for them to do or to feel like a failure at doing in a life replete with chaos and the experience of failure. We could shy away from assigning homework because talking about homework in session takes precious time that we may not have to spare. After all, the standard session lasts only 45 to 50 minutes, and a lot needs to be done in that time. The bottom line is this: When treating multidiagnostic clients, it is tempting to avoid talking about times when clients have not completed psychotherapy homework. Talking about other things may seem not only the easier path but also the one more justified. Just when you are about to talk about when and how to make change outside the therapy session, the client may begin sharing new information, pivoting to new topics that can be unearthed. With new conversational content to mine, homework discussion can wait. The client wants to talk about something other than homework, so is that not what you should do? This can be fool's gold. Although avoiding homework noncompliance may be rationalized by clinicians and clients as the right thing to do in the moment, we believe it may not always be the most helpful thing to do.

COMMON BARRIERS TO HOMEWORK COMPLIANCE

In DBT, we ask a lot from our clients, including homework assignments every week. Like non-DBT clients, those in DBT also can be noncompliant with homework. They do not do their homework, they do their homework, and they do some of their homework. We have seen it all, but because we nonjudgmentally expect noncompliance in our clients, we come to the clinic prepared and confident. Thinking dialectically about homework, therapists both expect imperfection and know that we can move toward increased homework compliance even in the most noncompliant clients. How can you ensure that your clients will be more likely to do the psychotherapy homework? To begin, we quickly summarize some of the main reasons why clients do not do therapy homework. Exhibit 6.1 is not a comprehensive list, but it covers many of the common reasons.

There is no need to belabor these common, fairly straightforward barriers. Strategies and techniques from DBT can help therapists overcome these barriers to increase the probability that (a) clients understand the homework; (b) the homework is aligned with goals that matter to them; (c) they have the skills to complete the homework; (d) they do not let emotions interfere with doing homework; (e) they are intentional about decisions to do homework; (f) they develop attitudes, rules, and beliefs consistent with accomplishing the homework; (g) they remember to do the homework; and (h) they prioritize and structure their environment to complete therapy homework despite competing priorities or constraints. In other words, psychotherapy noncompliance TIBs can be shared across psychotherapies, as can the intended eventual outcomes in overcoming these TIBs.

EXHIBIT 6.1
Common Reasons Clients Do Not Do Therapy Homework

- They do not understand the homework.
- They do not value the homework.
- They do not know how to do the homework.
- Emotions interfere with doing the homework.
- Indecision interferes with doing the homework.
- Attitudes, assumptions, rules, or beliefs interfere with doing the homework.
- They forget to do the homework.
- The environment or other priorities get in the way of doing the homework.

Clinicians might respond to any of these or other reasons for homework noncompliance in a number of ways. In the remainder of this chapter, we break down the issue of how to address TIB related to homework across three kinds of common psychotherapy interactions. First, we explore the critical early conversations that involve orienting the client to the process, function, and structure of therapy homework. Second, we share insights about ways to optimize how to target specific kinds of homework with the client. Third, we discuss how to review homework, including when clients have and have not been compliant.

ORIENTING CLIENTS TO HOMEWORK

The process of orienting clients to psychotherapy homework is critically important. In DBT, we begin to orient our clients to homework in the first sessions, and then we reorient them to homework again and again as needed, all the way until treatment ends. At first, the orienting may be general and abstract, connected only to what little information we have in the early part of the first session. Over time, orienting becomes more specific and contextualized, connected to the things that matter most to clients. As discussed in Chapter 4, orienting is a highly collaborative and client-centered process. And as we detail later, one of the key things that makes orienting to homework in DBT unique is the use of dialectics. That is, orienting in DBT is done using both a dialectical worldview and dialectical process of change. When homework is discussed, orienting usually occurs. When homework is completed and important changes in treatment outcomes have begun to take place, orienting often occurs again. And when TIB involves homework not being completed, orienting almost always occurs.

Why all of the orienting? At the outset of therapy, clinicians are swimming upstream against a historical current of negative associations with the word *homework*. As clinicians, we know that *homework* is simply a psychotherapy buzzword for doing something different outside the session that is an extension of what was learned inside the session. Homework is a synonym for behavior done outside of psychotherapy with intention that is aligned with one's life values and treatment goals. Literally, homework is doing the work of psychotherapy—behavior change, learning to respond in new ways to stressful events, practicing ways to relate to others and one's own internal experiences more effectively—somewhere outside the clinic setting. Homework is not always done at home, but think of the looks you would get if you talked to your client about doing "office-work," "places-work," or "with-friends-work." Thus, we end up using the word *homework*, even with all of the associations that inevitably arise. Think about this: When you think of the word *homework*, what are the first few things that instantly come to mind? Did you think of sunshine and roses? Roller coasters and first kisses? Or could it be that you thought of mean Ms. Smith, the middle school science teacher who you thought graded unfairly and gave you a *D?* Did you think about school work, grades, or worries about performance? *Homework* is a word that can elicit unpleasant connotations. It is a wonder that we do not use other terms as clinicians.

It is probably safe to say that *homework* as a word or as a stimulus will elicit negative emotions in many clients. That does not mean that clinicians should avoid using the term, but it does mean that use of the term may elicit client reactions that are important and could be associated with subsequent homework noncompliance. To clients, homework can equal perceived expectations from the therapist and, perhaps as in school, evaluations of performance. All of this triggers a range of emotions: worries, shame, hopelessness, a sense of being different from everyone else, a desire to please or impress, and so on. But you are not a "teacher" in the secondary school sense of the term, and although helping your client learn is at the core of what you do, this is not schoolwork. All this means that therapists can choose to avoid using this term to prevent reactions that may increase psychotherapy noncompliance. Although this may be a short-term tactic, we recommend the longer term strategy of exposing the client to the cue, in this case the word *homework*, repeatedly over time to allow the client opportunities to develop newer and more flexible psychological responses (i.e., more diverse ways of responding) to homework in a psychotherapy context. Avoiding the term altogether can functionally be a way of fragilizing the client. With attention to orienting to homework—and the common TIB that it brings—clinicians can get a leg up on homework compliance and, ultimately, treatment outcome.

ORIENTATION TO STRUCTURE AND SELF-MONITORING

In DBT, the "first session" of therapy is considered to functionally take about four sessions (Linehan, 1993a). There is a lot of ground to cover with complex multidiagnostic clients, so it may take that long to address everything that for less complicated clients can be discussed in fewer sessions. When orienting to homework, we often begin in these first sessions by reviewing the structure, function, and process of homework.

Structurally, the DBT treatment hierarchy is introduced as including targets for change, in this order: (a) harm to self or others, (b) TIB, and (c) any other behavior interfering with one's quality of life (e.g., anxiety and avoidance, substance use, reckless or impulsive behavior, problems with relationships; Linehan, 1993a). Collaboratively, the therapist and client identify targets that are germane to each of these areas. The therapist introduces some ways that therapy homework (e.g., using certain cognitive or behavioral skills) might be used to address these treatment targets, and in this process, the client begins to understand the basics of what is being asked of him or her outside the clinic.

Another structural aspect to homework in DBT is the way in which homework is tracked each week. A diary card is introduced as a homework-tracking tool in the first session, and as the client talks more and more about what he or she wishes to change in therapy, the therapist facilitates a collaborative process wherein the diary card is populated with personally relevant targets. With days of the week as rows and targets specified in columns, this one page grid conveys a wealth of information to prevent excessive TIB. Over time and the first few sessions, the diary card is iteratively refined to include the most relevant treatment targets for that client. It may begin by tracking, for example, daily self-harm urges or events, urges to drink or use drugs, or peak emotional misery. Over time more targets are added to help track progress meeting treatment goals. Importantly, the diary card becomes the stimulus that is used to structure what is worked on between sessions as homework.

Introducing this in the first sessions is done in a straightforward way once the client's treatment goals are discussed. The goals (e.g., to be less depressed and more satisfied in relationships) can be met by changing certain things (e.g., approaching, rather than avoiding some contexts; thinking more flexibly about one's self, others, and the future), and the diary card has targets that tell both the client and therapist if the planned treatment outcomes have occurred. The dialogue with a new client around homework completion in DBT can begin like this:

> *Therapist:* OK, Mario, so we have talked about how you would like to be less depressed and how this treatment can help you be less depressed.
>
> *Client:* Uh-huh.
>
> *Therapist:* Now let's talk about how we will know when you are less depressed and how we will be sure to make this happen as fast as possible.
>
> *Client:* That sounds good.
>
> *Therapist:* One way to make changes faster is to use something we call *self-monitoring.* This is simply the idea that if you pay attention and track how often a behavior that you don't want to happen occurs, the behavior is likely to decrease. So, for example, if you had a history of getting many speeding tickets and really didn't want to get another one, keeping track of how many times per day you drive 5 miles or more per hour

past the speed limit would likely lead to you driving over the speed limit less.

Client: If I want to cry less at work, I should keep track of how many times per day this happens?

Therapist: Yes, you got it. The same thing is true if you want to increase a behavior. Self-monitoring how often it happens can increase the desired behavior. What behaviors could you pay attention to that you want to increase?

Client: Maybe how often I go out with friends? Or how often I try to think about a situation in a way that doesn't make me feel like I am totally inadequate?

Therapist: Those are great ideas! So, we can decide on those things later, but for now, since it is our first session, it is really important that we consider whether you would be willing to keep track of these kinds of things each day, each week, as long as you are in therapy with me, to try to help you be less depressed by changing how you live your life.

Client: I am totally open to doing this. I want to get better. This sounds good.

Therapist: Excellent, Mario. We are going to use what we call a *diary card* as a tool to change what you do in between sessions. The diary card is simply a piece of paper like this [*holds one up*] that has days of the week and things to track each day. We can fill out the targets together, and we can change them whenever we need to. We also can do this using an app if you prefer to do it that way. It doesn't matter to me, as long as you choose to self-monitor in way that is most likely to work to help you get better.

Client: I'll do it. But what should be on the diary card?

Therapist: Well, we know several things need to be on it, such as thoughts about self-harm (yes or no for any given day), highest level of misery for the day on a scale of 0 to 10, and number of times you did things that were pleasant, such as talking with friends. But we don't have to figure out everything just yet. Let's keep talking about your treatment goals and as we go along we can keep updating what we put in the diary card. Sound OK to you?

Client: Sure.

Once a client begins to use the diary card, it functions as stimulus control to structure the first portion of each session. When the clients walk into the room, the therapist asks for the card and begins the session by reviewing it carefully and in a collaborative dialogue with the client. The highlights and low points of the past week should pop out on the diary card. The therapist looks for patterns, evidence of psychotherapy homework, medication compliance, symptom worsening, skills use, changes in treatment outcome, and the like. When clients do not bring the card into session, the therapist can then begin the session discussing how this happened. When clients do bring the diary card in but it is not completed, therapists can spend time at the beginning of the session reviewing and completing the card. When it is completed, the therapist is likely to reinforce this behavior in a kind and compassionate way. It does not need to take a long time, but diary card review does need to be done toward the beginning of each session as a way to manage the contingencies associated with treatment compliance and noncompliance, to monitor successes and struggles, and to keep the overall direction of the treatment trajectory clear.

As in DBT, therapists who use self-monitoring orient the client early (and often) to the function of this technique. For example, the therapist might say,

> The diary card is going to be our way of communicating quickly at the beginning of each session about your past week. We'll put anything important to you on it, and we can always modify it if we think there is something we somehow missed together.

As a shortcut to identifying key targets to discuss in the session, the diary card helps the therapist stay on track. If the dialogue veers into a new area and the therapist is unsure how what is being talked about is relevant, he or she can ask the client whether this is something that should be added to the diary card. The diary card is where the primary treatment targets appear in writing. If a client was feeling more depressed in the previous week, the diary card should reveal this change. If a substance use slip has occurred, the clinician does not need to talk for 10 minutes before learning about the slip; it will be on the diary card. The diary card sets the stage for the session, helping the client and therapist to structure the session, use time most efficiently, and monitor homework completion.

In addition to the diary card, therapists orient the client to weekly homework that arises spontaneously in the context of discussions occurring in therapy. For example, a therapist may conduct a behavioral analysis to identify the function of recent impulsivity. After sorting through the antecedents and immediate temporal consequences of the recent impulsive behavior and learning that the behavior functioned as an escape from acute emotional distress, the therapist may begin orienting to the need to practice distress tolerance skills. The orienting is done even though it likely has been done before. The therapist might say something such as, "So which skills would you be willing to try to use this week when you have similar urges to do impulsive things to escape from your emotional pain?" Or the therapist could say, "Now that we know the function of what you did was to escape from what was unbearable emotional pain, let's consider some solutions for this next week so that you are ready to use skills to prevent this from happening again."

In both examples, the clinician steered the conversation toward homework, without necessarily using the word *homework*, by linking what was just discussed to the broader treatment targets. Notice in these examples that orienting to homework is neither infantilizing nor fragilizing the client. The specifics of the homework have not been explored and will not be begun in earnest until the clinician is confident that the client is oriented toward the homework. Orienting to homework is the bridge between the narrative of the past week and plans for the next week. Orienting brings the clinician and client together for a moment to pause before collaboratively deciding the what, when, and how of this week's psychotherapy homework. Although it is easy to overlook, we believe orienting is a critical step in each session that sets the stage for targeting specific homework assignments.

TARGETING SPECIFIC HOMEWORK IN DIALECTICAL BEHAVIOR THERAPY

Identifying what homework to do in which contexts can be quite hard with some clients. The client may be oriented to the concept of homework; you may have talked about it before, perhaps many times; and in any given session you might have oriented the client to the importance of homework to address this or that problem just discussed, but then comes the time to talk about and agree on exactly what he or she will do between now and the next session. That is when the therapist and client are targeting homework, and it is in the process of targeting that a client makes a commitment to change. Targeting homework in usual psychotherapy can be a quick process, such as when a clinician asks the client at the end of a session, "How about you think about that over the next week, and we can keep talking about this when I see you next time?" Homework targeting can be driven prescriptively by a treatment manual, as is the case when a clinician doing cognitive therapy might say, "So, for this next week, the homework will be to use this thought record as a sheet to self-monitor dysfunctional beliefs." There are lots of ways a therapist can choose specific homework assignments. How do you as a therapist manage this process? Think about your approach to targeting homework as complemented or contrasted by how this is done in DBT.

BEING DIALECTICAL ABOUT HOMEWORK

Let us consider when homework is identified in DBT sessions. After reviewing homework and the diary card in any given session, the individual therapist spends a lot of time exploring chains of behavior from the previous week, identifying functions of problem behavior or recent successes changing patterns of dysfunctional behavior. Throughout the session, the therapist balances acceptance and change using a dialectical worldview and process of dialogue to identify targets for change—homework—over the next week. That is, he or she uses the therapy process to identify relevant homework targets for the next week and help the client remain motivated for change.

This organic process means that therapists do not always wait until the end of the session to talk about specific homework. Instead, at any point in the session the therapist may target homework. This approach requires clinicians to be mindful of possibly useful changes that can be made in the client's life as these opportunities appear. It can be particularly effective for the clinician to use this mindful awareness to fuel spontaneous explorations about possible avenues for change. In our experience it is best when the homework discussion organically arises after problem solving, analyzing the solutions to problems, and practicing skills as solutions in the session. When the client has experienced during the session how, for example, mindfulness practice can change the way he or she experiences unpleasant thoughts and emotions, it is an opportune time to begin discussing how to use this skill outside the therapy session. Similarly, after a client learns to reduce shame or guilt using emotion regulation strategies, the time is ripe for planning ways to use this same skill until the next therapy session.

Sometimes the therapist does this with gentle curiosity and expressions of emotional validation. Other times, initiating the homework targeting conversation is done with bold irreverence, even exuberance, about the possibilities for change. Recall that the primary function of individual DBT sessions is to motivate the client to be willing to try to change. Accordingly, when the therapist observes a prime homework target early in the session, there is no rule that this must be introduced. Instead, the therapist must weigh the pros and cons of homework discussion with helping to motivate the client to take behavioral steps toward a life worth living as an overarching function of the session.

How this process unfolds practically depends on the client, the behavioral treatment targets, and the context of the session. If talking early in a session about sleep hygiene as part of the solution to reduce depressive symptoms, a clinician could take time, before moving on to another topic, to target homework using approaches to improve sleep. If in the middle of the session with a client who has attention-deficit/hyperactivity disorder a clinician identifies an important context to use organizational skills to improve performance at school or work, he or she might take additional time to further target when and how to use specific skills. When working with a client who struggles with emotional reactivity and begins a session with an emotional outburst, a clinician might help the client process and regulate the emotion using a skill that the clinician would like the client to use outside the session (see also Chapter 7 on anger). Once the client has emotionally recovered, it can be effective to immediately discuss how she or he can use that specific emotion regulation strategy in specific contexts before the next appointment when it is highly likely that negative emotions might occur and ineffective behavior could follow.

In other words, one way to ensure that psychotherapy homework targets clinically relevant behavior important to the client is to build from demonstrable changes observed in session. But this can be challenging. We have learned from many training experiences with community clinicians that the temptation is often to move in a linear fashion from historical topic to topic, covering narrative content from the past or about the future that is rationalized by the client and/or therapist as important. And to be sure, sometimes it is important to keep moving to another topic after change occurs in the session, to listen intently and support without steering the conversation to changes that could result from homework. But sometimes this is not the most effective approach, and even though the session is nowhere near ending, the time is right to extend into homework for the week what has just been discussed or has just happened. Willingness to explore emergent issues and to pull out effective interventions and homework assignments as needed is part of the dialectical style in DBT of "movement, speed, and flow." Portions of sessions at times proceed in an organized, linear, lockstep fashion, as if the client and therapist are walking side by side down a trail, and at other times, the therapist and client are dancing, skipping, taking side trails to learn about new terrain, and then returning to a path that takes the client where she or he wants to be.

The dialectical synthesis between rigidly waiting until the end of the session versus taking the first opportunity early in session to identify possible psychotherapy homework is this: Be mindful, intentional, and willing to try targeting psychotherapy homework earlier in the session. It may be awkward at first, but soon you will realize the benefits in mitigating homework noncompliance, because the homework will have come up naturally, and there will be time to think through and deal with the details of the homework. If there is more time left to talk about something else after homework problem solving has concluded, terrific! Keep on working!

USING VALIDATION EFFECTIVELY TO PROMOTE HOMEWORK COMPLIANCE

Another strategy therapists use when targeting homework is to authentically highlight, using validation techniques outlined in this volume, how difficult it might be to make any changes to dysfunctional patterns of behavior. For example, a therapist might say,

> You know, we have just come upon something that could be really important for you. If you can use these skills to change how you relate to this person, then it could change your life. But I want you to know something. No matter how much making these changes could help you, I don't think it will be easy. If it were easy to change, you would already have done so. We will figure this out together.

In this example, notice how the therapist language is genuine in validating how hard it will be to change. Homework is change, and change is difficult.

Validation is used not only when first identifying homework but also throughout the process of determining and agreeing about the homework plan. The seeds of noncompliance are often planted when clinicians inadvertently emotionally invalidate clients when discussing homework. Invalidation occurs when the client's internal experience—in this case, his or her experience associated with psychotherapy homework (e.g., "I don't have enough time to do this homework!")—is minimized, trivialized, criticized, or rejected as invalid. Clients are not going to change their lives because a clinician has told them what to do. They have had people telling them what to do their whole lives. Giving them information or psychoeducation about why this or that homework assignment will change this or that process is a poor and incomplete recipe for change. Telling them what to do is not the solution to their misery. Similarly, hurriedly assigning psychotherapy homework or assigning homework that sounds like a simple solution to a complex problem invalidates how hard it is to make changes. And when people are emotionally invalidated they are prone to respond with negative affect, sympathetic physiological arousal, and narrowed attention. Some respond with anger or distrust, others simply shut down. In all of these responses, the net subjective result is the same: not feeling understood. Use validation when talking about how hard the homework is. Use it genuinely, because there may be lots of valid reasons why change will be difficult.

USING TROUBLESHOOTING STRATEGIES

Another strategy therapists use to mitigate homework noncompliance is to troubleshoot and iteratively refine the homework flexibly. This means that the therapist is willing to change the homework if needed. Let us say that the targeting of homework began with a plan for the client to use mindfulness skills with her partner in an effort to reduce emotional reactivity to the partner and build intimacy. The client initially thought this was a good idea, but then as the two of you talked it through she changed her mind and decided that it simply would not work. She thought about it and imagined what it would be like to observe and describe, nonjudgmentally, in the moment, her experience of watching TV on the couch with her partner. She visualized the homework, and though she understood logically that this kind of thing would be wonderful if she could do it, she decided against it. Her partner is too invalidating, too difficult, too full of himself, and the like. You can give up on this homework, or you can dig in deeper and try to resolve the problem.

In DBT we might do either, but usually we troubleshoot a bit before abandoning a solution. Like compassionate bulldogs, therapists will not let go of a solution easily, yet go about this by leaning into the problem-solving process with validation, soothing, and recognition that it could be difficult. The therapist might validate the emotion in the therapy room during that moment. For example, the anxiety about change may be real, but that does not mean that the thoughts accompanying the anxiety are 100% accurate. There is a lot to validate without agreeing about the truth of any dysfunctional thought or without changing course. The trick in this process is to speak from the heart with authenticity when acknowledging the anxiety and unwillingness to try the homework. From this context the probability of change increases, and any problem solving about the details of the homework practice becomes more likely to succeed. Validation is the machete cutting a path through a dense, anxious jungle, opening up space to refine the direction change will take.

REVIEWING HOMEWORK IN DIALECTICAL BEHAVIOR THERAPY

Now let us turn to how therapists review homework. In psychotherapy the basic and most fundamental dialectic is that of acceptance and change. Applied to homework, acceptance and change is an essential dialectic to consider. When thinking about acceptance as it pertains to homework completion, there are several factors to consider. What exactly are you to accept, and what exactly are you not to accept? Should you simply accept that the client did not do his or her homework without trying to change this TIB? Should you move on and not discuss this? What should you try to change when clients do not complete their therapy homework? Should you try to change how they think about the homework, change the homework itself, or change your approach to talking about the homework?

One thing we believe is important is that being mindful of this dialectic inherently means that clinicians can accept in one moment that the TIB has occurred and in the next instant may work to change the TIB. Once the TIB is observed and a decision made about how or whether to try to change it, the clinician has already recognized the TIB as an event that occurred. The next step is critical because therapists can notice but choose not to attend to TIB for a wide range of reasons, some of which are therapist TIBs (discussed in Chapter 12). A primary point is that acceptance is not antithetical to change; acceptance and change can happen nearly simultaneously, and sometimes acceptance without trying to change the TIB is itself a change in how the TIB is managed. Acceptance is at minimum a necessary precursor to therapeutic change. We have found that many clinicians and clients get confused about these points and incorrectly come to think that if they choose to accept that something has occurred, they will be unable to change. Like so many other dialectics described in this book, the distinction between managing noncompliance TIBs with either acceptance or change is a false dichotomy. Instead, therapists can seek ways to mindfully accept reality as it is, with decisions then made about whether or how to target changing TIBs.

The decision making about responding to this TIB is complex and need not be governed by any rules. However, a principle in DBT is that if homework has not been completed, it is the therapist's responsibility to try to understand what got in the way. Recall in Chapter 3 that we outlined some basic steps in managing TIB, including highlighting the problem, assessing and understanding the problem, solving the problem, obtaining a commitment for behavior change, and troubleshooting. The idea is that therapists can approach homework noncompliance from a problem-solving framework. Lack of homework completion becomes a problem to solve, even if part of the problem solving is to accept that the homework did not occur or that talking about this means time will not be spent talking about other things. Resolving homework noncompliance means talking about the fact that the homework was not done, but it can be done with gentle compassion and kindness.

It is important to keep in mind that trying to carefully understand the problems interfering with homework completion allows therapists to connect this TIB and barriers to the client making important changes in his or her life. In fact, one way you might know that the homework you are using is not important or relevant to the client is if you are not able to directly link the homework to goals and values that are central to the client's life. To the extent that the therapy homework is out of alignment with the client's values and goals, it is increasingly less likely that it will be completed (or that, once completed, it will actually help). This means that the therapist has to be open to flexibly changing homework when new goals and/or values are identified. Homework noncompliance as TIB can be evidence that the homework is not well-aligned with goals and values. Of course, however, this TIB may not at all mean that the homework has to change. It could be by virtue of this being TIB that the perfect homework target has been found, and it just so happens to be the one that is causing major and intractable life problems.

Highlighting the Problem

As discussed in Chapter 3, often a good place to start in discussing problems with homework or other TIBs is to find a way to highlight or bring the problem to the client's attention. In DBT, highlighting may occur in an irreverent or reciprocal style. *Irreverent* communication includes clinician verbal responses in therapy that are appropriate but unorthodox, something other than being warm and gentle, including anything from being playful to matter-of-fact. Irreverence should be genuine, nondefensive, and compassionate, but it can also be direct and plain-speaking or slightly unpredictable and different from what other therapists in the past might have said.

In the case of homework, a client could say, "Well, I should let you know that I failed to do my homework this week." Some irreverent responses to this could include the following:

- "Hey, 'fail' is a judgment. Let's talk about what you actually did, and I'll promise not to judge you if you promise not to judge yourself."
- "Did you fail or did you not do the homework?"
- "Well, I think it might make sense for us to talk about this today to make sure that we don't get a third or fourth week in a row without doing your homework."
- "This is a problem we need to solve. I have to say I'm afraid you're not going to get much better in this therapy if you don't begin to try making change in your life."

There are countless irreverent ways to respond when clients acknowledge not doing their homework.

The flip side to irreverence in DBT is to use a *reciprocal* communication style. If the client looks sad and slowly says, "Well, I should let you know that I failed to do my homework this week," a reciprocal response might be to slowly say something such as, "I'm sure there are good reasons why you were unable to complete the homework this week, and I trust we will figure this out." Another response that is reciprocal in this instance could be for the clinician to say, "Thank you for sharing this with me. I'm wondering whether you are feeling some sadness or hopelessness as you tell me this?"

Which style of communication should you use to respond to clients when they tell you that they have not completed their homework? From a DBT perspective, the answer is that it depends. There is no one correct style of communication that should always be used. In DBT, the clinician is encouraged to use a wide variety of communication styles in response to similar types of client behavior. There is certainly much to validate and to seek to explore with the client in understanding why homework was not completed. There may be important emotions to recognize and validate when the client tells you that he or she has not completed the homework. However, it may be important and useful to be matter-of-fact or straightforward in response to homework noncompliance. A principle in DBT is to try using both of these approaches, selecting a response style that makes sense given the moment without being out of balance in being either excessively reciprocal or irreverent.

Assessing and Understanding the Problem

Assessing why homework has not been completed should, from a DBT perspective, be a highly collaborative process. As discussed in Chapter 3, using chain analyses to understand why homework was not done, the client and therapist are detectives on the same investigational team trying to solve a case. Working carefully and critically analyzing all of the relevant information, the detectives unravel the mystery of how the homework did not get completed. This kind of truly collaborative process requires that the therapist embrace a nonjudgmental stance. For example, the therapist's attitude about homework completion has to be nonjudgmental. If you think about this outside the context of psychotherapy, it also makes perfect sense. If you go to see your primary care physician, and the doctor tells you that you need to do something as homework and then later on you come back to see the doctor and have not done your homework, do you really want that doctor to give you a hard time and be judgmental about not doing your homework?

Using a dialectical philosophy involves the therapist maintaining a humane and compassionate stance, validating the difficulty in completing homework and, at the same time, trying to understand how the client can do the homework next time. One way to maintain this compassionate stance is for the therapist to try to do the homework her- or himself. We have often had our team members try to complete daily diary cards, and even when the issues are not challenging or emotionally charged, the compliance rate is not 100%. Therapy is, for some clients, one of the most difficult things they will do.

The process of being collaborative in discerning the barriers for homework completion is perhaps as important as, if not more important than, identifying the barriers themselves. As a clinician, you may be able to identify barriers to homework quickly. You might be right in your assessment of what got in the way. But none of this will matter if your insights come at the cost of a rupture in the relationship. In DBT, there is a basic principle we use to help us in these situations: When reviewing homework, try to use validation before any emphasis on change. Understand the problem before you try to solve it. Do it from your heart with depth and authenticity, and then, when the time is right, begin considering what to do differently.

In previous chapters, we discussed extensively the use of problem-solving strategies for TIBs. We do not review all of these strategies again here. However, it may be useful to highlight how strategies such as contingency clarification, contingency management, shaping, and skill building all can be useful to directly try to solve the problem of homework noncompliance. Table 6.1 lists examples of these approaches.

MOVING FORWARD

We do a fair amount of training with clinicians who work in community mental health and substance use treatment programs. This includes teaching about cognitive behavior therapies in general and DBT in particular. One of the things we are asked all the time is how to get clients to do therapy homework. Actually, what we are usually asked is whether our clients really do therapy homework. In other words, is this just one of those things that is taught in graduate school, is written about in books and journal articles, but does not truly happen in everyday practice?

A healthy dose of curious and compassionate skepticism about clients' willingness and ability to complete psychotherapy homework is not only sensible but it can also help keep clinicians from becoming demoralized. However, clinician assumptions and beliefs about psychotherapy homework can be part of the problem underlying noncompliance. For example, the assumption that a client cannot or will not do his or her psychotherapy homework can, at times, be a patronizing stance that undermines progress. Did the client come to you to help him- or herself make changes in how he or she thinks, feels, relates to others, regulates emotions, responds to psychosocial stressors, and so on? And is psychotherapy homework not, in the end, about making those changes? We believe that clients can make difficult life changes gradually and with practice, and clinicians can motivate clients to do this by avoiding the fragilizing assumption that clients will not or cannot do homework.

TABLE 6.1

Examples of Ways to Use Problem-Solving Strategies in Dialectical
Behavior Therapy to Enhance Therapy Homework Compliance

Problem-solving strategy	Example
Contingency clarification	"I understand that it's hard to try to use these skills. They are new to you, like learning a new language. It makes sense that it may take time, on the one hand, and on the other, it is something that we will need to figure out. As hard as it is for you to find the time to practice these skills, we are going to need to spend some time problem solving in here together. I am confident we can do this, though it will take some time to sort through all of the details."
Contingency management	"Before we talk about what happened with your boyfriend, I think we need to take the time to review how it went last week practicing the mindfulness skills as homework. And I know from what you said earlier in our session that you are having a hard time staying focused in our session. So, before we go any further, how about we do a mindfulness practice?"
Shaping	"OK, so that wasn't so bad practicing mindfulness, was it? You really did a great job staying with the practice, you didn't try to talk with me during the practice like the last couple of times, and when we stopped to observe and describe our experiences from the practice you did a really skillful job. This all means you are well on your way to this mindfulness work. Next time when we practice, I think I will let you take the lead and choose the kind of practice we do."
Skill building and troubleshooting	"OK, so let's plan to improve how you do your therapy homework by considering which skills can be used to increase the chance that you are successful. We just completed a mindfulness practice, and you did a great job. So I am thinking that this week you might use mindfulness to help you be more likely to do your therapy homework. Let's consider this. I could be wrong, but it seems to be that mindfulness skills practice may be the way to stack the cards in your favor so that the other things you need to do get done. How about we take a few minutes and think through together when and how mindfulness practice could be most effective for you this next week?"

What can any clinician take from all of this? First, orient the client to TIB with compassion and genuine acceptance of imperfection. Consider using a diary card or self-monitoring and the contingencies of starting each session with this form as a way to review homework. Do not wait until homework noncompliance begins to establish this norm for beginning sessions. Orient to this process in the first session. Second, reorient to specific TIB as needed over and over again. Do not be afraid to use orienting as a strategy to bridge the gap between the narrative of the session describing past events to the plan to implement specific and targeted homework for the future.

Third, target specific homework that directly addresses why the client is in treatment, if feasible, and that can be reviewed the next week. Do this using behavior change strategies (see Chapters 2 and 3) and communicate acceptance of non-change when appropriate. Target change using validation before asking for commitment, and once clear targets for homework are identified and agreed on, continue to troubleshoot and analyze the solution until a newer and better version of the homework emerges. This requires thinking flexibly, searching for homework early in the session, and using the therapy process to elicit natural homework targets for the week. Fourth, when reviewing homework and highlighting problems with homework, do so being dialectical, balancing irreverence with a reciprocal style of communicating. To understand noncompliance and reduce TIB, use chain analyses, have multiple hypotheses, and problem solve. Remember when reviewing noncompliance there are often clear insights to be made about the link between TIB and life-interfering behavior. Look for these connections with curiosity and patience, love and authenticity, all while tenaciously seeking to make change.

7

EFFECTIVELY RESPONDING TO ANGER

Intense expressions of hostility or anger, whether directed toward the therapist or otherwise, are among the most stressful and challenging behaviors that therapists encounter. Behaviors commonly associated with hostility or anger, such as scowling; glaring; expressions of contempt; changes in demeanor, posture, or voice tone; verbal or physical aggression; or shutting down, often interfere with therapy and provoke fear and alarm whether they occur within or outside a therapy session. Moreover, when angry behavior occurs, therapists can sometimes be reinforced for ineffective treatment (e.g., withdrawing from or avoiding problem solving when the client becomes visibly angry) and punished for effective treatment. Therapists also might find that their own frustration, irritation, or anger toward particular clients impedes their effectiveness.

http://dx.doi.org/10.1037/14752-007
Managing Therapy-Interfering Behavior: Strategies From Dialectical Behavior Therapy, by A. L. Chapman and M. Z. Rosenthal

If managed effectively, however, anger-related behavior can also present opportunities to improve and even transform therapy. Among the core mechanisms cutting across many of the problems associated with borderline personality disorder (BPD), for example, is difficulty regulating or managing emotions (Lieb, Zanarini, Schmahl, Linehan, & Bohus, 2004; Lynch, Chapman, Rosenthal, Kuo, & Linehan, 2006; Rosenthal et al., 2008). Intense anger provides an opportunity to help clients gain practice in the effective management of strong emotions. A therapist's frustration or irritation regarding a client's lack of attendance, criticism, or judgmental statements may provide an opportunity to model the effective expression and regulation of emotions, as well as motivate the therapist to solve therapy-interfering problems. In this chapter, we emphasize strategies to use anger as an opportunity to strengthen and improve therapy.

KEY PRINCIPLES

A couple of key principles provide a useful guide to the management of therapy-interfering anger problems. First, it can be helpful to conceptualize anger and related behavior from within an emotion regulation framework. Within this kind of framework, anger and related behaviors, thoughts, and sensations are viewed systemically. Along these lines, Kassinove (1995) defined *anger* as a negative feeling state characterized by specific patterns of cognitive distortions, physiological changes, and action tendencies. Cues for anger and related emotions (e.g., frustration) generally tend to include situations involving threat (physical or otherwise) and interruptions in goal-directed behavior (Linehan, 1993b). Anger also serves important social and behavioral functions (Lemerise & Dodge, 2008), often functioning to motivate action, encourage attempts to master or control the environment, and to protect or defend against threats or danger (Izard & Kobak, 1991; Lewis, Sullivan, Ramsay, & Alessandri, 1992). Anger also is associated with the efficient activation of relevant sets of actions (e.g., self-protection or defense) without the individual having to think through and plan out such actions cognitively (i.e., "ready repertoires of action"; Oatley & Jenkins, 1996). Anger and related emotions also can help to communicate needs, preferences, and dislikes. Anger, of course, goes awry when the individual experiences inappropriately intense anger and chronic levels of hostility and engages in angry behavior that is ineffective in the current context (e.g., yelling at one's boss to secure a raise).

Second, it is also helpful for the therapist to maintain a dialectical stance regarding anger. Anger serves important functions and may be dysfunctional at the same time. A client who becomes enraged with a therapist for her lack of availability by phone during a vacation may appear to be acting and thinking in an unreasonable manner. When the therapist looks further into this problem, however, she or he may discover that the client's anger is serving a self-protective function. Perhaps the client feels hurt and rejected when the therapist goes away and is unavailable, and anger is motivating the client to express displeasure about this, reduce emotional vulnerability, or create distance from a person who may not be a reliable source of support. In this way, intense anger may be understandable and is serving important psychological functions. At the same time, it is dysfunctional to feel enraged whenever someone is unavailable to provide support, and actions related to rage can harm the therapeutic relationship (e.g., yelling, threatening, criticizing, refusing to return phone calls). Maintaining a dialectical stance involves the therapist mindfully observing the situation, seeing both sides of the issue, and even conveying this "both-and" to the client (Linehan, 1993a). To do this, the therapist often must jump into the client's shoes, see the world from her or his perspective, validate the valid (the anger is understandable in the context of the client's learning history and is serving a function currently), and invalidate the invalid (the intensity of the anger and the hostile behavior are problematic).

Another aspect of the dialectical stance on anger is that the therapist may be both attached to the client working on and reducing her or his anger and also willing to let go of this attachment. Angry behavior is aversive and may create problems in the client's life. At the same time, the therapist accepts the client's anger and lets go of the need to change it. When anger leads to problems in the therapeutic relationship, this is challenging. For therapy to proceed effectively, the therapist may require the client to reduce anger and also have to accept that the client is angry and unwilling to reduce it. The following is an example of the therapist taking a dialectical stance regarding anger, both pushing for change and letting go.

Therapist: As we've discussed, this anger really doesn't seem to be working too well for you. Feeling 10/10 anger when someone gives you constructive feedback at work shuts down your thinking, makes it hard for you to learn from the feedback, and has led to interpersonal problems.

Client: Yeah, I know, but people really just need to get the heck off my case. I'm doing my best, and they just keep picking at little details.

Therapist: I know you're doing your best. You've often told me how hard you're working. It is hard to get that kind of feedback when you're already trying so hard. The thing is, though, that, I'm afraid you're going to be at risk of losing your job if you don't work on the anger.

Client: Right, you've said that. I know—it's just so hard. Why do I always have to be the one to work on things? I don't really want to have to manage my anger.

Therapist: Well, you don't really have to. Nobody is saying that. You could keep feeling this angry whenever you get a performance review. That's an option. If you want to work on the anger, I'm here to help you do that, and I've got some strategies that I really think will work for you. But, of course you know it's up to you.

TARGETING, THERAPEUTIC MINDFULNESS, ASSESSMENT, AND VALIDATION

With these principles in mind, effective management of therapy-interfering anger also often involves appropriate targeting, therapeutic mindfulness, assessment of the anger problems, and validation. In terms of targeting, the therapist must first identify and prioritize anger and related behavior as an important target. Following this, another step is often for the therapist to mindfully observe and describe the behavior, associated antecedents and consequences, and the therapist's emotional reactions to the behavior. Assessing and understanding the essence of the problem contributing to the client's anger and angry behavior and focusing on how the behavior (and the anger) functions can facilitate accurate validation and illuminate directions for intervention.

Targeting: Identify Therapy-Interfering Anger

As discussed in Chapter 3, one of the first steps in managing therapy-interfering behavior (TIB) is to identify and recognize the behavior and consider why and how it interferes with therapy. Sometimes the problem is obvious. When clients vent and yell at length or engage in threatening or aggressive behavior, angry behavior clearly has the potential to interfere with therapy. In other cases, however, signs that something is awry might be more subtle, including emotional reactions on the part of the therapist, such as dread, fear, or anxiety about an upcoming session; frustration with the client during the session; or a pattern of the therapist backing off or acquiescing in circumstances when continuing to move forward with problem solving or other such interventions would be much more beneficial. Targeting involves being alert to both the form of the behavior and its effect on the therapy process.

Therapeutic Mindfulness: Observe and Describe

Another important step in managing anger-related TIB is for the therapist to mindfully and nonjudgmentally observe and describe the client's behavior, her or his own reactions, and the effects of the behavior on treatment. It can be easy to judge angry behavior because it can be aversive, extreme, and challenging to manage. The therapist may feel threatened, perhaps both personally and professionally, and feelings of being threatened can lead to judgments of the source of the threat. Indeed, it is normal and sometimes adaptive to feel alarmed, threatened, or afraid in the presence of aggressive and agitated people. The challenge is to maintain compassion, composure, and effectiveness even in the middle of this type of storm. This first step—stepping back mentally and observing and describing nonjudgmentally—can help to reduce the alarm response and allow the therapist to react wisely.

One of our students, for example, was seeing a client, "Amanda," who began yelling and swearing about social injustices and her past mistreatment by her mother from the waiting room, all the way down the hallway, and into the therapy room. The student's attempts to interject, set an agenda for the session, or even to validate the client's experiences often went nowhere. Amanda continued to yell, interrupted the therapist, often rose from the chair, paced around the room, and on a couple of occasions, threw a cup of coffee. The student was feeling demoralized, concerned about whether she was really helping the client, and afraid that the client would do something to harm herself or someone else.

The student first brought up this pattern of events during her supervision sessions, and the supervisor encouraged her to begin by observing and describing the client's behavior, sticking as closely to the facts as possible and avoiding assumptions or judgments. The student began with, "She just wants to vent the whole time and doesn't want to actually talk about how to improve her life." Although this is a start, it is important to remember that the mindfulness skill of describing involves sticking to the observable facts. This means assumptions about what the client "wants" to do are off limits. A more accurate description, for example, was:

> As soon as I greet her, she begins talking loudly, swearing, and stating that the government has ruined her life. When I speak, she continues talking, or she interrupts me, yelling and making statements about the government and how her mother is responsible for her involvement in prostitution.

It is also helpful for the therapist to observe and describe the effect of this behavior on the therapy session: "When this happens, we spend the first 25 minutes trying to get started, Amanda stops yelling in about the first 35 minutes, and we are often left with little time to address her problems." In addition, the therapist might also describe her own reactions to the situation: "I feel stuck, frustrated, and ineffective when this happens, and I'm not sure how to steer Amanda back on track or what to do to help her." Therefore, when dealing with angry behavior, the first step is to observe and describe, clearly and nonjudgmentally, (a) the behavior, (b) the effect of the behavior on the therapy session, and (c) the therapist's own emotional reactions and thoughts in response to the behavior.

Highlight and Discuss In-Session Behavior

Using highlighting strategies, the therapist can bring the behavior to the client's attention in a clear, behaviorally specific, and nonjudgmental manner. We recommend that therapists discuss anger-related behavior in a manner similar to how she or he would discuss any other behavior—the behavior of sleeping in, missing therapy sessions, avoiding public places, and so on. Angry behavior, as outrageous as it can be, is simply behavior. One way to obtain practice at this is to think about outrageous or unusual behavior that would elicit judgments and shock, and then to practice describing and highlighting it in a clear and matter-of-fact manner. If a client, for example, stated, "I've begun to have sexual relations with cows," the therapist could practice highlighting or discussing this behavior in the same way in which she or he would discuss any other behavior. The following is an example of a therapist highlighting anger-related behavior with a client.

> *Therapist:* I'm noticing that your muscles appear tense, your fists are clenched, and you're breathing heavily. Also, your voice is raised and has an edge to it. Are you noticing that as well?
>
> *Client:* Well, yeah, but I'm really pissed off. I mean, you said you'd be able to see me every week, and I'm going through a really hard time right now. This is the worst time you could ever choose to just take off on me and go on vacation!
>
> *Therapist:* I know this is bad timing for you, and you need a lot of help and support right now with all that you're going through [*losing her job, boyfriend cheating on her*]. It makes perfect sense to me that you're angry. In fact, anger is a normal reaction when something or someone is preventing you from getting your needs met. But I'm a little concerned that if you stay this angry, I might have a hard time helping you.
>
> *Client:* Yeah, well, I don't know how you expect me to get through this alone. It just seems like, if you really cared about me, you wouldn't be doing this.
>
> *Therapist:* I see—that thought is going through your mind. Do you think there's anything else besides anger that you're feeling right now?
>
> *Client:* I don't know.
>
> *Therapist:* I could imagine myself feeling a little afraid, being without a major source of help or support. Are you, by any chance, also feeling afraid, like you're not going to be able to manage or cope? Or, maybe hurt that I'm leaving you for a bit?

Client:	I am, well, I guess, hurt, yes. I don't know—it seems like you don't care about me if you're willing to go away [*in a teary, softer voice tone*]. I am maybe a little afraid that I'm going to really lose it. I've been trying so hard, and I feel like it's only going to take one small thing to really push me over the edge.
Therapist:	I thought that might be the case. I know this is so hard for you. Let's talk about what we can do.

Sometimes anger is hardest to manage and most distressing when it is directed toward the therapist, particularly in reaction to something she or he may not be willing or able to change. Following the basic steps we have discussed will help the therapist to regulate her or his own emotions while responding effectively to the client. In the example just described, the therapist starts by observing and then describing the client's behavior in a specific manner. The therapist models exactly the type of behavior that she or he wants the client to learn: observing and then describing physical sensations and expression of emotion. The therapist also uses validation to express understanding of the client's concerns and then highlights a contingency: that, if the client were to stay this angry, it would be difficult to have a helpful session.

Although not displayed in this clinical example, another useful strategy is to ask the client whether he or she is willing to work on reducing the anger. We have found that providing the client with a choice regarding whether to work on anger can help to avoid power struggles that might emerge if an angry client feels pushed into regulating or reducing anger. Anger is an activating emotion, and when people who are already angry feel like their freedom is being limited, angry behavior often escalates. In addition, clients who "buy in" by agreeing to work on anger may be more likely to follow through and take a collaborative stance with the therapist.

Assessing and Understanding the Essence of the Problem

Following highlighting of the behavior, another common next step is to assess and understand the essence of the problem. In the case of angry behavior, the therapist's aim is to understand what is contributing to the client's anger, the link between the anger and the angry behavior, and the client's full emotional experience (often involving emotions other than anger, as is seen in the example). It is important to understand precisely what is contributing to the client's anger, and a good starting point is to conceptualize anger as multifaceted, including external prompting events or triggers for the emotion, thoughts, appraisals, and interpretations that both influence and are influenced by the emotion, biological changes and physical sensations, and emotional expression (Gross, 1998; Linehan, 1993a, 1993b, 2015). If the therapist understands the terrain of the client's experiences and behavior, she or he can help to intervene on a variety of fronts, including helping the client change his or her thoughts, actions, expressions, and so on.

As discussed in Chapter 3, one way to assess anger-related TIB is through functional analyses of angry behavior. A functional analysis might focus on anger reported both between and within sessions. For example, a client might come to session having recorded an anger outburst with his partner, and the functional analysis could focus on that episode. When it comes to angry behavior occurring within session, a therapist might, for example, highlight that a client has engaged in threatening or verbally aggressive behavior in session and use a functional analysis to better understand how this happened and how to intervene. Generally, if this is the case, we recommend that the therapist initiate the functional analysis after the client's anger has reduced enough so that she or he is less likely to act aggressively and is more able to focus cognitively on the task at hand. A therapist might say the following, for example.

> Earlier this session, you said that if I don't write that letter to your university for you, you will quit therapy. I think we should talk about this a bit to better understand how you ended up feeling so angry or frustrated with me that you threatened to quit therapy. Sort of a chain [functional] analysis of what just happened a little while ago. Would you be willing to do that?

Clearly Defining the Problem Behavior

As discussed in Chapter 3, it is important to anchor the functional analysis on a specific instance of a target behavior. The therapist observes and may describe the specific behavior as follows, "The client had his fists clenched, got red in the face, and began breathing heavily. He said in a loud voice that he can't stand it when I ask about his homework and that he wants to leave." This is the behavior targeted for functional analysis. Often, therapists become confused when conducting a functional analysis because they move back and forth between analyzing a general pattern of behavior and a specific instance. It is important, therefore, to remember that a specific instance, on a particular day, at a particular time, is the target of the functional analysis.

Assess Prompting or Triggering Events for Anger

Another important area of assessment includes the precipitants or triggers for anger. This is yet another opportunity for the therapist to model and help the client practice mindfully describing the facts of the situation without judgments, inferences, assumptions, and so on. When the client states judgments, assumptions, inferences, guesses, and so on, instead of facts, the therapist coaches the client on sticking to the facts. The following example illustrates some of these strategies.

> *Therapist:* So, tell me a little about what was happening when you started feeling angry.
>
> *Client:* Well, I'm really angry because my wife doesn't even care about me enough to support my therapy. I mean, she takes no interest in it whatsoever and just seems to want me to come in and get fixed. She has no idea how hard this is!
>
> *Therapist:* It's really hard to feel unsupported when you're going through a lot of pain and stress. To help you with this, I think I need to get clearer on the facts or what's actually going on with your wife. Do you remember the mindfulness skill of describing?
>
> *Client:* I think so—is that where you state the facts or label things?
>
> *Therapist:* Yes, exactly—describing involves stating the facts as you have observed them. So, if your wife walked into the room, said "Hello," and sat down, you'd say, "My wife walked into the room, said 'Hello,' and sat down." Just the concrete facts, with no judgments, assumptions, guesses, hunches, et cetera. Do you think you could do that with what you're seeing with your wife?
>
> *Client:* Yeah, I guess, but it's hard, she's just so . . . OK, I guess before I came in today, I was talking with her about something that was really upsetting me. My coworkers just seem to get all wigged out when I come into the room, and it seems like they've been talking about me. I was telling her this, and she just said, "You're just being paranoid again, dear, and I think you should talk to your therapist about that."
>
> *Therapist:* Oh, I see. So, let me guess, you would have preferred it if she actually talked with you about it. What did you really want from her?
>
> *Client:* Right, I mean, I really just wanted her to listen to me. I feel like an outcast at work, and I wanted someone to listen and maybe tell me I'm not a freak, but she just refers me to you.
>
> *Therapist:* And what emotions did you feel? And what was going through your mind when that happened?
>
> *Client:* I guess I felt hurt first. I was thinking, "She can't even give me the time of day, and she just doesn't care enough to deal with my problems." Then, I felt really angry. I do a lot for her, and she's not even willing to do this!

Therapist: OK, let me get this clear. You were hurt and had the thought that she doesn't care about you, and you were angry because it seems unfair that you support her and she didn't spend time listening to or helping you. It's like this is just another one of your mental health problems that you should see your therapist for. Or, that's your thought, at least.

Assessing Vulnerability Factors

A functional analysis of angry behavior also focuses on factors that might have made the client vulnerable to the prompting or triggering event. What is it about this particular day and time that made it so the client reacted with such strong anger or frustration? How is it that today the client ended up engaging in an outburst, whereas at other times the client did not? The key idea here is to determine what made the client so responsive to a prompting event. Common vulnerability factors for anger episodes might include chronic pain, recent stressors or interpersonal conflict, poor sleep, problematic eating, drug or alcohol use, a build up of daily hassles and inconveniences, or perhaps rumination about past events. When examining vulnerability factors, it is generally helpful to focus on events occurring over the past day or two, but longer term factors, such as coping with chronic pain over many weeks or months, or more sustained, major life stressors, such as losses (e.g., of relationships, jobs), moving, and so forth, also are important to consider. Determining vulnerability factors can help build awareness of warning signs and encourage the client to engage in prevention in the future.

Assessing and Validating the Client's Emotional Experiences

The previous clinical example demonstrates how the therapist might closely assess and validate the client's emotional experience. A shift occurred from anger and criticism to the client describing and explaining feelings of hurt and fear in a way that would facilitate continued work. As is suggested in other approaches (e.g., emotion focused therapy; Greenberg, 2010), delineating both primary (in this case, possibly fear and hurt or sadness) and secondary emotions (anger) can facilitate emotional processing. One way to conceptualize the example is that the client felt afraid and hurt and then became angry as a secondary emotional reaction. Anger is indeed a common emotional reaction to other painful emotions or physical sensations (fear and hurt or sadness) or to threats (in this case, the loss of support). In some cases, once clients become aware of and attentive to primary emotions, the secondary emotions tend to reduce. This, however, is not always the case, and it is important for the therapist to avoid assuming that anger is always a secondary emotion; sometimes it is the primary emotion.

Assessing Cognitions

The therapist might also assess the client's interpretations or thoughts. In the example the client had the thought, "If you really cared about me, you wouldn't be doing this." Typically, in dialectical behavior therapy (DBT), the therapist would first help the client identify this as a thought, as in the example when the therapist says, "That thought went through your mind." Other thinking patterns might include thoughts or rules related to the cause or expression of anger (Farmer & Chapman, 2016; e.g., "When I get angry, there's nothing I can do to stay in control," "It's other people's fault when I get angry."). Brief interventions that orient the client to observe her or his thought as a thought, if performed consistently over time, can encourage the client to observe thoughts as thoughts rather than facts. It is important to remember that, when people are very angry, cognitive change strategies may be ineffective because emotional arousal often impedes information processing. Often, with clients with BPD in particular, episodic and intense emotional reactivity can interfere with clients' ability to process corrective information about thinking patterns, solve problems, or control impulsive behavior when they are emotionally distressed (Chapman, Dixon-Gordon, Layden, & Walters, 2010; Chapman, Leung, & Lynch, 2008). Therefore, the therapist might consider being judicious about when or how cognitions are addressed.

Assess Consequences or Function of Angry Behaviors

Another important area to examine includes the events or consequences following angry behavior. When anger erupts in a therapy session, what happens afterward? How does the therapist change her or his behavior in reaction to the client's angry behavior? What kind of internal changes occur in terms of the client's emotional state, physiological state, or thinking? What are the short and longer term consequences of angry behavior? Table 7.1 lists some helpful

TABLE 7.1
Types of Consequences of Angry Behavior

Locus of consequence	Positive	Negative
Internal	Feel charged up, energized Feel powerful	Feel agitated Feel afraid of saying or doing something wrong
External	People do what I want quicker because they don't want me to get angry. People stop bugging me to do things.	Isolation, aloneness, people avoid me

ways to guide the client toward a better understanding of consequences. The therapist can use this as a tool to help the client understand the short- and long-term effects of angry behavior, as well as the internal or external effects. The therapist might explain the role of consequences in angry behavior as follows:

> All behavior has consequences. Angry behavior is no different. When you express anger, things change internally, such as with emotional states, thoughts, urges, desires, and physiological changes in your body. Things also change externally. People might react to your angry behavior in a variety of ways, such as by backing off, asking what's wrong, changing the topic, leaving, getting angry and criticizing you, and so on. Also, externally, if you engage in angry behavior, other things may change, such as if you're angry and driving quickly, you might get into an accident or you might get home or to work more quickly. If we understand the effects of your angry behavior, we will know how it works (or does not work) for you. And if we really understand how it works, we can find a way to make it work less well or to replace it with something else.

STRATEGIES TO MANAGE ANGER-RELATED PROBLEMS

In this section, we review common components of anger management–oriented interventions applied to TIB. Common components of such interventions include psychoeducation and interventions to enhance motivation to change, self-monitoring, strategies to avoid anger-provoking situations, identification of alternative behaviors in which to engage when angry, reducing physiological arousal, role-playing and exposure-oriented strategies, letting go of resentment and anger regarding past events, and reducing vulnerability to negative emotions (Farmer & Chapman, 2016; Kassinove & Tafrate, 2002; Novaco & Jarvis, 2002). Both DBT and cognitive behavior therapy oriented interventions have been associated with moderate to large improvements in anger-related problems within a variety of client populations (Del Vecchio & O'Leary, 2004; DiGiuseppe & Tafrate, 2003; Sukhodolsky, Kassinove, & Gorman, 2004), with findings on DBT including improvements in subjective experience of anger and reductions in self-directed aggression (Cavanaugh, Solomon, & Gelles, 2011; Koons et al., 2001; Linehan, Heard, & Armstrong, 1993; Linehan et al., 2006). In addition, we have found that the effects of these strategies can generalize outside of therapy and the therapy relationship to other relationships, and outside of anger to the effective management of other emotions.

Psychoeducation About Anger

Once anger is identified as being related to TIB, it can be helpful to educate the client about anger. Talking with clients openly about anger and normalizing and clarifying anger can sometimes be disarming and facilitate the perspective that anger-related issues are just one more problem to solve collaboratively. Education might address the systemic nature of emotions more broadly, the fact that angry thoughts and urges do not mean that angry action is inevitable, and the influence of intense anger on the client's ability to think clearly, solve problems, and use coping skills. All of these points can help provide the client with a better understanding of their anger and a place to start in terms of working on it.

Reducing Vulnerability to Anger

One set of emotion regulation skills in DBT is the ABC PLEASE skills (Linehan, 2015), focused on helping clients to reduce their vulnerability to negative emotions. The ABC stands for accumulating positives (engaging in pleasurable activities), building mastery (engaging in efficacy-enhancing activities), and coping ahead of time (proactive coping and practice of effective coping with regard to future stressors). The PLEASE skills involve several strategies to enhance self-care, such as effectively managing physical illness, balancing eating and sleeping, exercising, and avoiding mood-altering substances. In addition to BPD, anger difficulties are common among people with bipolar disorders, where interventions to establish lifestyle balance, regular routines, and consistent rhythms have been found to improve mood stability and reduce vulnerability to anger (e.g., Frank et al., 2005). It can be helpful to periodically check in with clients about their self-care regimen, challenges with eating or sleeping, and so on, as well as other factors increasing emotional vulnerability, such as life stressors. The consistent use of skills to reduce vulnerability and improve self-care may reduce anger episodes over time.

As an example of one of these strategies applied to TIB, the strategy of coping ahead of time can be used to plan ahead to avert anger-related TIB. For example, one of our clients ("Joan"), engaged in a fairly egregious verbal outburst during a group session. During group, a particularly anxious client who was often reluctant to share her experiences practicing new DBT skills had begun to talk more but still had difficulty articulating herself, likely due to anxiety, and she sometimes spoke more loudly or for longer than was socially appropriate. During these times, Joan would periodically snicker to the person next to her. The group therapists and her individual therapist talked with her about this and helped her reduce this behavior in group. One day, however, when the anxious client was talking about her difficulties with her boyfriend, Joan suddenly exclaimed, "You're a fucking bitch!" The anxious client and some of the other clients began to cry, and the two group leaders had to "divide and conquer" to speak individually with a few clients and help them regulate their emotions. The group leader asked Joan to leave and speak with her individual therapist. Subsequently, the DBT consultation team met to discuss the situation and decided that Joan would not be permitted to return to that group but would be allowed to "apply" to get into one of the other available groups.

Applying to get back in involved Joan working with her therapist to (a) devise an appropriate repair for her behavior and (b) come up with a plan to cope ahead of time to prevent this from happening again in the new group. These requirements followed the behavioral principle of *overcorrection*, whereby Joan was asked to provide an apology letter to the group and to the wronged client and to repeatedly practice her coping ahead plan. The plan involved Joan first noticing cues for anger. She often felt irritated with other group members but did not notice her irritation until it had become too intense for her to cope effectively. Much of this preliminary work involved her attending to bodily sensations of emotional arousal using the mindfulness skill of observing. Subsequently, Joan practiced breathing and muscle relaxation and other arousal reduction strategies that could be used in a group context, distraction skills to divert her attention from the anger-eliciting stimuli, and later, the skill of opposite action (Linehan, 1993a, 1993b) to foster compassion for the persons with whom she was irritated. Joan successfully put this plan into action, and although she did engage in periodic disruptive behavior in group, her verbal aggression stopped, and she successfully "graduated" from group about four months later.

Avoiding Anger-Provoking Situations

One common intervention in anger management treatments involves teaching the client to avoid cues for anger. Often referred to as *cue elimination*, this strategy also is one of the steps in the DBT skill of opposite action applied to anger, which involves "gently avoiding" anger-provoking people or events (Linehan, 1993b, 2015). The client gently avoids triggering events for anger, for example, by gracefully leaving the situation or taking a time-out when involved in interpersonal conflict, avoiding e-mails or texts that provoke anger (taking a brief vacation from electronic devices), avoiding people with whom she or he is angry, and even gently avoiding angry thoughts by labeling such thoughts as angry or ruminative thinking and redirecting attention to something distracting in the present moment. A common strategy for couples is to encourage partners to take a time-out when anger is intense enough to interfere with the discussion. Two important rules regarding time-outs are (a) both partners have to agree ahead of time to the time-out and (b) partners must agree to resume the conversation once they have calmed down and are able to talk effectively. Sometimes triggers are difficult to avoid, and in those cases, clients are often taught to insert delays before responding (e.g., by counting to 20 before saying or doing anything), to temporarily walk to another area of the house or room, or to use mental distraction strategies to temporarily disengage attention from the anger-provoking situation or events.

When it comes to anger-related TIB, this strategy may be helpful when the client is unable to engage in a productive discussion with the therapist (because of high levels of anger) and other attempts to regulate anger have proven unsuccessful. The therapist and client might, for example, apply the time-out strategy, whereby the client takes a brief time-out to regulate anger and then returns to the session. Another strategy is to temporarily avoid discussing anger-provoking topics, with the understanding that these topics will be gradually revisited later on. In group settings, the client may temporarily leave, practice emotion regulation strategies, and then return to group.

Reducing Physiological Arousal

Anger can be an intense, motivating emotion, affecting attention, cognition, and the client's ability to communicate skillfully. As a result, even skillful clients (or therapists) can appear unskillful when angry. The problem is not that the client is unable or unwilling to communicate in a nonhostile manner; rather, the client is too upset to think clearly. Arousal reduction strategies can help the client bring emotional arousal to the point where she or he can think clearly and act effectively. In addition, angry behavior sometimes functions to down-regulate emotional arousal (reducing tension, "blowing off steam"), and it can be helpful for clients to have alternative arousal reduction strategies available.

In DBT, one set of physiologically oriented skills that can be especially effective for anger is the TIP skills. TIP stands for temperature, intense exercise, and progressive muscle relaxation (Linehan, 2015). In terms of *temperature*, skills involve strategies to regulate arousal by changing body temperature. One method of doing this is for the client to dunk her or his face in a bowl of ice water, a strategy said to induce the dive reflex and stimulate activity in the parasympathetic nervous system (the "rest and digest" system). Other strategies might involve the client holding cold ice packs on her or his face, taking a warm footbath with aromatherapy oils (e.g., lavender), taking a warm or cold shower, or performing other actions that shift body temperature. *Intense exercise* that is nonaggressive (i.e., not punching, kicking, or other aggressive exercise) can be helpful in reducing anger-related arousal. Muscle relaxation strategies, including *progressive muscle relaxation*, have been used for decades (Goldfried & Davison, 1976) to help clients reduce aversive arousal states, and generally involve the sequential tensing of isolated muscles to about three quarters of their potential tension for about five to 10 seconds, followed by a release of the muscle tension for about 20 seconds. This process is usually repeated twice for each muscle group. After practicing this skill repeatedly, the client may also pair a particular word (e.g., *calm* or *peace*) with the relaxation response, such that the word may eventually come to elicit relaxation in circumstances where more formal practice of this skill would not be possible (e.g., a job interview). This strategy is called *cue-controlled relaxation*. In addition, other relaxation strategies might include diaphragmatic (Hazlett-Stevens & Craske, 2008) or paced breathing (Bornas et al., 2006).

We have coached clients to use these strategies many times in both group and individual therapy contexts in which anger threatened to interfere with therapy. We often describe these physical strategies to clients as the *too-upset-to-think skills*, strategies to use when anger and other emotions are strong enough to interfere with adaptive problem solving. In addition, it is helpful to let clients know that these strategies will not solve the problems leading to anger, but that they will allow clients to approach the problems later on with a clearer mind.

Improving Effective Communication

One of the primary functions of any emotional behavior is to communicate. Effective strategies to reduce anger-related TIB, therefore, often involve training and coaching the client in the use of specific assertiveness skills to communicate her or his needs. The following example illustrates how the therapist might coach a client in some specific DBT interpersonal effectiveness skills, the DEAR MAN skills (Linehan, 1993b, 2015).

Client:	[*Appearing angry, red in the face, with muscles tense.*] I think I'm going to quit group. I don't see the point of going anymore.
Therapist:	This is the first I've heard of this. What's happening with group?
Client:	I leave every week and try to do the homework, and I really don't have any idea what you guys are talking about. Then when I can't do the homework, you all ask me why in front of everyone. It's totally unprofessional, and I don't see why I should keep coming.
Therapist:	OK, it looks to me like you're feeling really frustrated about this. And I can get that if, from your perspective, we're not even giving you what you need to do the homework, and then we ask you why you didn't do it. That would be very frustrating.
Client:	Well, that's what's happening. It's like I don't even get a chance to ask questions, and then I leave all confused.

Therapist: I agree that this is not a recipe for success in group. And I really want you to go to group and learn all the skills we're trying to teach you. So, we've got to come up with a way to make this work for you. In fact, come to think of it, this might be a great opportunity for you to practice some of the interpersonal effectiveness skills we talked about a couple of weeks ago.

Client: Well, I guess, but I'm not sure what you're talking about.

Therapist: OK, so, do you remember the DEAR skills?

Client: I remember DEAR, but I haven't really had a chance to practice or anything.

Therapist: Well, why don't you try now, with my help? Here's the first thing: The *D* stands for "describe the situation," sticking to the facts, and the *E* stands for "express how you feel." Remember?

Client: Sure.

Therapist: Let's just start with those two, *describe* and *express*. Why don't you go ahead and give it a shot. I know you just told me why you're frustrated, but I'd love it if you could take this opportunity to practice.

Client: OK, describe, huh? Well, I leave group confused and not understanding the skills. Then when I sit down to do the homework, I don't know what I'm doing. It's really frustrating!

Therapist: OK, nicely done! You described the situation and your emotional reactions really clearly and concisely, and you left out judgments or inflammatory statements like we talked about in group—not easy to do when you're frustrated or angry, right?

Client: OK, well, thanks.

Therapist: The next thing is to *assert*, or ask for what you want. Think for a moment about whether there's anything you'd like to ask me to do differently. I can't promise I'll be able to do it for sure, but you can ask, and we can discuss it.

Client: OK, but I'm really not good at asking for things. Hmm, could you please check in with me, or with everyone, every once in a while to make sure I'm getting what you're saying and understanding what I'm supposed to do for homework? I think that would help me so I don't leave so confused. Sometimes I am a little shy about speaking up and asking questions.

Therapist: Definitely, I can certainly do that, and I'll mention this to Barb [*the group coleader*] as well, if that's OK with you, so she can do it as well. You know, for someone who says she doesn't understand the skills, you're doing very well! You asked specifically for what you want, and even before that, you came up with a possible solution to the problem. You also did the final skill, the R part, without my asking you to. Do you remember what the R stands for?

Client: Reward or reinforce or something?

Therapist: Exactly. The R is reinforce ahead of time. This means that you tell the person what's in it for her or him if she or he does what you ask. In this case, you know that I want you to succeed and understand the skills. I don't want you to leave confused. And, you let me know that I could help with that by doing what you asked. Right away, I'm much more motivated to do what you've asked me to do. Can you see how this might work better at getting what you want than your other strategy of saying we're unprofessional?

Empathy Building and Perspective Taking

One of the opposite action strategies for anger in DBT involves having the client foster a sense of compassion for the person with whom she or he is angry (Linehan, 1993b, 2015). This strategy involves the client taking the other person's perspective, seeing the world through the other person's eyes, and trying to understand how the other person could feel, think, or act in a particular manner. Empathy and compassion are often incompatible with and may lead to reductions in anger. In the context of TIB, if the client is angry with the therapist, she or he might encourage the client to understand the therapist's perspective. One way to do this is to literally switch seats and have the client pretend to be the therapist. Another strategy is for the therapist to engage in *self-involving self-disclosure*, stating her or his ongoing reactions in the situation; for example, "I get that you're feeling hurt and angry about my being away next week, and I also notice myself feeling hurt and a little scared when you get up and raise your voice at me." Often, clients who seem callous or otherwise uninterested in others' feelings are surprisingly concerned when their therapists express vulnerability in this way. One of our colleagues recently was seeing a client who repeatedly directed harsh criticism at the therapist, and when the therapist stated that she felt hurt when the client described her opinions in this way, the client backed down immediately, apologized, and said she never meant to be hurtful.

Role-Playing and Exposure-Oriented Approaches

Although in the shorter term it can be helpful to encourage clients to avoid anger-eliciting events, in the longer term it is effective for clients to learn how to tolerate these events and the ensuing angry reactions without acting in a dysfunctional manner. This brings us to the principle (previously discussed) of *not removing the cue*. Essentially, when given the choice between removing the cue for emotional distress and helping the client tolerate the cue and cope effectively, it can be most effective to do the latter, because the real world is full of cues for anger. This approach is consistent with exposure- and acceptance-oriented approaches to emotions.

Interventions emphasizing exposure have shown promise in the treatment of anger (Brondolo, DiGiuseppe, & Tafrate, 1997; Tafrate & Kassinove, 1998). As mentioned in Chapter 3, exposure interventions typically involve arranging conditions for the client to encounter stimuli that trigger strong emotional arousal and occasion emotion-consistent behavior. The goal of exposure therapy is for the client to learn new associations with triggering events so that a previously threatening event (e.g., encountering a spider) comes to have a larger array of learned associations (Abramowitz, 2013; Bouton, 1988). In the case of a phobia of spiders, the association of spiders with threatening consequences (e.g., being bitten, infected, or harmed) may persist, but the client also learns "safety" associations.

Similarly, with anger, exposure interventions aim to help the client (a) learn new associations with anger-provoking events, moving from threat, inconvenience, or harm to relative safety, and (b) reduce problematic anger-related behavior. Exposure interventions for anger tend to involve repeated exposures to anger-eliciting events while limiting the client's engagement in anger-consistent expression or actions and, consequently, accompanying reinforcers for these actions (see Tafrate & Kassinove, 1998). One example of this approach to exposure for anger involves *verbal barbs*, or brief statements that trigger anger (Kassinove & Tafrate, 2002).

Another approach that has elements of exposure therapy and skills training is to engage in within-session role-playing of anger-eliciting situations. The therapist assumes the role of a person who engages in anger-provoking behavior, coaching the client on how to effectively cope with the trigger (e.g., through arousal reduction, breathing, and other skills) and effectively communicate in the midst of the angry reaction. This approach, whereby the therapist prompts skillful behavior from the client, can be helpful as an assessment strategy (to better understand exactly what factors trigger anger and what the client experiences) and as practice of new behavior for the client. The therapist also may model effective behavior and coach the client, providing behaviorally specific feedback (Farmer & Chapman, 2016).

Letting Go of Anger and Resentment

Persistent resentment or anger directed toward the therapist or others regarding past events can become therapy-interfering. In these cases, it is particularly important for the therapist to assess and understand the functions and maintaining factors for persistent anger. Often, rumination, repetitive thinking, and holding onto resentment about past events function to maintain the anger in the present and increase vulnerability to angry or aggressive behavior. Persistent anger and resentment may also help the client avoid other emotions, such as shame or sadness. In these cases, mindfulness strategies can help the client reduce rumination (Teasdale et al., 2000), attend to activities in the present moment, and experience and process primary emotions blocked by anger. Interventions addressing persistent anger also involve the client's letting go of grudges and the desire for retribution, revenge, or justice and transitioning from a self-view of oneself as a victim to that of a survivor (Farmer & Chapman, 2016). In addition, as mentioned earlier, it can be helpful for the client to engage in perspective taking to better understand (and possibly foster empathy or compassion) the behavior of the other person or persons with whom he or she is angry.

Contingency Management Strategies

Another helpful set of strategies for anger-related TIB includes contingency management. As discussed in Chapter 3, a first step in contingency management involves the determination of which behaviors to increase and decrease. Sometimes with anger the behaviors to decrease are rather obvious—yelling, screaming, threatening, stonewalling, complaining, criticizing, and so forth. To determine behaviors to increase, the therapist must attend to the function of the angry behavior. Does the client's angry behavior (e.g., yelling, silence, harsh criticism) function to elicit reinforcement in the therapeutic relationship that the client does not receive when she or he communicates in another way?

One way to use contingency management is to extinguish angry behavior and provide differential reinforcement of other or alternative behaviors (Farmer & Chapman, 2016). At times, angry behavior functions to divert the discussion onto another topic or to halt ongoing problem solving or problem discussions. When this is the case, the therapist might gently ignore the angry behavior and return to the topic at hand. If the client is engaging in hostile behavior in session, the therapist might largely ignore this behavior, only providing reinforcement when a more skillful, alternative behavior emerges. This sometimes involves selectively attending and responding to some, but not other, aspects of what the client is saying. A client in a group session, for example, might say, "All of these mindfulness skills are useless! There's no point in this, and I don't know why we keep talking about it. I just don't understand any of this, and it's driving me crazy!" One option is for the therapist to attend to the valid, effective aspects of this client's communication (the communication that not understanding the skills is driving him or her crazy) and to largely ignore the more extreme statements (e.g., statements that the skills are useless). The therapist might say the following, for example:

> You're not getting the point, and it's really frustrating. That makes a lot of sense to me. It might help if we spent a little more time discussing what these skills are and how they are supposed to help. To begin with, do you have any specific questions?

In the case of a client who threatens to engage in harmful behavior of some kind, the therapist must strike a balance between risk management and avoiding the reinforcement of extreme behaviors and threats. When a reinforcer is initially withdrawn, the behavior may temporarily increase in intensity or variety—an *extinction burst* (Miltenberger, 2011). When trying to avoid reinforcing a child's tantrum at the grocery store, a parent might notice that the child temporarily increases the intensity of the tantrum, engages in other aversive behavior, and so on, before she learns that the tantrum does not "work" (i.e., she does not get the cookies that have been denied). In cases where the extinction burst may include serious, self-damaging, or suicidal behavior, the therapist must strike a difficult balance between avoiding the reinforcement of threatening behaviors and managing risk effectively. An example might be a client who states, "I'm going to kill myself if you don't take my calls while you're away on vacation." The behavior to decrease here is suicide threats. There is no simple solution to this problem, but the therapist might remain focused on the behaviors she or he would like to see the client display, such as effective communication of thoughts and feelings about the therapist's unavailability, and then prompt these behaviors by, for example, stating the following:

> Can we rewind just a bit? I can see that this is really important to you, but I'd like to hear you say how you feel about it without the threats. I'm willing to listen to you and talk about this, but not if you're going to threaten to kill yourself. Let's start over. Tell me how you feel about my not being available while away.

This situation presents an opportunity for the client to learn how to state and discuss how he or she feels in an effective manner, without suicide threats. The therapist, of course, must have in place an adequate crisis plan, a solid suicide risk assessment, and must know when and how extra measures must be taken to ensure the client's safety.

MANAGING AGGRESSIVE OR THREATENING
BEHAVIOR IN SESSION

Sometimes angry behavior might involve aggression, threats, or other such actions that must stop immediately to ensure safety or prevent further damage. In these cases, the therapist's top priority is to (a) maximize the safety of the client, clinician, and other clients, if applicable; (b) block and prevent the behavior from continuing; and (c) elicit and reinforce alternative behavior. The therapist must strike a balance between firmness in the message that the behavior needs to stop and a compassionate and nonjudgmental stance. One way to do this is to quickly highlight the behavior (e.g., "You're threatening to hurt me," "I see you have your fists raised") and instruct the client to stop (e.g., "I'd like you to put your arms down, rest them on your lap, and open up your hands," "OK, start over. Please say what you want to say to me, but leave out the part about hurting me"). Another example is the following:

> OK, first, the threats need to stop. When you threaten to hurt me, I feel afraid and frustrated, and I end up focused on how to protect myself rather than how to help you. You're in a lot of pain, and you need me to stay focused on how to help you. So, let's have you start over what you were saying, without the threat, and if you're having a hard time getting it across to me, I'll help you find a way.

Assuming the client has stopped the threatening behavior, the therapist's role would be to coach the client in how to apply skills to regulate or tolerate emotions or more effectively communicate her or his needs. As discussed earlier, ideally, the therapist would then provide a natural positive consequence contingent on the presence of the more effective behavior (e.g., increased warmth, nonverbal communication of interest, nodding; see Farmer & Chapman, 2008, 2016, and Kohlenberg & Tsai, 1991, for further examples), in the hope that this would serve to reinforce the alternative behavior.

It also is likely that threats or verbal or physical aggression, because of their extremity and possible threats to the therapist's safety, will cross the therapist's limits or suggest that the client needs a different level of care. One of our colleagues, for example, was seeing a client who struggled to maintain life outside of institutions (both forensic and psychiatric). She struggled with transient psychotic symptoms, was diagnosed with BPD, had repeatedly engaged in serious suicide attempts, and had previously assaulted a treatment provider. At the beginning of treatment, the clinician conducted a thorough risk assessment, reviewed past files, assessments, and reports, and discussed his own limits regarding physical and verbal aggression. The therapist and client also devised a plan for what the client could do (and specifically which skills she could practice) if she were to feel aggressive urges during group (which she frequently did). Unfortunately, the client arrived one day distraught about interactions with one of her caregivers. When the therapist tried to help her to better understand her emotional reactions, she began to appear agitated, fidgeting, looking away, and saying, "Why do you keep saying that!" Suddenly, she got up and lunged toward the therapist, pinning him in his chair. He extricated himself from the situation, alerted the client's care workers, and explained to the client that he might not be willing to continue to see her for treatment but would first discuss the situation with his treatment team. The team provided support to the therapist and assistance in thinking through the pros and cons of continued work with the client. They also discussed what factors would have to be in place for work with this individual to proceed safely and effectively. Ultimately, however, they decided that her needs would be best met in a different setting. As in this example, we highly recommend that therapists working with aggressive clients seek support, consultation, and assistance from colleagues both regarding the emotional toll this type of work takes and also for assistance in making balanced decisions and pursuing the most effective course of action.

Although generally rare, clinicians sometimes end up in situations such as this, whereby the client either becomes physically aggressive or threatens to. In some cases, these situations are avoidable if the therapist notices the signs of increasing agitation as they are occurring. The following are a few pointers for how to effectively manage clients who are highly aroused and are engaging in threatening behavior:

- Use a calm but firm voice tone. Lower the voice tone somewhat so that the client must stop yelling, and so forth, to listen, but remain firm and emphatic.
- Use the client's name to get her or his attention, but avoid doing so excessively or in an overly soothing or patronizing manner.
- Use a confident, direct posture, and make appropriate eye contact.
- Ask the client to stop the behavior and prompt a new, alternative behavior immediately.
- Redirect the client to another, ideally distracting, topic or activity.
- Provide the client with coaching and assistance in how to stop, how to tolerate her or his level of distress, and how to perform the alternative behavior. Relaxation strategies, such as progressive muscle relaxation or diaphragmatic breathing, as well as self-soothing, can be helpful in reducing anger and arousal in the moment. In addition, physical strategies, such as exercise or having the client hold an ice pack or splash cold water on her or his face, also are effective.

- Orient the client to behavioral skills that she or he can use to regulate and tolerate distress, and actively drag out these behaviors in the moment.
- If the client's behavior continues or escalates, consider (a) instructing the client to leave and use skills to regulate emotions before returning to talk; (b) creating space between the client and the therapist, making use of objects or furniture in the room, if necessary; and (c) leaving the room and finding a colleague or security person with whom to consult.

SPECIFIC STRATEGIES FOR GROUP TREATMENT

Angry behavior sometimes occurs in group and can have a demoralizing effect on both the group members and the therapists. In this discussion, we comment on strategies that therapists would use for groups similar in goals and format to the DBT skills training group (Linehan, 1993b, 2015). Anger-related behaviors in group might include refusing to talk, criticizing the therapist(s) or clients, storming off and out of the room, using verbal aggression or judgmental statements, or being physical aggressive.

There are a few key principles to keep in mind when highlighting and managing angry behavior in groups. First, ideally, highlighting should be done in a light manner and be minimally shame-inducing or embarrassing. This might involve irreverence, humor, stating the unexpected, using a gentle voice tone, or highlighting in a nonverbal or less obvious manner.

Second, the therapist must remember the treatment hierarchy as it applies to groups. Unlike in individual therapy (where life-threatening behavior is the highest priority target), in DBT groups, therapy-destroying behavior (when relevant) is the top priority, followed by behavioral skills and therapy-interfering behavior. *Therapy-destroying behavior* is that which prevents the group from functioning effectively. Examples might include verbal aggression, severely judgmental statements or threats toward other group members, lewd or lascivious behavior, physical aggression toward the therapist, and so on. The top priority in these cases is to stop the behavior; hence, the therapist would use the strategies and tips discussed earlier, and if the behavior is severe or the client does not stop, he or she might ask the client to leave the room or group. If, however, the client's angry behavior interferes with her or his treatment but does not threaten to destroy therapy, the therapist might instead temporarily ignore the behavior in hopes that it may extinguish. If this does not occur, the therapist may have to take the client aside during a break to coach her or him on strategies to better manage anger in group. It can also be helpful to encourage the client to speak at greater length with her or his individual therapist about how to get through group more effectively.

Third, it is important for the therapist to remember that the primary goal of skills training is for the group of clients to learn the skills. As such, if a client's behavior makes it difficult for others to learn the skills or if it precipitates serious frustration or demoralization on the part of other clients or therapists, these behaviors should be addressed sooner rather than later. Prevention of worsening problems should be a primary goal. To engage in effective prevention, the therapist has to be attentive to and observant of the client's behavior and must consider the potential longer term impact of such behavior should it persist or worsen. The following is an example of this with regard to a client making extreme and angry statements (along with sighing, eye rolling, etc.) about the skills she was learning in one of our groups.

> *Therapist:* You know, I can tell you're having a really hard time with the mindfulness skills, and I really want to help you with that. The problem I'm having is that the vehement way in which you bring up your frustration could start to become a problem. Think about what it might be like if you were in a class, and one student in the class kept saying to the professor, "This material really sucks! I'm not learning anything!" How would you start to feel as a student?

> *Client:* I guess I'd have a hard time and be annoyed with the person. Like, why can't she just keep her comments to herself or talk with the prof or something.

> *Therapist:* Exactly, I'm thinking you'd probably also have a hard time concentrating on the class when someone is doing that. So, I'm worried about that with our group. It's OK to be frustrated about the skills; a lot of people are frustrated and have a hard time understanding mindfulness at first. I think we need to work on you saying it differently, though. How could you say it differently?

> *Client:* I guess I just feel frustrated because I waited for this treatment and really thought it could help me, and I'm struggling so much. It's just so hard, I can't really have a blank mind.

> *Therapist:* I know you've been wanting help for so long, and it must be demoralizing to feel like you can't even take full advantage of it. But wait a second—did you say you thought you had to have a blank mind?

> *Client:* Yeah, I mean, isn't that what mindfulness is all about?

Therapist: OK, I see the problem here. I've been practicing mindfulness for 15 years, and I can safely say that I rarely ever have a blank mind! Let's talk about what mindfulness is really about.

MOVING FORWARD

When managing anger-related TIB, there are several important principles to keep in mind. First, it can be effective to approach angry behavior from an emotion regulation framework. Second, remember that angry behavior often serves important social and behavioral functions. Third, it is effective for the therapist to maintain a dialectical stance, remembering to balance acceptance and change, to acknowledge that angry behavior is both functional and dysfunctional, to step into the client's shoes and understand her or his experience, and to both hold onto and let go of the desire for the client to work on anger. Strategies to reduce anger-related TIB (and anger problems more broadly) often first involve the therapist observing and describing the behavior nonjudgmentally and specifically, clearly highlighting and precisely assessing the behavior (e.g., through functional analysis) and looking for opportunities to validate valid aspects of the client's reactions. Skills training can help clients to reduce vulnerability to and physiological arousal associated with anger and to replace angry behavior with effective communication. Other interventions might encourage perspective taking, letting go of resentment, and tolerance or reduction in anger through exposure-oriented approaches. Close attention to contingencies within and outside of the therapeutic relationship also can facilitate effective work on anger-related TIB. Finally, we discussed a few strategies that are more specific to group treatment and to the management of aggressive or threatening behavior.

8

HOW TO CONFRONT THERAPY-INTERFERING BEHAVIOR

"Do you mind if I drink this beer in here?" These were the first words, in the first moment, of the first group psychotherapy session one of us conducted in graduate school. It was a dialectical behavior therapy (DBT) skills training group, and the client was one of the most difficult-to-treat people any therapist could ever have. "Alicia" was a mid-40s Hispanic single mother who met full diagnostic criteria for borderline personality disorder (BPD), polysubstance abuse, posttraumatic stress disorder, and as it would turn out, dissociative identity disorder. She had been hardened by an interminable series of life traumas, beginning in childhood and continuing—sexually, physically, emotionally—throughout her life. Listening to her story, it was as if a shadow had been irrevocably cast early on, darkness following her every step, shifting in shape and size over time but never leaving her alone. She had suffered mercilessly through chronic and unrelenting childhood sexual abuse,

http://dx.doi.org/10.1037/14752-008
Managing Therapy-Interfering Behavior: Strategies From Dialectical Behavior Therapy, by A. L. Chapman and M. Z. Rosenthal

emotional invalidation and frequent beatings by her father, and rapes, many of them, throughout her adolescence and adulthood by at least a dozen men.

During all this suffering, Alicia had no choice but to adapt, to learn how to escape, even if temporarily. Substance use, dissociation, suicide attempts, and nonsuicidal self-injury had emerged as her primary ways of coping with acute emotional distress. Long before the day she asked permission to drink a beer in group therapy, these had become her survival strategies. From a DBT perspective, she was, on the one hand, doing the best she could do given everything she had endured, whereas on the other, she had to learn to do better.

Alicia had been hospitalized for psychiatric reasons too many times to count, was known all over the region by emergency department personnel from her attempts to obtain pain medications, had no job, had few friends, and was significantly emotionally labile and impulsive. In any instant during psychotherapy she could swiftly move from expansive emotional incoherence to stone-faced dissociative immobility, and anywhere between. She was as likely to be calm and serious as she might be agitated, unpredictable, or flippant. Being in the room with Alicia, one had a sense that she just might say or do anything. Interestingly, as therapy-interfering as her actions could be, they never seemed to be deliberate. It was easy to see how her therapy-interfering behavior (TIB) made sense, no matter how egregious and stunning it could be.

Alicia's life experiences had undoubtedly affected her biological makeup. Recurring traumatic experiences and lifelong interpersonal invalidation had affected the basic processes needed to skillfully live her life. Central nervous systems underlying sensation, perception, attention, and emotion had all surely been altered, and this meant TIB of the unintentional sort could be expected. This was not because she was trying to be manipulative but because dramatically distressing events had changed the nature of her biology and behavior. Using the framework of Linehan's (1993a) biosocial model, DBT therapists would humanely conceptualize her TIBs as accidental byproducts of emotional dysfunction resulting from the back and forth between her reciprocally transacting lifetime of biological vulnerabilities and environmental invalidation. Problems regulating emotions made it hard for her to be skillful, which made it difficult for the world to respond to her well, which exacerbated her emotional dysfunction, which made it increasingly difficult for her interpersonal needs to be met, and so on. These biologically and socially mediated influences begetting each other endlessly, her TIBs naturally occurred along the way.

Alicia's case illustrates how TIB can nonjudgmentally be thought of as conditioned responses to stimuli inherent to the process of psychotherapy. Although hers is an extreme example of such conditioned responses, this way of thinking about TIB allows therapists to comfortably and compassionately talk with clients about their TIB. It is not that she was necessarily trying to interfere with her therapy progress, wanting to be this way or that way, or purposefully getting in her own way. Instead, one way to conceptualize why Alicia's TIBs were highly probable is that her ability to sense, make sense of, and respond to emotionally evocative cues was severely impaired.

Talking to her about this could go as follows:

> Alicia, as we think about how we can collaboratively plan on ways to help you dissociate in here less often, I'd like to share with you how I think about this. From my experience knowing you, I don't think you are trying to dissociate in here on purpose. Not at all. I think it is more likely that when certain things happen in here, you are taken by surprise and have a hard time knowing what to do skillfully. So, for example, some things I say or do might trigger an automatic and unplanned response that leads you to respond in the best way you have learned to, which can be dissociation, urges to hurt yourself, or other ways to escape. These therapy-interfering behaviors make lots of sense. It's as though over time from your experiences your brain has grown a long antenna attuned to detect danger in your environment. The antenna is there to protect you, and when it senses danger the emotional center of your brain hijacks other parts of your brain. This means that even the everyday and nondangerous sensory cues—what you hear, see, touch, smell, and taste—all of these things can be processed as signals of danger, like false alarms. Your brain then activates its survival circuitry to protect you from being harmed, except that when you truly are safe, as you are in here with me, this means your survival circuitry overrides some of those other parts of the brain—like paying attention, thinking, and problem solving. With those parts of your brain being overridden, you are at risk for saying or doing things that end up interfering with therapy, like dissociation. Our job together is to notice when these things are happening so that we can catch the survival circuitry from overriding those other parts of your brain, and over time you will learn to predict these things and have new and more skillful ways of responding using your DBT skills. If we do this well, it will mean that the therapy-interfering behaviors we catch and change in here, like dissociation, will happen less both during our sessions and outside of therapy.

In conceptualizing TIB as conditioned responses to stimuli evaluated as aversive or dangerous, Alicia's request to drink alcohol in group psychotherapy could be thought of both as TIB and as a way of coping with the unpleasant internal experiences elicited by an unfamiliar male therapist entering the room. The surprised therapeutic response to her request was an irreverent, "No, you cannot," but it led to others in the group being distracted and talking to each other. Fortunately, the more senior cotherapist took over and initiated the mindfulness practice, standard as a way to begin the group. Everything settled down quickly. The TIB had not derailed the group process.

Over the next few years, Alicia's TIB in group continued. It was unpredictable, often startling the clients and cotherapists with its intensity and magnitude. Her TIB included, among other things, instant and seemingly unprovoked agitation, unresponsiveness and dissociation, impulsive behavior, inconsolable sobbing, and inappropriate boundaries with others in the group. The question of whether this was culturally influenced was explored, and her second-generation Mexican American perspective was considered. It is important to point out that Alicia was as likable as she was impaired. When lucid, she was irrepressibly sweet, tenderhearted, grateful for treatment, and even hopeful. Sadly, from her perspective she was living a life that was not worth living. Alicia had learned that, sometimes, physical escape from acute negative emotions was not an option. The frequency of such torturous moments early in life had taught her to flip the dissociative switch to reduce acute psychological distress. Her primary alter, Anthony, had developed over time as her protector, a way for her to make it through the slog of everyday emotional misery, an ally ready to help in the event of unpredictable and uncontrollable traumatic events. Often during group therapy sessions, Alicia's face would wear the signs of the oncoming dissociation that would produce Anthony. First, her eyes began to stare as if seeing through the walls of the clinic, far into the distance. Then, her emotionless blank expression would be arrested by the violent twitches of staccato eyeblinks. This TIB lasted 10 to 20 seconds. As dissociation neared, Alicia seemed like a balloon being untethered, readying to float away and surrender to the winds until coming back to the ground somewhere far away. When the onset of these TIBs was complete, everything about her comportment would predictably shift. Her "other personality," Anthony, would show up in the room to continue the therapy session.

Anthony was a man who sat straight, stood tall, and looked people in the eye. He behaved like a caricature of masculinity, powerful and dominant over anyone in the room, in charge of the therapy process, subject to no one's agenda or rules. He did not put up with anything inside or outside the therapy session that he did not want to. Anthony was confrontational, unwilling to show vulnerability, a hardened and uncompromising shell. In treating Alicia, the most difficult-to-manage TIBs occurred when Anthony was in the room.

It is not every day that the average clinician encounters someone with the frequency and severity of Alicia's TIBs. In considering Alicia and her fundamentally distinct repertoire of behavior she called Anthony, what were the TIBs that had to be targeted? When? How? Should the TIBs related to dissociation and Anthony have been targeted before trying to help her be less impulsive and disruptive, as Alicia, in the group? Should agitation and hostility have been the most important things to address first so that the other group members could feel safe in the room? Or should the substance-use-related TIBs have been prioritized over everything else? Maybe it would have been best to begin by targeting the prevention and containment of sudden emotional outbursts that could become hopelessly protracted. Lots of TIB means lots of tough choices for the therapist about what to confront and what to avoid, what to challenge and what to ignore, what to target for change and what to allow and accept. These kinds of choices commonly are made in psychotherapy clinics all over the world by therapists with clients far less impaired than Alicia.

The remainder of this chapter is intended to help clinicians develop a plan and process for how to confront TIB not addressed in other chapters. As mentioned in Chapter 2 and discussed next, often the first step in such a plan is to use the DBT target hierarchy to determine what TIB occurring in session to target, and when. When highlighting or confronting in-session TIB, another important consideration is how to use a dialectical worldview to guide the synthesis of acceptance (e.g., validation) and change-oriented (e.g., direct confrontation, problem solving) strategies. We discuss these and other steps and strategies next.

EFFECTIVE TARGETING OF IN-SESSION THERAPY-INTERFERING BEHAVIOR: WHAT TO TARGET AND WHEN

The model for managing TIBs in DBT is designed to help clinicians know what to do in highly complex and severe multidiagnostic clients. With extremely impaired clients such as Alicia, there is simply no way to be effective without having some kind of approach for TIBs. The approach used in DBT to attend to and manage TIB, however, need not be specifically limited to managing erratic and dramatic behaviors among those meeting diagnostic criteria for BPD or other personality disorders. The approach also does not have to be restricted to those examples detailed in other chapters of this book. TIBs occur across clients, across therapists with different therapeutic orientations, and across clinic settings.

Recall that in DBT, a structural heuristic is used to provide a framework for therapist decisions about what, in any given moment, has to be targeted. The treatment target hierarchy dictates the first step in considering whether it makes sense to address any TIB during the psychotherapy session. Put simply, if problems related to self-harm or harm toward others are present, any and all TIBs unrelated to harm can be ignored. The priority in those moments is to reduce the risk of harm to self or others. If TIBs are present at the same time as problems with harm toward self or others, such TIBs can be addressed as a component of reducing the risk of self-harm or harm to others. This could be the case if a client reports increased suicidal ideation related to a relationship ending and this relationship ending explains why the client missed recent therapy sessions. In this case, the therapist can help the client reduce suicidal ideation as the primary target, consistent with the DBT treatment target hierarchy. As part of the plan to stay alive and reduce risk of self-harm, the therapist can at the same time work toward obtaining a commitment from the client to come to therapy sessions no matter how upset she or he is about events during the week.

In the absence of any concerns related to self-harm or harm to others, the next level of targets on the DBT treatment hierarchy involves attending to and working with the client to reduce TIBs. The TIBs that are most important to target are those that are therapy-destroying, which we discussed in Chapter 7 and elsewhere. Also, as discussed in Chapter 7, there are important considerations in selecting which TIB to attend to, such as the degree to which the TIB is directly interfering with the client attaining their treatment goals, life goals, and the goal of living consistently within their core values. Once the TIB is observed by the therapist and the decision is made to target it, many different approaches from DBT can inform what the therapist says or does. We have dedicated chapters in this book to specific kinds of TIB, including when clients push up against the therapist's boundaries or limits (Chapter 4), are late or miss psychotherapy appointments (Chapter 5), become angry or hostile (Chapter 7), engage in avoidance (Chapter 9), or behave in a sexually inappropriate way (Chapter 10). In this chapter, we introduce key considerations that therapists can use to respond to other kinds of TIB in the psychotherapy session.

NOT CONFRONTATION: COMPASSIONATE, COLLABORATIVE, AND INTENTIONAL TARGETING OF THERAPY-INTERFERING BEHAVIORS

An organizing principle DBT therapists use when managing TIB is that the therapist has to aim for effectiveness. The therapist has a target in mind when she or he attends to the TIB during session, leading the client to, ideally, overcome this TIB to help move closer to his or her treatment goals. Effectiveness as a principle is inherently pragmatic, focused on the therapist's searching for and inching closer toward what works. This is what the philosopher of science Stephen Pepper (1942) described as a *contextualistic approach to truth*. What works in the dynamic context of the moment is what is true. Being right is only possible if it means the contextual truth—workability, effectiveness—is observed. This is how the DBT therapist is trained to think. It means that, as therapists observe TIB, they are likely to immediately consider whether and how to effectively orient the client to and target changing these behaviors.

Chasing effectiveness as the bull's eye criterion for the management of TIBs means that therapists must discern and communicate how TIB is clearly linked to the client's treatment goals. The TIB can sometimes be an exemplar of the very things the client would like to change, making a straightforward case for why such behavior has to be observed and attended to during the session. Clients who would like to have better relationships with others, for example, might demonstrate clinically relevant in-session interpersonal behaviors (e.g., unwillingness to be vulnerable or trusting) that are similar to what they do with others and that make it difficult for meaningful relationships to develop or be maintained. This is a common clinical example. In such cases, the TIB is the quality-of-life interfering behavior. To not attend to it may be a disservice to the client. Similarly, clients who have difficulties regulating emotions will have this problem during psychotherapy, those who are impulsive in decision-making will demonstrate a high sense of urgency to make quick decisions in session, and so on.

To be effective in response to most TIBs, DBT therapists attempt to use a nonjudgmental therapeutic frame. Seeking what is valid and what is not in the TIB, the trained clinician commonly responds using validation before trying to seamlessly orient the client to the TIB as a treatment target. After nondefensively observing the TIB and highlighting how it makes sense that the TIB has occurred, the therapist then actively and directly orients the client, usually in a gentle manner, to ways that the TIB can be attended to in the therapy session. The narrative content that was being talked about can be revisited soon after, but the opportunity is there to shift targets toward the process of what is happening in the session and the emergent TIB.

Sometimes, without wilting in distress or defensively responding, the DBT therapist does this with delicate and soothing precision to ensure the client's response is open and willing. At other times the therapist is matter-of-fact and straightforward about the need to consider changing the focus of the session for a few minutes. And at other times this orientation and redirection of the session is done with enthusiasm, excitement, and demonstrative optimism:

> I am so glad to see this therapy-interfering behavior has finally happened! I know how badly you want to be able to change your relationships with people, and this is one of those moments when we have a chance to directly work on the very thing getting in the way of your relationships!

(This is an example of the dialectical strategy of "making lemonade out of lemons"; Linehan, 1993a.) Irrespective of the interpersonal style the therapist uses, organizing principles of orienting the client to TIB targets include being intentional, nonjudgmental, compassionate, collaborative, and clear about what can be targeted, why, and how it will be helpful to do so.

This active response to TIBs can be contrasted with therapist passivity, affirmations of the client, or efforts to encourage the client to share more details about their experience associated with the TIB. There is nothing inherently problematic about responding to TIB with what has been defined elsewhere as *Level 2 validation* (i.e., reflecting, paraphrasing, or summarizing what the client has said). Indeed, these microlistening skills are essential to psychotherapy and vital to the nonspecific common factors that account for much of the success in psychotherapy.

When responding to TIB, however, we suggest that clinicians keep in mind that this particular strategy often functions to encourage the client to talk more about whatever might be associated with the TIB being observed. Sometimes, getting clients to talk more about this or that TIB is a smart strategy, but at other times, talking about TIB is not part of the solution to the TIB. Sometimes, talking about TIB can be itself TIB, as when the client talks tangentially or in an avoidant manner. At other times, clients are not sure what to talk about and talk discursively or without intent. Their thought processes can be ruminative, disorganized, or paranoid. Accordingly, more rumination, more disorganized thinking, or more paranoia may not be helpful. Instead, it is possible that learning to identify and change these TIBs might help clients get some relief and learn to change these dominant psychological processes. The bottom line is that it is wise for therapists to use Level 2 validation mindfully, and not habitually as a rule. This requires considering, irrespective of the TIB, whether to passively or actively respond. Passive responses may be experienced as validating but may not lead to decreased TIB. Active responses, however, may include both validation and orienting toward ways to change the TIB therapeutically. Table 8.1 offers several concrete examples of how passive responses to TIB can be compared with more active ones.

In all the examples in Table 8.1, the active and direct response to TIB is anything but confrontational. In fact, it is soft, from the heart, validating, and then and only then includes orientation to TIB. All of the examples connect the TIB in the room to a problem interfering with the client's life. This connection is the secret to success in these moments. In the following transcript, we take a deeper dive into the trenches of how one of these TIBs could look. In this case, the client is a depressed and anxious young man who has difficulties coping with stress during the week. The client is afraid his wife will soon leave him, is afraid he will be fired, and is unsure whether he wants to continue working as a computer programmer. He is a devout Christian whose faith is important to him, yet he is unhappy about

TABLE 8.1
Comparing Passive and Active Therapist Responses
to Therapy-Interfering Behavior

Therapy-interfering behavior	Passive response	Active response (validation + orienting)
A client with generalized anxiety disorder behaves in a highly distracted way, checking his mobile phone and sending texts in the session while talking discursively.	Therapist ignores the therapy-interfering behavior (TIB), focusing instead on the content of what the client is saying, reflecting, paraphrasing, summarizing, affirming the client for coming to therapy, working hard, or asking the client to "tell me more."	Raul, I can't help but notice how you seem very distracted today. I know there is a lot going on at work and at home, and my guess is that you are feeling worried that you need to keep up with it all, even in here for our session. This is the kind of therapy-interfering problem, being unfocused and distracted, that we talked about could happen. And you may remember that when we talked about it, we agreed together that if this happens we will notice it in here and try to change this process. If we can do that in here it will help you be less stressed and more focused in your life.
A depressed client is unresponsive to questions, sitting and thinking for minutes at a time.	Therapist sits in silence, leaning toward the client, taking notes, nodding head, or displaying facial expressions suggesting the therapist is interested.	As you think about these things, I'd like to make an observation, and I want you to know this is coming from a place of caring for you. I can see that it is hard for you to answer the questions I am asking, and with your permission I'd like to see if we can turn our attention to what is making it difficult for you in here. It's possible that if we can solve this problem in here, we can help you be more skillful in dealing with your wife and boss when they ask you things and you are unsure how to respond.
A socially anxious client is excessively agreeable with the therapist and neglects to ask for what he wants or needs.	Therapist ignores the TIB, waits, and hopes this will change over time as the client learns to be less socially anxious about evaluation by others.	Before we keep going, let's be mindful together of something that is happening in the room. I am noticing that you have agreed so quickly to what I have asked of you that I am not sure I am connected to what you are really wanting or needing. Based on everything I know about you and our work together, I am wondering if you are feeling anxious, in here, with me, about how I might think about you if you were to say no to something I ask of you. It would make sense if you felt that way, since that is what we are working on together as something that happens at work and feels terrifying. Can we turn together to look at this, and we can come back to what we were just talking about in a few minutes? Would you be willing to do this? And I won't be offended if you say no.

(continues)

Therapy-interfering behavior	Passive response	Active response (validation + orienting)
An emotionally upset client with multiple diagnoses and many treatment targets comes into session and talks superficially about events in the past week, insisting the therapist needs to hear about things that happened, and descriptions of these events takes most of the session.	Therapist listens, validating the client's request to be heard, periodically trying to talk about other topics, and then relenting again to silence as the client shares additional details about different events that have been stressful in the past week.	You know, all of these things sound very upsetting, and I can see how distressed you are in here as you talk. I think everything you just shared would be pretty upsetting to most people. Certainly I would be upset if this stuff happened to me. And here is the thing I'd like to observe, right now in this moment: I am having the thought that in all of what you have told me, I understand the facts of the events, but I do not know how you are feeling in here. So I am sitting here and noticing to myself that my mind is asking me to check in on you. And you know what, the other thing is that by doing this, by being mindful of your emotion in this moment, it may help give you a tool to use when you need to be mindful of your emotions outside of this room. Would you be open to taking a minute, stopping, and being mindful of your emotions, here and now, and then we can choose together the most effective next step in the session?

the church he has been attending since moving into the area 2 years ago from another state.

> *Client:* So, as I was saying, it's just, I mean, it's everything these days. I don't know where to start. This last week was totally emotional for me. My wife won't even look at me, my subordinates at work don't listen, and my boss doesn't give me the time of day. And then I go to my church—remember I was telling you about this last week—and so the pastor delivers this sermon about hope, how faith is hope bestowed by Jesus Christ. How we all need to allow Him to be a part of our daily lives with our faith, which you know I believe in, and how this is the path to true hope [*shaking his head*]. I mean, should I tell you more about this? Is this what you wanted us to talk about today? Because it really, really stressed me out, and I could just vent the whole time about it. Probably

make me feel better if I did, too. Right? But first I have to tell you about what my wife said this morning, because it was so unbelievably hurtful. I know I am kind of rambling here.

Therapist: [*Validation*] You are feeling really stressed and it sounds like there is a lot to talk about, and so I am wondering if we can stop for a moment, breathe, be in the here-and-now together, and be mindful of what you are feeling. Maybe a mindfulness exercise would be a useful thing for us to do before we get too far into our time today?

Client: Yeah, I guess. Sure. But before we do that, can I tell you what happened this morning? I promise it will be quick [*client tells the story of what happened, and it takes 10–15 minutes.*] So, can you believe that? I don't even know what to do about this one. Oh, and the other thing. I can't believe I haven't told you this yet. This is ridiculous. You are not going to believe it.

Therapist: [*interrupting gently but decidedly*] What happened with your wife this morning was important, and how you are feeling about all of this is important. I'd like to suggest that we pause, together, and take a minute to consider what we might want to accomplish in our appointment today. Before we do that, would you be open to us doing a mindfulness practice?

Client: I am so sorry—you asked me to do this a few minutes ago and now you are asking me again [*sighs*]. This is the story of my life these days. I feel like I am disappointing everyone around me, and no one seems to get what I am going through. It's getting old, this feeling that I am failing at everything I do. I am failing at work, obviously. I am failing with my marriage. Why? What did I do to get into this mess? Why am I so damn stuck? And you know what? Nothing seems to help me feel better. Nothing at home. It's like a morgue in there. She is so cold to me, you have no idea. Work? I used to like what I do—you know? I should never have gotten this degree, my parents were right. And now, like I was telling you, this pastor and this church. I have always found solace and peace in my faith. Not even this is helping me anymore. I think I'm having a midlife crisis. But I'm not even that old, right? What does middle-aged mean anyway? You know?

Therapist: Lots of questions and lots of emotions right now. I'd like to observe that we are in this same space together, swirling around and around in all that you are experiencing right now. It's a lot for anyone to have at once. A lot to sit with and observe. And I'd like, if you are willing, to help you with all of this right now. I have suggested we practice mindfulness together, and you have said you are open to this. But each time this happened in the first half of our session, you shared more details about what has been bothering you.

Client: Isn't that what I am supposed to do in here? Tell you about the things that have been bothering me? I'm sorry, but I'm confused. I am just disappointing you, right? I'm a train wreck.

Therapist: If I observe my experience right now, it is anything but judgmental of you. In fact, I am feeling a lot of sadness about all of the emotional pain and suffering you are experiencing. I want to help you. And I think I can, if you are able to practice a little willingness and try out a mindfulness practice to stay present for a few minutes. I really think this will help anchor you, and then we can really dive in and work on what's important to you.

Client: OK.

Therapist: See, mindfulness can bring you into the present moment, to [allow you to] stand back from the past and the worries of the future, to let go of the truth of all the thoughts in the emotional vortex of your mind. And I think this tornado of rumination that is happening in here is similar to what you have told me happens outside of therapy. I think—and you tell me if I am on to something—that this kind of thing happens a lot, and that it is hard to live your life the way you would like to when you are overwhelmed with all of these stressful things and the ways your mind tries to handle the stress.

Client: Yeah, you're right.

Therapist: So this moment, in all of its misery and suffering, is an opportunity for you to learn how to change how you experience yourself and relate to your struggles. Mindfulness practice right now can help you take a step back from all of these upsetting thoughts and can help us then use the rest of our session effectively.

Client: You don't want me to tell you about everything that happened this week?

Therapist: I want us to change the way you experience your distress, and I want us to figure out together what we want to work on so that when you leave here in 15 minutes, you have learned to do something with this emotional vortex in your mind that you can bring with you, into the moments of your life between our sessions when you are upset. I am confident that mindfulness is a way in here for us to catch your mind spinning, to observe it without getting taken by it, and to move you forward toward your life goals. Talking about the past is a part of that, but I want to help you learn to talk about the past in a way that is effective, skillful, targeted toward your goals.

Client: You don't want me to come in here and vent? I thought that is what I was supposed to do.

Therapist: Good question. On the one hand, venting is going to happen in here sometimes. Sure. And on the other hand, there is no reason to believe that venting is the solution to all of your problems. It may help you feel slightly relieved while you are here, and you might feel like someone understands you, which is very important. The thing is, there are other ways I can show you to talk about things that are upsetting, ways that are not about venting only, ways of experiencing yourself, ways of problem solving, ways of changing how you process your thoughts. If venting was the solution, you would have gotten better a long time ago, because you have some people in your life who you can vent to, right?

Client: That's true. OK, I think I get what you are saying.

Therapist: So shall we practice mindfulness?

Client: Sure.

SOME THERAPY-INTERFERING BEHAVIOR MUST BE DIRECTLY CONFRONTED

Although most TIBs are attended to in a nonconfrontational manner, the dialectical antithesis is that, in some instances, it is entirely appropriate and reasonable for the therapist to confront a TIB as being significantly problematic. This, too, often begins with his or her validation of the valid. And although we emphasize throughout this volume the value therapists place on validating the valid when responding to and attempting to help clients change TIB, it is also important to point out that therapists do not always validate first. This could be intentional or inadvertent. It may be that the therapist responds to TIB without thinking, acknowledging that the TIB is a problem that has to be solved without first validating the valid aspects of the TIB. This is akin to what happens when driving a car and realizing that the tires have begun to lose air pressure. The first thing to do is recognize there is a problem, but immediately after this it is usually most effective to get to the gas station as quickly as possible to fill the tires with air. After doing this, the driver keeps a watchful eye on the air pressure, the tires may or may not stay inflated for a long time, and the driver may or may not have to follow up with a visit to the mechanic.

When therapists respond to TIB without validating first, it is done from a stance of compassion, nonjudgment, and openness. This means that the words themselves may be direct and clear, but the way in which the therapist frames the words is not pejorative, but is collaborative and with the client's interests in mind. In such cases, the issue is less about whether the therapist remembered to validate first than about whether she or he was able to respond to TIB with curiosity, seeking the kernels of truth in the client's experiences associated with the TIB. What are some examples of TIBs that may be difficult to first validate? Imagine a client after the first few sessions suggesting that you, the clinician, are not the kind of therapist he wants, stating,

> No offense, but I thought you were going to be an expert, not just your typical shrink. Can you suggest a therapist who can help me? I need help, and I don't see how in the world you are going to be the one.

And let us imagine in this example that his style of saying this is not kind, that it is judgmental and hostile. Let us also assume it is the kind of interpersonal request that the client learned might get him what he needs from people in his family when he was younger, but that few people in the client's current life would respond to this behavior favorably. Should you respond with warmth or validation? It could be, on the basis of your theoretical orientation, that you respond to these statements with a set of assumptions, hypotheses, or interpretations, that you respond with warmth and understanding and refer the client to another clinician, or that you reflect back what you are hearing to encourage him to share more of his thoughts, to feel more of his feelings, maybe to vent his emotions, or to learn to trust you will not respond the way others do when he expresses himself this way. In other cases, therapists may choose not to observe the TIB for valid reasons guided by their case conceptualization or theoretical orientation.

A response therapists might have to this case is to directly and matter-of-factly attend to the TIB. The therapist might say,

> This is something we should talk about for a minute. I'm glad you brought it up. On the one hand, I think this treatment can help you. And on the other, I am willing to help you find another therapist. With that in mind, I also would like to observe that asking others to help you, skillfully, is something that we have talked about as a goal of our work.

In this example, the dialectic of how helpful the treatment will be was highlighted and it was set up for the client and therapist to collaboratively synthesize. Because the client asked for help in an ineffective manner, the therapist answered the question directly, without explicitly validating anything, and then shifted the target to the way in which the question was asked. Put another way, therapists can directly and effectively respond to TIB without much validation first. Table 8.2 illustrates a few examples of TIB that might

TABLE 8.2
Contrasting Passive and Direct Therapist Responses
to Therapy-Interfering Behavior

Therapy-interfering behavior	Passive response	Direct response
Client with opioid addiction is nodding off.	Therapist asks the client to share more about her or his thoughts and feelings.	Can you look up while we talk? You look like you might be nodding off or really tired. Are you on the nod? [*Client affirms and then sighs.*] What can you do right now to be more present and attentive?
Client who has narcissistic features is highly disrespectful, making an exceptionally unreasonable request of the therapist.	Therapist ignores the therapy-interfering behavior (TIB), capitulates to the client request, and decides to talk about the TIB another time.	I am not willing to say yes to your request. However, I am having the thought that this kind of request is the kind of thing that, even though it seems reasonable to you at the time, sometimes gets you into trouble with others because it is not received well. It is not appropriate for me or any therapist to say yes to that request. Would you be willing to take a look together at what led you to ask me that question as a way to look into the window of this process for you? I think that if we do this, we might find a way to help you make some changes to get what you ultimately want—others to understand you better.
Client with severe obsessive–compulsive disorder insists repeatedly when ruminating in session that the treatment is being done incorrectly.	Therapist tries to satisfy the client by recurrently making small changes to the therapy.	I understand that this treatment does not always look the way you expect it to. I assure you, this is the treatment. We can take a look at the research behind it or the treatment manual on my bookshelf. I would not make this up, and even though it is not what you expect, it is an approach that has been found to be safe and effective. It can work. Would you be willing to notice the urges to ask me to change the treatment in our session today, and instead of acting on those urges, would you be open to the idea that you could observe the thought without saying anything? I suppose I am asking you if you are willing to let go and trust me, to allow me to provide this treatment to you.

not be met with heavy doses of validation; it also includes examples of possible passive therapist responses and the way a therapist might respond directly.

In addition to these strategies, it is important to point out that therapists sometimes redirect, interrupt on purpose, or explicitly block TIB because it might be effective to prevent a particular behavior (e.g., a client beginning to cry and then saying, "See, I am a total failure") in a class of behavior (e.g., declarations of self-loathing) that is similar to what the client does outside therapy (e.g., being self-judgmental with people close to the client in their personal life) and functions to keep she or he from moving closer to the life they value having (e.g., others are distressed by this and distance from her or him whenever self-loathing behavior occurs). In this example, the therapist could choose to redirect the client by alerting her or him to another topic to discuss that is unrelated. This could be subtle, as when a therapist ignores the self-loathing and says, "You know what, I realize we have not yet talked about your promotion at work. Last time we met you said we needed to talk about this. I think now might be a good time to do that." Alternatively, the therapist could interrupt the self-loathing as soon as it gets started and suggest a skill be used instead. This could happen if the therapist were to say,

> Let me stop you before you get any deeper into this pit of self-loathing. I see you have picked up the shovel and are digging, and we have been here together before, so I know what is about to happen. What do you say we break this habit by doing something totally different right now? How about we use a distress-tolerance skill for a few minutes? Then we can come back to talking about this and we will see if you are any less self-judgmental.

Still another response the therapist might have is to block this self-loathing TIB altogether. This could happen if the therapist were to say,

> You know, today I want you to know that I am not willing to allow you to begin talking about yourself in a self-judgmental way. I care about you too much and have seen it happen too many times, so I won't let it happen. I certainly can't control what you think or feel, but I will do everything I can to block you from talking about yourself in a way that is self-judgmental.

When using these direct approaches, the tone is compassionate and client centered; the therapist might lean in and show care and support, all while making it crystal clear that these behaviors are problematic and will be prevented at all reasonable costs in the service of helping the client meet his or her treatment goals.

ATTENDING TO THE PSYCHOTHERAPY PROCESS

Psychotherapy sessions involve a lot of talking. If you ask clients who have never received psychotherapy what they imagine the process will look like, almost all of them will say they expect to talk about their problems and the therapist to help them. If you ask clients who have been in therapy before about their expectations, they say something similar. Clients talk, and therapists listen. This is the convention in psychotherapy in most parts of the world. Through this process, the client gains insight and soon begins to make changes. And along the way, there are TIBs. Therapists work with clients early in treatment to orient to TIBs and to construct the concrete bridge between the TIBs that occur inside the clinic to the quality-of-life interfering problems outside the clinic. But clients do not walk into the session and simply tell therapists, "Today we will be working on my TIB. I am feeling angry with you and considering dropping out of therapy," although both of us have had clients say that before (they were DBT clients, though, so that does not really count).

The more typical process of attending to TIB begins by collaboratively identifying near the beginning of the session a couple of targets to work on together. After deciding that there is no higher order target of self-harm or harm to others, there is a discussion about the various topics that could be addressed in the therapy session. If any of these topics are TIBs, they are prioritized accordingly. As an example, it is possible that a client has been thinking about ending therapy prematurely. The therapist could assess this by asking, as we often do in our clinics, the client to rate her or his urges to end therapy on a scale of 0 to 10. If this number goes up from session to session, it may be an important topic to discuss. But let us say that the therapist and client began the session without having identified any clear TIBs, and the decision was made to talk about events of the previous week that were stressful. The client shared what happened, and as the session continued, the therapist looked for ways to solve problems with the client so that new skills could be identified to help respond to recent life stressors. This client was depressed and upset about feeling rejected by his boyfriend, and the client and therapist decided to spend time examining the automatic thoughts, assumptions, and interpretations about the situation leading to him feeling rejected. As this was being done, the client started to talk about something else altogether. He segued into this new discussion by saying, "I really need to tell you about something else," and continued in this way, making it difficult for the therapist to observe the shift in conversation as TIB without interrupting the new story that was being told. We think this is something most clinicians experience. Frustration about not feeling comfortable interrupting is the most common reason clinicians we train tell us they choose not to attend to TIBs, but there are many other reasons as well. Exhibit 8.1 offers some of the common reasons for not attending to TIBs.

We now take a couple of these examples and explore them further, with approaches that therapists might use to overcome these barriers. We have already reviewed several key principles underlying therapists' decision making about whether or when to attend to TIB. The therapist attempts to (a) be mindful of TIB as it occurs; (b) be intentional about targeting TIB by considering whether there are other targets higher in the treatment hierarchy that have to be attended to first; (c) understand the client's experience by being compassionate, curious, and/or validating of the valid when observing TIB has occurred; and (d) maintain a compassionate and collaborative stance when directly orienting the client to the TIB as a target. Mindful, intentional, validating, compassionate, and collaborative—we think it is safe to say that DBT does not have the patent on these therapeutic approaches. So if all of these steps are things that all therapists are capable of doing in response to TIB, and the barriers listed earlier are what get in the way of doing so, what does DBT offer to help clinicians?

DBT-trained therapists, in an effort to be effective in the ever-changing context of each moment, must be flexible in their thinking. All therapists may feel uncomfortable at times interrupting clients when they are talking about something that seems important to them. The DBT therapist is willing to be flexible about interrupting if he or she believes

EXHIBIT 8.1
Common Reasons Clinicians Do Not Attend
to Therapy-Interfering Behavior

- The client has not finished talking about something that they have said is important to them, and the therapist does not want to interrupt.
- It is early in the session and the therapist is afraid attending to the therapy-interfering behavior (TIB) will take the session into a conversation that is not part of the agenda.
- It is the middle of the session, and attending to the TIB could prevent the client and therapist from finishing what they began talking about.
- It is late in the session, and the therapist is afraid there is not enough time to talk about the TIB.
- The therapist is afraid talking about TIB will be upsetting for the client.
- The therapist thinks that TIB is unrelated to why the client is in treatment.
- The therapist is afraid that openly talking about TIB will result in the client leaving the session or quitting therapy altogether.
- The therapist is afraid talking about TIB directly will result in the client harming themselves.
- The therapist worries that the client may not enjoy the treatment or like the therapist as much if TIB is confronted or challenged.
- The therapist lacks skill in confronting or bringing up TIB.
- The therapist fears she or he is too irritated or emotionally distressed to respond directly to TIB and may therefore come across as judgmental.

in the moment that this is what is needed to be effective. It could be at the beginning, midway through, or near the end of the psychotherapy session. The DBT therapist is not constrained by rules about never interjecting, interrupting, or directing clients. If it makes sense to do so, given that a clear target is in sight, it may be effective to actively redirect.

There is no rule that client problems will be solved by talking about whatever topics or events they choose to talk about. Of course, the converse also is true: There is no rule that client problems will be solved by the therapist always choosing what to talk about. This dialectic is resolved by the DBT therapist seeking the space between extremes in any given moment of the session that is most likely to be effective. The following is an example of a conversation highlighting this process with a community therapist being trained to attend to TIBs:

> *Therapist:* The problem I have is that this client has been coming to therapy for a long time and is not getting better. She is really frustrated about this, and so am I. What do I do?
>
> *Trainer:* That is really frustrating. I have been there before many times myself. Let me ask you, what do you think is one of the main reasons she is not getting better?
>
> *Therapist:* I don't know, but she is kind of a talker. You know, she talks a lot, and once she gets going, it is hard to stop her. She always has lots of examples about the things that are upsetting to her. But it is hard to redirect her.
>
> *Trainer:* What makes it hard to redirect her?
>
> *Therapist:* Well, you know, she is telling me her story. I don't want to interrupt her.
>
> *Trainer:* What do you think might happen if you interrupted her?
>
> *Therapist:* I don't know, I just don't think I should. When clients are telling their story, I like to listen. I think it helps them feel safe, so they can trust me. I was trained to be a supportive therapist, and I don't feel comfortable interrupting clients.
>
> *Trainer:* That makes sense—it is hard for you to interrupt because you believe it will be unsupportive. You believe interrupting might make the client trust you less.
>
> *Therapist:* Yeah, but I don't know—because sometimes what she is talking about just keeps going on and on. Sometimes she will start a story and then the next thing I know, the session is just about over, and I don't really know what we have worked on.

Trainer: Oh, I know that experience. It happens to most therapists, as far as I can tell. So is this rule about interrupting your clients something you are willing to be flexible about, maybe something you might be open to experimenting with by loosening up the rule, even just a little bit?

Therapist: What do you mean?

Trainer: Well, it seems that your client isn't getting better, and one of the major therapy-interfering problems in the psychotherapy process is that she talks a lot and you are not attending to how this could be slowing her progress. So, one thing you could do is consider the dialectical opposite approach to what you are doing. Now, let me be clear—I am not suggesting you interrupt her every time she talks. What I am saying, however, is that if you think dialectically here, you will think more flexibly about the rule you have about interrupting. The rule says interrupting is bad. But maybe that is only a rule and not the truth with a capital T? Maybe sometimes, in some ways, interrupting could be exactly what is needed? Let me take this one step further. What if interrupting skillfully might be the most supportive thing you can do? What if this is exactly what is needed to help her trust you even more? Could it be possible that by letting her talk ad nauseam without redirection, she could end up feeling unsupported and lose trust in your ability to help her? This would be a different way to look at the process, and I don't know what is right, but I am interested in helping you be more effective by being a bit more flexible.

Therapist: You know, I never thought about it that way. You are saying that, ironically, by me not ever interrupting, she might be getting worse and feeling unsupported? I hope that's not happening.

Trainer: Me too, and I don't know what her experience is. But sometimes, with some clients, therapists need to help shape what is happening in the therapy session. Listening is a powerful elixir, but listening alone is sometimes not enough to help clients get where they want to be with their lives.

MOVING FORWARD

In this chapter, we explored ways that non–DBT therapists can use DBT strategies and techniques to manage TIBs not extensively detailed in other chapters. We reviewed common barriers that get in the way of therapist willingness to attend to TIB. Examples included the clinician believing he or she does not have enough time to deal with TIB, having too many other topics to discuss, and believing that clients do not want to talk about TIB. A key point of this chapter was that DBT therapists attend to and target TIB without always being confrontational. We emphasized the use of targeting strategies and validation as principles that yield specific techniques suitable for these difficult therapy sessions. More generally, we addressed ways to target in-session TIB without letting this TIB targeting automatically become the focus of the session. The goal is to attend to TIB effectively without derailing the session.

We hope this chapter helps therapists learn to be mindful in observing and compassionately intentional in managing the therapy-interfering process. This focus on expecting, noticing, and skillfully responding to therapy-interfering processes during psychotherapy is suggested as an approach that can be used irrespective of theoretical orientation, presenting client problem, and the content of what is being talked about in the session. This process-oriented approach does not devalue the importance of the narrative content of the psychotherapy session. Instead, the therapist's willingness to let go of controlling the narrative of what is talked about, and to instead focus on TIBs that emerge during the session, is a way to provide clients with a sense of safety and reassurance that they are able to talk about things that matter to them the most. When TIB occurs during this process, the therapist highlights, targets, and validates before moving on to using other core strategies, such as assessment, problem solving, contingency management, skill training, and use of commitment strategies to enhance motivation. TIB can occur in many forms, and as outlined in this chapter, therapists can make choices to be intentional, direct, and active without compromised or diminished empathy. The therapeutic relationship matters and so does attending mindfully and compassionately to TIB to help the client improve.

9

HELPING CLIENTS OVERCOME AVOIDANCE

Psychotherapy is an emotional context. Our clients can feel frustrated, hopeless, shameful, guilty, angry, empty, alone, and other negatively valenced affective states. Of course, they also feel hope, peace, happiness, vitality, and other positively valenced affective states. Between it all there is vulnerability and willfulness, doubt and excitement. Sometimes there is a meaningful interpersonal connection with the therapist, sometimes there is mutual admiration. However, at times there can be mistrust and suspicion from clients or therapists toward one another. With all these emotions that come and go, therapy can be an unpredictable and uncertain experience for our clients. Though the benefits can be life-changing and the hope for change is what brings our clients to the clinic, the perceived unpredictability and uncontrollability of psychotherapy can lead to anxiety and avoidance. Approach and avoidance is the classic ambivalence dilemma. When it comes to psychotherapy, ambivalence is more the rule than the exception.

http://dx.doi.org/10.1037/14752-009
Managing Therapy-Interfering Behavior: Strategies From Dialectical Behavior Therapy, by A. L. Chapman and M. Z. Rosenthal

Psychotherapy is a place to learn new ways to relate to oneself and to others. It is a unique context in which vulnerability, willingness, and authenticity from clients can yield the fruits of a genuine and trusting relationship. When people sense that they might soon be unsafe, avoidance behavior is sure to come. It is no wonder that one of the most common therapy-interfering behaviors (TIBs) we see in psychotherapy is avoidance behavior. Put in a slightly different way, the context of psychotherapy elicits emotions and ambivalence about experiencing or expressing emotions; ultimately, when these things happen, avoidance behavior is sure to follow.

Most therapists have observed how avoidance interferes with psychotherapy. We have seen many examples over the years and expect to see more each week and each year. We have seen clients avoid talking about the things that are most important to them, only to find many years later that adverse consequences happened, in part because they were unwilling to address issues earlier in life. We have seen psychotherapy last for many years with little success, in part due to clients avoiding having the discussion with us about why they cannot seem to embrace core elements of the treatment. We have seen clients quietly struggle, never revealing things to us that they sometimes wished they would, their shame tamping down topics for months or years. Sometimes these things are never revealed until therapy is nearing an end. At other times we have had clients end treatment only to return years later and admit that all along they had secretly wished we could have talked about a particular experience in their life.

As an example, long ago I (MZR) treated a socially isolated young man who was depressed. In addition to longstanding problems managing depression, "Bill" also had obsessions related to harming others. He had become obsessed with mass murders in the wake of the Columbine massacre. Feeling disenfranchised from what he called "normal people," Bill talked openly about his desire to pay everyone back for how they had treated him. He was resentful but not psychotic or embittered and was prone to elaborate fantasies about ways he would massacre others. Naturally, treatment targeted these obsessions as well as his depressive symptoms, and after nearly a year of dialectical behavior therapy (DBT), Bill was less depressed and had successfully learned how to manage his urges to harm others. The fantasies were conceptualized as escape behavior, and he learned new ways to regulate his affect instead of obsessing about hurting others. He let go of the idea of committing a mass murder. The thoughts about harming others were carefully assessed as having no intent, no clear plan, and no steps taken toward acting on the thoughts about harming others. This, along with Bill reporting no history of harming others or violence and along with ongoing clinical supervision, led to the conclusion that there was no duty to report his thoughts about harming others. Treatment was a success.

Except that all along, Bill had waited to unveil a secret he had kept hidden throughout therapy. It was something he felt deep shame about, something he had never told anyone, something he believed was grotesque and was evidence that he was fundamentally flawed as a human. Bill was sexually aroused by sadistic and masochistic acts. He denied ever acting on this behavior, said he had never harmed himself or others but instead fantasized about these sexual experiences. For this attraction, he heaped shame and dehumanizing feelings of disgust on himself. He kept it hidden until he felt safe; after a year of psychotherapy with a lead ball around his ankles, his actions and eventual improvements slowed but not stopped. He avoided disclosing his secret, but when he did, he reported feeling unburdened and released from his self-imposed emotional chains. Bill's avoidance was private and unverbalized until the end, when he thought the time was right and expressed his self-loathing directly. At other times avoidance is a bit easier to see.

Avoidance is the conjoined twin to ambivalence about receiving psychotherapy. All psychotherapies have to account for avoidance. On one hand, clients want and need change, sometimes desperately. On the other hand, like Bill, they may be afraid, embarrassed, or have other emotions that interfere with the ability to engage fully in the treatment. They may be able to see the destination in psychotherapy, like an island in sight across a body of water, but the journey requires them to traverse the channel between land and this island of hope. Even as clients wade out in the water, even as they make great strides, the things that swim in the water with them can be scary. The perspective shift along the way is different. No longer is it an intellectual exercise to imagine crossing this channel. Now the sightlines bob up and down, the island looks different during the act of swimming, saltwater gets in the eyes, the progress seems slower than anticipated. All of this leads to the client being highly likely to avoid or escape, returning to land and recalibrating the next approach. Progress can be made, but until that island is reached, the client may feel exhausted and skeptical or, worse, may feel like a failure and become paralyzed by hopelessness and anxious rumination. In this chapter, we discuss how to conceptualize avoidance in the context of TIBs and offer strategies therapists can use to help clients continue to navigate that journey.

CONCEPTUALIZING AVOIDANCE AS THERAPY-INTERFERING BEHAVIOR

Avoidance makes sense in the context of psychotherapy and can be conceptualized as a set of behaviors related to human neurobiology. Neurobiologically, some of the processes inherent to psychotherapy are likely to trigger responses in the emotional center of our brain, the limbic system, which initiates downstream effects in the form of observable behaviors. Thus, for example, when a client is worried about what the next therapy session will include, the appointment reminder the night before the clinic visit can function to elicit neural activity in the amygdala and other neural substrates of what LeDoux (2003) and others have called our *fear or survival circuitry*, triggering a cascade of complex events in the central and peripheral nervous system, culminating with behavioral avoidance of the anxiety-evoking cues (i.e., not showing up on time, if at all, to the psychotherapy appointment). Defensive motivational responses can occur when humans, all humans, clients and nonclients alike, encounter cues that elicit negative affect. These responses can activate what Gray (1987) termed the *behavioral inhibition system*, putting the brakes on efforts to take risks and make changes. This avoidance, when reinforced over time, can become something the client does across contexts, may be thought of as being consistent with the personality dimension called *harm avoidance* (e.g., Cloninger, 1986), and can be a risk factor for mental health problems.

Avoidance and escape are related but different kinds of behavior. *Avoidance* occurs when the client does anything that functions to prevent encounters with an aversive stimulus. The stimulus can be internal (e.g., thoughts, feelings) or external (i.e., things that are observable) and is often thought to be experienced as aversive because of direct conditioning. As an example, one client, "Holly," said at the outset of therapy that she was looking for an active and directive therapist after having some disappointing experiences in the past with therapists who had offered little direct guidance and were quiet during sessions. Holly let it be clear that she wanted to have fewer panic attacks as soon as possible and that she wanted therapy to offer the solutions. By using cognitive behavior therapy (CBT) for panic, in this case the empirically supported panic control therapy developed by Barlow and colleagues (Craske & Barlow, 2007), it seemed easy to be responsive to Holly's request. This is a manualized approach that works for many people with panic disorder with or without agoraphobia. As with any CBT, it can be delivered in a supportive way but is not best defined as primarily being a supportive therapy. After several sessions of assessment, Holly became frustrated, saying that this was no different from what she had before with her previous therapists who had been supportive but who had not directly helped her to reduce her panic attacks. After addressing this worry, it became clear that Holly's worries about this were triggered specifically by moments in therapy that were less directive. When asked an open-ended question or when encouraged to share more using reflection or summary statements, Holly became increasingly irritated. This example illustrates how the therapist's questions and emphasis on support reminded Holly of previous ineffectual therapies. Certain classes of therapist behavior had become conditioned stimuli for her conditioned responses, in this case her memories of past therapy and the associated worries.

Sometimes avoidance occurs because of direct classical conditioning, as in this example. However, at other times avoidance occurs when the client responds to cues in psychotherapy sessions that were never directly paired with the same therapist behaviors in the past. This can occur, for example, when clients avoid talking about certain topics because those topics, although not directly paired with negative outcomes, are similar functionally to other topics that have been linked to aversive outcomes. A client, "Annika," once told one of us that she did not ever want to talk about her job. She kept saying, "It is going very well," and then shifting topics. She eventually realized that her job was going so well that she was afraid talking about it would lead to her feeling worried that it could not continue to keep going so well for much longer. Things that had been successful for her in the past, including relationships with men, had gotten precipitously worse as soon as she began feeling comfortable. Annika had derived the functional response of avoiding talking about success at work because of her verbal association between success in other contexts with subsequent and major problems. It did not matter that she had always been successful at work. She did not want to talk about things that were going successfully, as a broad class of topics, because this class of things had been coupled with negative outcomes. This type of derived verbal responding can sometimes explain client avoidance in psychotherapy sessions and can be a useful way to conceptualize avoidance as TIB.

Avoidance in psychotherapy can be classically conditioned or occur through derived verbal relational responding (Hayes, Wilson, Gifford, Follette, & Strosahl, 1996). In addition, avoidance can be cognitive (e.g., not listening to the therapist, daydreaming, dissociating) or behavioral (e.g., asking the therapist not to talk about a certain topic before it is brought up, showing up late, therapy noncompliance).

If avoidance functions to distance oneself from impending aversive stimulation, *escape* is the behavioral process in which one distances oneself from an aversive stimulus when it is present. Like avoidance, clients commonly engage in escape behavior. This includes such things as choosing to change topics when the emotions are too painful to experience, redirecting the conversation, and the like. Escape behavior also can be cognitive or behavioral and can be triggered automatically through classically conditioned responses with or without conscious intent or can be elicited by derived verbal relations between cues in the psychotherapy session and those in the client's learning history. Generally speaking, similar DBT strategies can be used to manage avoidance and escape TIBs. Table 9.1 gives several common examples of ways clients avoid unpleasant stimuli across psychotherapies using the common scenario in which clients do not share many details about a past life event that was upsetting. In this table, consider the scenario wherein a client has hinted to you that something unpleasant happened several months ago, and

TABLE 9.1
Common Ways Clients Avoid in Psychotherapy
When Asked About an Unpleasant Life Event

	Cognitive	Behavioral
Automatically elicited	Inability to remember (e.g., "I don't remember much of what happened.") unpleasant events when feeling upset after being asked to recall these events by the therapist	Conditioned emotional responses (e.g., anger, shame) when asked a specific question, leading to emotional dysregulation and a change of topic away from the question being asked about the unpleasant life event
Consciously chosen	Deciding not to talk about an unpleasant life event but to instead zone out, ignore, or otherwise not listen to the therapist to reduce the chances of feeling upset	Insisting that the therapist has to hear many details about other events, delaying a response to the therapist's question about the unpleasant event

avoidance is evident when asking the client to share more details and he or she is unwilling to do so. The question signals to the client that negative emotions may be nearing, and the avoidance functions to reduce the probability that the aversive response occurs.

STRATEGIES TO MANAGE THERAPY-INTERFERING ESCAPE AND AVOIDANCE

In this next section, we suggest and describe ways in which non–dialectical-behavior therapists might address avoidance and escape behaviors that interfere with therapy. We focus on a variety of strategies and skills, including dialectical strategies, mindfulness, interpersonal effectiveness skills, emotion regulation skills, brief exposure techniques, and suggestions for managing avoidance when it is therapy-interfering in the context of group psychotherapies.

Using Dialectical Strategies to Engage Clients and Increase Commitment to Change

A critical challenge to any psychotherapy is the need to overcome avoidance of commitments and actions that can help the client have the life that they value having and, not coincidentally, have hired you to help them create. When clients are having difficulty engaging in psychotherapy, these approaches can be used to help improve client motivation to change.

All efforts to enhance motivation are tied directly to several things: (a) motivation is as motivation does, as it is evidenced by behavior and not by what clients say alone; (b) clients have the inherent ability to make change, though they often need help with change; (c) DBT skills can help clients make changes; and (d) behavior change among clients occurs through the same basic processes that underlie behavior change in non-clients. Table 9.2 offers ways in which these DBT strategies can help manage avoidance as TIB.

Using Mindfulness Practices to Reduce Avoidance

Mindfulness practice is the antidote to avoidance of internal experiences. Many of our clients have developed context-insensitive patterns of avoiding their thoughts, feelings, and physical sensations. They try not to have the internal experiences they have; emotions are avoided. Thoughts that are distressing and unwanted are avoided too. Who wants to have unpleasant physical sensations of distress when you can avoid them? DBT does not have the patent on mindfulness; indeed, the practice of mindfulness meditation is thousands of years old. Today it has been packaged by DBT and other contemporary CBT interventions as part of empirically supported treatments. Mindfulness meditation, however, is something that any clinician can weave into his or her practice. You certainly do not have to be a DBT therapist to use mindfulness to help your clients stop avoiding internal experiences.

What can mindfulness do to help with avoidance? In DBT, mindfulness practices are standard at the beginning and/or end of each group skills training. The mindfulness practice is usually less than 10 minutes, includes a brief orientation to the specific practice, is followed by the practice itself, and ends with group members observing and describing their experience during the practice. These observations are specifically about what was noticed in the practice and do not include storytelling, processing one's experience hearing someone else describe their experience, or anything else. To directly shape the skill of observing and describing experiences as they are and not what the evaluative mind says they are through interpretations and appraisals, the sharing of experiences postpractice is intentionally descriptive and present centered.

Highlighting and Targeting Avoidance
With Interpersonal Effectiveness Skills

One strategy DBT therapists use to prevent or respond to avoidance behavior is to use the very interpersonal effectiveness skills clients are learning in group skills training. A number of interpersonal skills can be used to manage avoidance-related TIBs. For example, one of our favorites that can be extremely helpful is DEAR MAN (see Table 9.3; Linehan, 1993b, 2015).

TABLE 9.2
Ways That Dialectical Strategies Can Help Manage
Avoidance as Therapy-Interfering Behavior

Avoidance therapy-interfering behavior	Dialectical strategy	Example
Unwillingness to try to use mindfulness skills	Foot-in-the-door	I can see that trying mindfulness is something new for you, and that it doesn't sound like something you are feeling very open to. I have seen this before and I totally understand where you are coming from. I am wondering if you would be willing to try, just one time this week, for only 5 minutes, to use a mindfulness practice? Maybe you might even be willing to try in here with me, for a minute or so, to see what I am talking about? Is that something you could be open to?
Giving up early in therapy, saying it is hopeless and he or she can never change	Door-in-the-face	I get it. You have been to therapy before and this is not going to be a cakewalk for you. It is going to be hard to make these changes. And there is a part of you that keeps on saying that change is never going to happen. Let me ask you something though, since we are only at the beginning of therapy, would you be willing to commit to not harming yourself at all, as long as we are working together?
Missed appointments, homework noncompliance, repeated behavior demonstrating that therapy is going to be difficult	Making lemonade out of lemons	I agree, you have missed some appointments and are still learning how to use the skills you are learning. There is a lot of work in front of us. I'm in, though. I am committed to helping you. And you know, let's look at what you have done. You are here today when you could have chosen never to come back again. You did try to use the new skills you learned last time I saw you. So what it wasn't done perfectly? I have to say that I am pretty excited to see you again and that you are trying to do this therapy. I have never seen anyone do this therapy perfectly, and it is hard for everyone, so you know what, we are exactly where we should be. Let's agree, shall we, that there is an opportunity to address this problem of you missing appointments? We can figure this out. I am sure of it. And even though it may feel sour and unpleasant to problem solve this, when we get it figured out we will be able to create solutions in your life outside of therapy to help you make it to work on time, to be home to your girlfriend when she is expecting you, and to be better at following through on all of your commitments. We can make lemonade out of these lemons!

TABLE 9.3
Using the DEAR MAN Skill to Manage Missed Therapy Sessions
as Avoidance-Related Therapy-Interfering Behavior

Step in DEAR MAN	Description	How the therapist could use DEAR MAN
Describe	Briefly and concisely describe the situation that is directly relevant to the avoidant behavior without any judgments or interpretations.	We have come a long way together in the past year of therapy. The last time we met you told me you were afraid we might talk about being traumatized when you were younger. And since then, for the past 3 weeks you have not shown up for your appointment.
Express	Express feelings and/or opinions about the situation in a clear way.	I have wondered what has changed because you had been here each week, like clockwork, for so many months. I am hoping we can talk about this today so that we can understand what has changed and get you back on track.
Assert	Ask for what is wanted or say no clearly and with a level of intensity that is appropriate for the situation.	Would you be willing to talk today about what has made it difficult for you to come to our appointments?
Reinforce	Clearly state how the other person benefits from complying with the request.	By talking about this my hope is that we can figure out together what we need to do in here to keep us moving toward your therapy goals.
(Be) Mindful	Stay mindfully focused on the targeted request, even in the face of distractions.	[*If the client deflects the request by talking about something else*] I see. That sounds like something we can talk about, but before we do, what do you think, would you be willing to talk about what has gotten in the way of you coming to therapy the past 3 weeks?
Appear confident	Behave and speak in a confident manner.	Therapist looks in the client's eyes, sits straight up, speaks kindly yet plainly.
Negotiate (if needed)	If the person does not comply, consider negotiating in an effective manner. Be willing to meet the person half way, to give in order to get.	OK, then. Let's talk about what happened to you at work and we'll be sure to then talk about what has been making it difficult for you to come to therapy. It's possible the two things are related, and I will listen for ways in which that could be the case.

This is the acronym for the set of skills used to effectively ask for something or to say no to a request. It is the basic tool to teach clients to use in order to be taken seriously by others without having to be either passive or aggressive. It is the way to have an objective met during an interpersonal situation, when having that objective met is the priority that is identified in that context. Using the common example of avoidance of the therapy session itself as the TIB, take a look at Table 9.3 and then read the following transcript of how a therapist might respond to missed therapy sessions as avoidance TIB.

> Therapist: You know, as I'm listening to you tell me about what happened last week with your boyfriend, I have to say that not only am I feeling sad about this breakup, I also am mindful of how hard this must be for you. I'd like to keep talking about this. Here is the thing, though: We've been talking for the first half of our appointment about this really unfortunate relationship breakup, and as important as it is for you, I'd like you to notice that we have not talked about the fact that it has been 3 weeks since you came to therapy.

> Client: I know, I know. I really have wanted to come here but things have just been so . . .

> Therapist: I am glad to hear you have wanted to be here. We have done a lot of really good work together the past few months. And you have made some pretty amazing changes in your life.

> Client: Thanks. I just don't know what to do about my boyfriend. Or I guess now he is my ex-boyfriend [starts crying].

> Therapist: [Pausing, paying mindful attention to the emotion for a moment] There is a lot to talk about here, a lot to try to understand, and a lot of emotions to sort through. It makes perfect sense that you are feeling so sad and upset. Let's come back to how you are feeling in a minute, OK? I'd like to ask you something.

> Client: OK.

> Therapist: [Initiates DEAR MAN targeting avoidance of therapy session] It has been 3 weeks since you came to therapy, and each week you have not shown for the appointment. During those 3 weeks, your relationship with your boyfriend has fallen apart. The last time I saw you, as far as I recall, things with him seemed to be OK. [DESCRIBE]

> Client: That's true, but I guess looking back everything wasn't OK.

> Therapist: That may be true. But things started to really change over the past few weeks, right?

Client: Yeah, I mean I told you that I found out he cheated on me a few weeks ago and that he wants us to have an open relationship now. I didn't know what to do. I love him and want to be with him, but I don't want to be intimate with anyone else, just him! The whole idea makes me feel so gross. Why would he want to do that?

Therapist: Right. And that makes sense. You love him, and you have never wanted to have an open relationship. He is asking for something of you that is against your values.

Client: [*Nods head affirmatively*]

Therapist: In the past 3 weeks when you did not show up for your appointment and knowing how consistent you have been to your appointments, I really began to worry that something was going on making it difficult for you to be here. [*EXPRESS*]

Client: Sorry.

Therapist: It's OK. I am so glad you are here today. [*ASSERT*] Can we talk for a minute about what has gotten in the way of you coming to our appointments? [*REINFORCE*] I think if we can understand together what got in the way, we can figure out what we can do to make sure that when things are not going well for you that you are still able and willing to come to our therapy sessions. When things are at their worst, this can be a safe place to help you. It's like shelter from a sudden and massive downpour of rain, a place to cool off when the sun is beating down on you in the summer.

Client: I know. And I feel so bad that I missed our sessions. But it was just . . . things got so crazy with him. I hate myself for what I did. I couldn't show my face in here. I couldn't.

Therapist: You felt embarrassed or ashamed?

Client: I'd rather not talk about any of this.

Therapist: This is hard to talk about. [*Therapist being MINDFUL*] And it would be the kind of thing we could choose not to talk about to make things feel less miserable in here right now. On the other hand, us talking about this may help us understand how it came to be that during an incredibly difficult time for you—a monsoon of emotions was happening—you didn't come to our therapy sessions to keep up the great work you had been doing.

Client: I did some pretty horrible things. I gave in. I let him have his way, and it was awful. I did it for him, because that's what you are supposed to do if you love someone. I couldn't come in here and talk about what was going on. It's disgraceful, humiliating.

Therapist:	I'm so glad you're telling me about this and how you are feeling. This probably goes totally against the grain of what you feel like doing right now. It seems that when you felt ashamed you avoided coming to our appointments, which makes sense, because that's what people do when they feel ashamed, they hide from others, they go into their cave. And that's what you did, if I understand you correctly?
Client:	Yes, exactly. Can we please talk about something else? Talking about this just makes me feel so . . . dirty, so bad about myself.
Therapist:	It sounds like you feel shame right now.
Client:	Big time.
Therapist:	You are doing a great job not avoiding your emotions right now. Stay with this, and we will get through it together. [NEGOTIATE] I tell you what, we have about 15 minutes left. Let's talk for a few more minutes about how we can problem solve to help you come to our appointments when you are feeling ashamed, or when things are at their worst in your life. That's the time when coming here might help the most. Let's see if we can come up with a plan for the future to make sure that even when things are at their worst you are willing to come here. We can talk about this for a few minutes and then spend the rest of our time talking about something else entirely different. How does that sound?
Client:	OK.

In this example, there are a couple of key things to notice. First, the therapist does not use DEAR MAN in one fell swoop. *D* then *E* then *A* then *R* and so on, do not have to be implemented without interruption. Instead, the therapist can be patient and use each element in the transactional flow of the dialogue. In this case, the therapist used validation often, and importantly, validation was used before the therapist made a request of the client. Validation came before asserting and reinforcing, as well as before staying mindful and negotiating. Validation was brief, to the point, and was immediately coupled with the DEAR MAN steps. This sequencing is part of the art of using DEAR MAN and other change strategies to manage TIBs. Validation is reassuring and comforting; the client may feel heard or understood and may, as a result, become more open to the request to talk about what got in the way of coming to therapy the previous 3 weeks.

In summary, the DEAR MAN skill is used to help clients who have significant challenges in asking for what they want or saying no to others effectively. We think this is a skill that clinicians of all therapeutic orientations can benefit from using as a way to prevent or respond to client avoidance. In this case it was about missed therapy sessions, but because is easy to implement, DEAR MAN can be used for a wide variety of client TIBs that function as avoidance: coming to session late, insistently talking about off-topic issues, making idle chitchat, not doing homework, and so on. DEAR MAN is an effective tool therapists can use to persuade clients to stop avoiding in therapy. DEAR MAN can be used to block avoidance and encourage willingness to approach the emotionally difficult things that are fundamental to therapeutic success. Clinicians who use DEAR MAN can improve client outcomes by helping clients make more rapid change. DEAR MAN is simply an acronym for how to use basic persuasion skills. People, not just therapists, use this every day to get what they want, meet their objectives, and do what they need to do. If you are not so sure about this, try it a few times outside of therapy. Try it in your personal life and see how simple it can be. Then use it with your clients to manage avoidance as a TIB. If you are an astute observer, you may have realized that in this last paragraph we used DEAR MAN on you. Our objective is to get you to consider using DEAR MAN.

USING EMOTION REGULATION SKILLS
TO REDUCE AVOIDANCE

In addition to interpersonal effectiveness skills, DBT therapists use emotion regulation skills to manage avoidance as a TIB. Emotion regulation skills can be acceptance- or change-based. Acceptance-based interventions help clients experience their emotions without avoiding, escaping, or otherwise responding ineffectively to them. Change-based emotion regulation skills help clients alter the experience or expression of emotions. All these are cognitive and behavioral skills, ways to regulate affect in order to be effective in the moment in a way that brings the client closer to a valued life. In DBT, clients learn these skills in skill training groups, but these are skills that can be used outside of DBT by non–DBT therapists too. Indeed, as you read the following examples, consider how you might apply these skills to your own therapy approach. Consider how the examples of emotion regulation skills therapists can use to manage avoidance might be applicable to your own practice.

Acceptance-Oriented Emotion Regulation Skills

Acceptance-based emotion regulation skills include helping the client be willing to experience unpleasant emotions as they rise and fall, without trying to change the form or frequency of these experiences. Such skills can take many forms and can occur in many contexts during therapy eliciting avoidance, but consider the following straightforward and ubiquitous example, Therapy commonly elicits negative emotions, and clients—some more than others—may avoid or escape from unpleasant emotional experiences. Hayes et al. (1996) called this general phenomenon *experiential avoidance* and described it as ordinary, not inherently pathological, a product of how humans relate to their own thoughts and private emotional experiences. Therapists of all theoretical orientations can probably agree that the tendency to avoid internal experiences is ubiquitous across many mental health problems and all forms of psychotherapy. Experiential avoidance can help the client have temporary relief by keeping her or him away from something that is unpleasant or uncomfortable to experience. The avoided experience can be a negative affective state—shame, guilt, sadness, and so on—or it can be a positive affective state, such as hope, joy, or love. Avoidance and escape behaviors take many forms and are negatively reinforced, making them likely to occur again in similar therapeutic contexts in the future. Clients distract by changing the topic, they react to shame by expressing anger, and they avoid sadness and hurt by talking about minor daily hassles. Clients with all sorts of presenting problems and psychiatric diagnoses demonstrate experiential avoidance in therapy. The research on experiential avoidance has suggested this may be an underlying dimension common across a wide variety of mental health problems, including mood, anxiety, personality, eating, and substance use disorders (e.g., Hayes et al., 1996).

When a client is experientially avoiding in the therapy session, the therapist has many options. Is this a moment to be silent and to listen and allow the client to go wherever they go with the content of the session? Or should the therapist redirect the client to what they are avoiding? What if the therapist is afraid that attempts to redirect might be experienced as aversive by the client? What happens if the best therapeutic intentions result in the client becoming distressed? What should the therapist do if he or she is concerned that helping the client approach and experience that which they are avoiding might make the client feel distressed? This fear of making the client feel unpleasant is, in our experience, the most common reason therapists have for not directly talking about or otherwise managing the client's avoidance behavior in therapy. We want to help clinicians learn to overcome this barrier without in any way compromising the integrity of the relationship. Moreover, using emotion regulation skills to manage avoidance as TIB can not only prevent avoidance but it can also help improve the quality of the therapeutic relationship. These specific techniques can function to enhance the common factors of the therapeutic process, including trust, attention, respect, and understanding of the client.

One example of an acceptance-based emotion regulation strategy DBT therapists use to block avoidance is mindfulness. The emotions eliciting avoidance may feel dangerous, risky, or painful to the client. These emotions can ambush our clients, and like a fish suddenly ensnared, the client can automatically and reflexively take off in the opposite direction to danger. Mindfulness of emotions allows clients to learn to observe and describe, to feel and have the very emotional experiences that are already there. As a way to keep the client from fleeing, to help them retrain their brain and behavioral responses not to habitually move away from emotion, DBT therapists use mindfulness practices during therapy sessions. Table 9.4 illustrates this.

TABLE 9.4
Ways to Use Mindfulness to Manage Avoidance
as a Therapy-Interfering Behavior

Client avoidance	Mindfulness skill	Example of therapist use of mindfulness
Client begins therapy session by talking tangentially or about emotionally detached topics that take a lot of time	Mindfulness exercise to begin the therapy session	Before we get too far into our session, I'd like your permission for us to begin with a mindfulness practice. We can keep it brief, with the goal of helping us settle into this room for the next 45 minutes together, clear and oriented to the things we need to talk about to help you. The practice will help us both let go of the things that are in our minds about what has happened before this moment, before this session, as well as things that we might be thinking about that could happen after this moment, later in the day, and so on. Mindfulness practice will help us stay in the moment and aware of what is here and now so that we can do our best possible work today.
Client becomes upset during therapy session and avoids the topic that triggered his or her feelings	Mindfulness of current emotion, thoughts, or actions	I certainly understand why you don't want to talk about this. It is upsetting, and why in the world would you want to talk about something that makes you feel that way? I get it. Would you be willing instead to take a moment with me and observe the thoughts, emotions, and urges you are having as you feel this way? Let's take just a minute or two and lean into the emotional pain of this moment before we begin to talk about something else. If you are willing, I'd like to ask you to go ahead and close your eyes, breathe in and out, and observe your breath with all of the focus of your attention. Now, turn your attention to observing any internal experiences as they arise, like you are standing and watching cars go by you on a busy city street. Observe each thought as a thought, each emotion as an emotion, each urge to do or say something as just that—an urge.

(continues)

TABLE 9.4
Ways to Use Mindfulness to Manage Avoidance
as a Therapy-Interfering Behavior   *(Continued)*

Client avoidance	Mindfulness skill	Example of therapist use of mindfulness
Client becomes irritated or angry after talking about something that elicited sadness, grief, or shame	Mindfulness of the primary emotion	You are upset and seem to be feeling angry or irritated. You know what, though? I'm noticing that just a moment ago you were in a different emotional space, feeling what seemed to be sadness, and then from this sadness suddenly you were overcome by something else. This is an important process. Would you be willing to turn your attention, for this moment, to the emotions you are currently experiencing? You might close your eyes and observe the sensations in your body. Begin with your feet and move your mind's spotlight slowly over your body to the top of your head. Notice any bodily sensations. These sensations may give us clues about what emotions you are feeling underneath the anger. Observe these bodily sensations, here and now, and if any thoughts come up that take your focus away, please redirect your attention back to your body. Do this for a minute and then we can continue.
Client obsesses in a self-judgmental or critical way instead of addressing ways to solve a problem	Therapist observes mindfully this process and helps client let go of the truth of these thoughts	Can I comment on something that is happening right now? You are talking about feeling upset, and as we now are beginning to identify solutions to try to use to change the situation, you are becoming increasingly judgmental and critical of yourself. I'd like for you to try to be mindful, as we keep talking, of this self-judgment. When you notice the self-judgmental thought, before saying it out loud, would you be willing to let me know the thought is there? You can say "judgmental thought" and then keep talking, OK? The skill is to catch yourself having the judgment and to notice it without it passing by you unnoticed. It is a thought that is there, but it is not the truth when you notice it for what it is, simply a judgmental thought. Are you open to doing this right now? And we can keep talking.

TABLE 9.4
Ways to Use Mindfulness to Manage Avoidance
as a Therapy-Interfering Behavior

Client avoidance	Mindfulness skill	Example of therapist use of mindfulness
Client avoids trying new skills outside of session	Plan for use of mindfulness outside therapy	These are difficult things to try to do. It's one thing to practice these skills in here with me. And you have been skillful at doing that. But it is another thing to use them in the heat of the moment in your life outside this room, especially when you need to use these skills the most in stressful moments. I am thinking mindfulness practices during the day might help you. It could be at work or at home, and it could be really brief practice. I think mindfulness practices outside of here might really help you take that next step in being skillful with your partner. Is this something we can talk about for a minute?

Change-Oriented Emotion Regulation Skills

Emotion regulation strategies in DBT also include ways to manage avoidance as TIB by helping the client directly change their emotions. A classic DBT skill to help in this way is called *opposite action*. The opposite action skill is based on research suggesting that emotions can be changed by approaching the stimulus that elicits the emotion. This is a skill to help clients learn that emotions are not always a signal for true danger. Much like exposure therapy, opposite action permits the client to learn how to discriminate true alarms from false ones and signals of danger from harmless and unpleasant noise. Opposite action always must be done safely and collaboratively with the client's goals and values squarely and openly available for all to see at any given moment.

Exposure-based therapies, which are gold standard behavioral treatments for posttraumatic stress disorder (PTSD), obsessive–compulsive disorder, and anxiety disorders, use similar principles as DBT therapists use in opposite action. Whatever the emotion the client is having (e.g., anger at someone), there are action tendencies associated with that emotion (e.g., yelling at that person). Those action tendencies have a function (e.g., the person being yelled at apologizes), and as a result, acting with those tendencies reinforces the probability of the emotion–response pairing in the future. In contrast, acting opposite to the action tendency (e.g., being kind to others when angry, gently avoiding the person who elicited the anger) disrupts this reinforcement cycle. This can lead to the client learning, in each instance, that a particular conditioned stimulus does not always predict the previously conditioned responses.

Acting opposite can function to associate cues from the context of psychotherapy (and in the natural environment when opposite action is practiced in vivo) with a reduced probability of aversive responses. Take the example of using opposite action as a strategy to reduce in-session avoidance about things that elicit sadness. By repeatedly and consciously choosing to talk about a topic that has in the past elicited sadness despite urges to avoid talking about the topic, the client can reduce the intensity of future urges to avoid this topic or others that elicit sadness. In addition, the next time the client talks about this same topic, he or she may have a slightly lower intensity or shorter duration of sadness.

How might this work? One possibility is that cues from the psychotherapy session directly paired with the presence of the conditioned stimuli (e.g., questions about emotionally evocative events) but without the previously conditioned aversive response (e.g., negative emotions) can facilitate inhibitory learning. The therapy setting signals that the previously avoided conditioned responses are less likely to occur, the client feels as though it is a safe place to trust and be vulnerable emotionally, and topics related to sadness can be explored with less avoidance. More generally, this process of conditioned inhibition underlying opposite action may help describe why this technique can help the client in the future be more willing to approach rather than avoid conditioned stimuli (e.g., questions about one's family history that might be asked when out on a date or when meeting new people). This increased willingness to approach cues historically associated with aversive conditioned responses subsequently increases the chances that the client will learn experientially that such conditioned stimuli are infrequently likely to lead to the aversive responses. The result is that the client learns newer and healthier way to respond to emotionally evocative cues and has a broader repertoire of responses to things that in the past elicited emotions and avoidance or escape responses. This translates into enhanced motivation and willingness to avoid less and instead to approach more of the people, places, and things associated with his or her life values and goals. Table 9.5 illustrates examples of emotions, normative action tendencies to these emotions, and ways that these emotions and action tendencies can function as avoidance in psychotherapy.

Let us use these example emotions and their subsequent action tendencies during psychotherapy and imagine how a non–DBT therapist might apply the opposite action skill. With sadness, the client action tendency may be to avoid others, resulting in missed therapy appointments. The action urge coupled with sadness is to avoid people. The opposite action is to approach

TABLE 9.5

Emotions, Action Tendencies, and Avoidance as Therapy-Interfering
Behaviors in Psychotherapy

Emotions	Common action tendencies	Avoidance as therapy-interfering behaviors
Sadness	Social isolation, crying, rumination about events causing sadness	Missed therapy sessions, excessive rumination about life events causing sadness without allowing discussion of ways to improve functioning or reduce sadness
Anger	Confrontation or escape	Hostility expressed during session that functions to avoid discussion of certain topics
Fear or anxiety	Flight or freeze responses	Conditioned dissociative responses to cues during psychotherapy, such as therapist actions, or client thoughts, memories, sensations, or emotions
Shame or guilt	Hide, conceal oneself, or behave in a conciliatory way	Not looking at the therapist, non-responsiveness to therapist questions, or behaving with excessive agreeableness

people. Thus, if the target is to use opposite action to help reduce missed therapy sessions, lateness to sessions, or avoidance of psychotherapy in any other way, the therapist can try using the opposite action to sadness. The client might be asked to approach others as an opposite action skill whenever he or she feels sadness during the week. When sadness is present, the client is asked to call, e-mail, text, or instant message someone. Or the client could physically approach others when she or he feels sadness, instead of staying home alone, instead of retreating to the safety of their shell. Opposite action is a principle-based skill that is used to approach social contexts in an effective manner consistent with the client's goals and values.

In the case of anger, the action tendency is to either avoid the anger evocative cue altogether or to aggress toward this cue. If a client is angry that someone has put a barrier in the way of her or his achieving an important goal, anger is an expected emotion. If the anger is expressed during psychotherapy and is functioning as avoidance, such as often happens when a client expresses hostility by venting expressively throughout the therapy session without problem solving, the therapist may try using opposite action to change this avoidance behavior and help the client learn to feel less angry and more skillful managing her or his anger. For example, the client could be asked to do something opposite to cathartic venting of hostility. The therapist could gently ask the client whether he or she is willing to work on anger at that moment by trying out opposite action. The therapist could then ask the client to try any number of behaviors that are opposite to his or her anger-related action tendencies. These could include trying to understand the world from the perspective of the person with whom she or he is angry (compassion and empathy often are incompatible with and can inhibit anger) or talking about or doing something kind or nice for someone else, even if not the object of the client's anger. In all these responses, the therapist blocks the client's venting of hostility that is functioning as avoidance and is likely not helpful to the client.

Opposite action to fear or anxiety, when avoidance of the cues eliciting these emotions is present in the therapy session, can be facilitated by the therapist asking the client to be willing to try to approach or stay with these cues. Instead of changing the topic when anxiety is elicited by a therapist question, the therapist might encourage the client to come back to the topic, to stay with the thoughts that are associated with topic, and to suspend her or his belief that these thoughts are literally true, yet allow them to be present. By psychologically contacting the experiences that trigger experientially avoidant responses to anxiety cues, the therapist is directly training the client to learn through experience and not instruction to become more psychologically flexible. Avoidance as a response is problematic when it is a context-insensitive, rigid, and habitual automatic response to fear or anxiety cues. In therapy, experiential avoidance can be changed through staying with, approaching, or otherwise allowing the client to remain in psychological contact with aspects of the context eliciting avoidance.

With shame or guilt, opposite action can be used to manage avoidance as TIB by helping clients stop and think through whether these emotions are justified and how they can be changed immediately. Shame and guilt are similar moral emotions. However, shame is often considered to be an emotion characterized by a negative sense of self (e.g., "I am a bad person"), whereas guilt has been characterized by actions or inactions appraised as negative (e.g., "I did a bad thing"; Tangney & Dearing, 2002). Guilt is justified when a client has engaged in behavior that is inconsistent with her or his values, whereas shame is justified when the client would be rejected by an important person or group if her or his behavior were known to these individuals. Shame in the therapy session may be justified if a client has cheated on her or his partner, and the partner is considering divorce (i.e., the client actually is potentially being rejected by an important person). The client, however, might feel ashamed of disclosing this to the therapist, and if that were the case, the shame would not be justified, in that the therapist is not likely to reject the client for cheating on his or her partner. In this case, because the emotion is justified in relation to the partner, the skill to avoid avoidance might be an acceptance-based strategy such as mindfulness or the distress tolerance skill of radical acceptance. Another strategy to use when the emotion is justified is problem solving (see Chapter 3 for steps for problem solving), whereby the client and therapist actively approach and talk about the problem (which runs counter to avoidance) and consider options to lighten the impact of the problem or solve the problem. The client is not able to change the fact that the cheating occurred but may be able to take steps to reconcile with the partner, repair the damage to the relationship, or at least part amicably. In relation to shame in the context of the therapeutic relationship, the strategy of opposite action may be more appropriate, because the shame is unjustified, and having the client openly disclose what happened in a non-shameful manner can help run counter to the avoidance tendencies (e.g., hiding, concealing) associated with shame.

When shame and guilt are not justified, as is often the case, opposite action is a useful approach. When are these emotions not justified? If the same principle outlined earlier is applied, clients feel these unjustified emotions even after behaving in a way that is consistent with their values; does not violate any laws, rules, or ethical codes; and is unlikely to lead them to be rejected by others. Unjustified guilt or shame happens in psychotherapy when clients are especially conciliatory with therapists, are overly agreeable, apologize for things that are of minor important to the therapist, and the like. When the shame or guilt is unjustified, clients could engage in any number of avoidance behaviors in-session or outside the session. The opposite action skill is to help the client do over and over again the very thing they are feeling unjustified, inappropriate guilt or shame about, until the emotion decreases.

Let us take a straightforward example before examining a more nuanced way to do this. "Martina" goes into a shameful emotional nosedive every time she is barely and rarely late for the therapy session by less than 1 minute, sticking her head in her hands and then ruminating shamefully in a way that prevents movement on important and agreed-on therapeutic targets. It may or may not be planned, strategic, intentional avoidance, but it does not have to be. If the behavior functions as avoidance and this avoidance interferes with the therapy process or outcomes, it may be conceptualized as TIB. Opposite action in this example might include the therapist asking Martina to come to therapy sessions late for the next few visits, with the intention of helping her to compassionately and collaboratively learn that there are no adverse outcomes when this happens and that it is OK to be imperfect, that it is permissible, even ordinary. Over time, with this deliberate practice, the client and therapist can work together to directly train the client to feel less ashamed or guilty when these kinds of behaviors occur. Shame and guilt will extinguish when they are unjustified and repeatedly approached. With this TIB out of the way, the client and therapist now have more time during session to work together to help the client live the life she values living.

A more nuanced example might be if Martina is feeling ashamed of herself every time she talks during therapy about a failure to complete a task at work. She feels like a failure in life, and recently work is where she feels most highly ashamed. Whenever she talks about work, her head goes down, she loses eye contact, and she speaks so softly that she can barely be heard. In using opposite action to change this shame behavior, the therapist might gently ask Martina to sit up in her chair, look the therapist in the eyes, and maintain eye contact while talking more clearly about what has been happening at work. All of these behaviors linked to talking when feeling shame are ways to act opposite to the action tendencies associated with shame. In this example, it is not the event from work itself that the therapist asks Martina to do again and again, but instead opposite action includes disclosing in a manner that is inconsistent with shame.

USING EXPOSURE TECHNIQUES TO REDUCE AVOIDANCE

As mentioned in Chapter 3, exposure-based interventions can be effective when the driving forces behind TIB include fear, escape, and avoidance. In many instances, opposite action is similar to the techniques used in exposure-based therapies. By exposing clients to cues associated with negative emotions and avoidance responses, the client learns to develop a wider repertoire of responses to these cues and emotions. Instead of avoidance, clients can learn other responses that are more effective and help them move closer to a life consistent with what matters to them—to their values—in any given moment. In DBT, exposure therapy techniques are used to help reduce the probability of avoidance behavior; to help clients learn to think about their past, present, and future more flexibly; and to recover more quickly after emotions are elicited.

Exposure-based therapy as a treatment for PTSD is commonly used after the first stage of DBT is completed. This often means that for the client with BPD and PTSD, exposure therapy directly targeting PTSD begins after she or he has completed learning all skills modules in DBT group, no longer has any egregious and out of control behavior associated with harming themselves or others, and no longer has significant TIBs or major quality-of-life problems. Before these things have happened, the client is still in the first stage of DBT, and exposure therapy is unlikely to occur because it may be that this client has not learned sufficient skills for managing the psychological distress that is part and parcel of working through past traumatic events (although see Harned, Korslund, & Linehan, 2014, for a preliminary study on the application of exposure for PTSD in the context of DBT with clients who are highly suicidal).

Exposure therapy as a protocol-driven empirically supported approach for various disorders is not equivalent to using exposure therapy techniques to help with reducing avoidance as TIB. In other words, clients do not have to be receiving exposure therapy, per se, for therapists to use exposure therapy principles and techniques to manage avoidance-related TIBs. Brief exposures to thoughts, emotions, or sensations can be used by the therapist, in consultation collaboratively with the client and with previous orientation to this approach, to reduce avoidance as TIB.

Brief exposures can include the non–DBT therapist doing the following: (a) observing the behavior that is therapy-interfering; (b) describing the TIB and asking the client whether she or he is willing to work on it; (c) linking the TIB to a problem interfering with the client achieving treatment targets, values, and/or goals; (d) with the client's permission and willingness to proceed, orienting to the target that is being avoided, specifically; (e) for several minutes or longer, practicing experiencing the thought, emotion, or sensation, letting it come and go naturally without trying to do anything about it; (f) evaluating changes in distress, urges to avoid, or other clinically relevant targets resulting from exposure to the avoided target; and (g) discussing any changes that naturally occurred in the client's experience, such as changes in emotional intensity; newly observed cognitive attributions, assumptions, interpretations, or appraisals; or alterations in bodily sensations that occurred during brief exposures. When something is being avoided in session and it is safe to approach it, instead of talking about doing this, non–DBT therapists can try using brief exposures to help directly train new responses to the avoided cues.

USING SUPPORTIVENESS, VALIDATION, AND RECIPROCITY WITHOUT REINFORCING AVOIDANCE

Sometimes therapist efforts to be supportive can function to reinforce client avoidance. This is a problem that can be averted using strategies to reduce avoidance as TIB. Before exploring how to do this, it may be helpful to highlight a primary barrier confronting therapists when they have to address avoidance as TIB. This has to do with clinicians being supportive, or rather, clinicians being worried about not being supportive. This fear of being nonsupportive can lead to therapists inadvertently reinforcing avoidant TIBs.

One of the more interesting things both of us experience as we are training clinicians is that therapists often are reluctant to directly target client avoidance. This makes perfect sense. Clinicians value being supportive, kind, compassionate, and gentle, and they routinely worry that attending to avoidance as TIB can come across as unsupportive and mean, lacking compassion, and as insensitive to the client's experience. To be clear on this point: We support all clinicians being supportive. Careful listening, active listening, listening to help elicit change behavior, and skillful listening is an essential underlying process of support that elicits the trust required for successful psychotherapy.

In DBT, the therapeutic relationship is built on a solid frame of supportive listening. Supportive, warm responsiveness is often what we refer to in DBT as therapeutic *reciprocity*, which is essential to the therapy relationship. Indeed, many of the most emotionally rich and interpersonally curative moments of DBT come in the form of therapists behaving in a client-centered Rogerian manner. Nearly all DBT sessions, at least those that adhere to the treatment, include a significant amount of supportive and client-centered listening. Recall that the primary function of individual DBT therapy sessions is to motivate the client to change. DBT therapists motivate clients to change longstanding and difficult-to-change patterns using dialectical thinking, commitment strategies, and using heavy doses of validation. This includes support of the client's values, goals, wants and needs, limits, and the like. You cannot be an effective DBT therapist without being proficient at supportive therapy. Who is more sensitive to the experience of rejection, abandonment, failure, or feeling alienated and/or unwanted than those who DBT was developed to treat? For DBT therapists, the ability to be highly supportive is required but is insufficient to help clients change. On one hand, DBT is a highly supportive therapy, and on the other hand, as discussed next, DBT therapists targeting the reduction of avoidance behavior sometimes provide support in the form of helping the client learn to avoid avoiding.

Sometimes therapeutic responses to clients' distress that are intended to convey how supportive the therapist is can inadvertently lead to avoidance of important therapeutic processes. An example of this is when a therapist is treating a client with social phobia and has a planned treatment using exposure-based interventions. The client expresses ambivalence about learning to approach anxiety-evocative stimuli to learn new and adaptive responses to these cues. When the first few sessions begin, the therapist asks the client, "How are you doing today?" and the client responds by talking about a series of recent events, ruminating and feeling upset; in turn, the therapist encourages the client to share more about his or her feelings. The client then talks discursively for most of the session, perhaps a bit of problem solving happens, and then the session ends. This process happens repeatedly each session, but the social phobia does not improve. After a number of sessions like this, the client learns that by talking about various recent events, ruminating and expressing distress, the exposure therapy continues to be prolonged. It never begins in earnest, and eventually the client terminates from therapy, citing this or that reason. We have seen this same pattern of behavior many times in trainees and students, as well as with our own clients. Almost always, the therapist rationalizes his or her actions by saying that the client was not ready for exposure therapy, needed supportive therapy first, or would have been at risk of quitting treatment if exposure therapy began too soon.

How do DBT therapists attempt to avoid this problem? First, they try to be supportive without being rigidly and habitually passive or silent. The trick is to remember that being supportive is functional behavior, not formal. It is about supporting the client in moving closer to important goals and values, it is not about specific forms of behavior, such as sitting with legs crossed, head nodding, or softly encouraging the client to share more about their feelings, and it is not just about being warm and kind. Support can come in many forms. Thus, for example, when a client is unresponsive to attempts to talk about a painfully emotional topic, support does not only have to look like the therapist silently listening, paraphrasing, reflecting, or using other micro-listening skills. After all, when the client is headed in an avoidant direction, what response might you expect if you ask them to "tell me more about that" or you reflect back "you are having some other problems that you want us to talk about?" These ways of being supportive encourage further elaboration and, in many cases, backfire by eliciting additional avoidance.

Non–DBT therapists can attend to avoidance as TIB in a supportive way, without reinforcing avoidance and related dysfunctional learning, by (a) behaving with compassion and with authentic, heartfelt expressions of intention to help the client; (b) nonjudgmentally observing and describing the avoidance TIB; (c) clarifying gently that this avoidance-related TIB may or may not be a problem that has to be targeted immediately; (d) engaging the client to think collaboratively and mindfully about what is being avoided and if it is TIB; (e) seeking a clear connection and offering a simple explanation of how this avoidance contributes to the problems being addressed in therapy; (f) encouraging new approach-based responses instead of avoidance; (g) helping the client be willing and then approach that which is being avoided; and/or (h) reinforcing these approach responses and avoidance of usual avoidance TIBs by being especially warm, excited, or otherwise demonstrating genuine positive affect effectively. This process as a whole over time and with many different avoidance TIBs can be experienced as highly supportive and rewarding. Table 9.6 includes several examples of avoidance TIB and ways in which therapists might respond supportively with an intended outcome that is collaboratively agreed on by the client.

Many therapists fear what could happen if they respond to client avoidance without being supportive. Therapists may be afraid that active efforts to reduce avoidance will be too direct, will be disrespectful of what the client wants, or will not meet the client where they are in the moment. Despite

TABLE 9.6
Ways to Reduce Avoidant Therapy-Interfering Behaviors
Supportively Without Reinforcing Dysfunction

Avoidance therapy-interfering behavior	Example of a dialectical behavior therapy–based response	Intended outcome
Changing topic of conversation	Observe the behavior nonjudg-mentally, validate what is valid (e.g., the emotion that is present) without chang-ing the topic further, and collaboratively orient to the most effective target for the session	Enhanced mindfulness, efficient use of time toward targeting an agreed on process or outcome in the session
Venting angrily or ruminating in a long-winded way	Validating what is normative or makes sense given the client's history about the emotional response and immediately helping to label the emotion and associated action urges, assessing the effective-ness of acting on these urges or continuing to vent or ruminate	Gently turn the client's atten-tion and behavior away from venting or ruminat-ing and toward seeking effective regulation of this affect and mindfulness of actions that could result from these emotions
Quibbling ad nau-seam with the therapist about the details of a specific solution	Observe the process non-judgmentally, modeling mindfulness, validating the valid in the client's concerns and targeting an effective solution based on their stated values and goals by seeking commit-ment to changing a defined behavior in context	Dialectical thinking and resolution of apparent contradictions with a workable synthesis and genuine commitment to try that solution
Responding to attempts to prac-tice a new skill in the session with reasons why the skill will not help	Dialectical strategies to obtain commitment while labeling reason giving as a possible therapy-interfering behavior linked to other life-interfering problems	Openness to try new experi-ences to learn new solu-tions to familiar problems without reason giving functioning to prevent learning

these worries, it is safe to say that attending to avoidance as TIB does not sim-ply lead to clients feeling invalidated, angry, or more distressed or to harm-ing the therapeutic relationship. This might happen if therapists are highly insensitive, rude, or disrespectful. The irony is that the therapists who are most afraid of coming across this way are usually the last ones who would come across as unsupportive. The extremely kind and gentle, the warmest and sweetest of our field, the clinicians who are the most afraid of being unsupportive and who end up having the hardest time managing avoidance as TIB are the people who can probably be the most skillful at borrowing the DBT skills to manage avoidance.

MANAGING AVOIDANCE IN GROUP PSYCHOTHERAPY

Group psychotherapy brings some unique TIBs. Avoidance in group can be particularly challenging for group therapists to manage. This is especially true when there is only one group therapist. Even with two cotherapists, it still can be tough when erratic or dramatic avoidance behaviors occur. Whether it is a psychotherapy process group, a psychoeducational group, a cognitive behavior skill training group, a substance abuse group, or any other group-based psychotherapy, avoidance behavior is both common and difficult to manage. Table 9.7 offers common avoidance behavior that is therapy-interfering in different kinds of group psychotherapies.

What strategies can clinicians draw from DBT to effectively manage avoidance TIBs in group? One thing we suggest is to consider how the group therapy being conducted might conceptualize avoidance. If the therapy has some account of why avoidance is important, orientation can be used to discuss this and communicate that the group therapists will attend to avoidance. From the outset of each group member's time in the group, avoidance can be observed and explored in whatever form is appropriate for that theoretical model. In other words, group therapists can let clients know using a rationale germane to that therapeutic model that part of group therapy involves paying

TABLE 9.7
Common Avoidance Behavior in Group Psychotherapies

Type of group	Common therapy-interfering behavior	What is being avoided?
Psychoeducation	Chitchat, storytelling	Listening to new information and solutions to problem behaviors
Skills training	Not paying attention, cathartically talking about problems	Learning to practice new skills to help difficult life problems
Process group	Not talking, behaving as though one is busy or distracted, deflecting focus on oneself to others in the group	Considering one's own thoughts and feelings about what is happening in the group process
Substance use	Telling others in the group what to do, using hyperbole and platitudes that oversimplify things	Identifying with vulnerability one's own needs and next steps in substance use treatment

attention to and trying to decrease avoidance behavior when it interferes with group process. After orientation to this, the group members can be asked to commit to not avoiding as best as possible and to being willing to talk about avoidance when it is present and interfering with the group process. With this groundwork laid, it will come as no surprise to clients when the group therapist observes avoidance as TIB and works with clients to circumvent or mitigate the effects of such avoidance. It is true for individual therapy as well as for group psychotherapies: You do not need to be a DBT therapist to target and reduce the impact of avoidance as TIB.

MOVING FORWARD

In this chapter we described ways that DBT principles and strategies can be borrowed by DBT therapists and non–DBT therapists alike to help reduce and prevent client avoidance as TIB. An underlying premise was that avoidance behavior is a normal response to emotionally evocative contexts, such as psychotherapy. From this, it follows that many of our clients across various diagnostic presentations and treatment modalities have learned to avoid or escape from unpleasant emotions. And because therapy is itself an emotionally rich and dynamic context, our clients should be expected to avoid emotions during the therapeutic process. There are many ways in which avoidance takes center stage in therapy, and we emphasized how therapists try to overcome the challenge of avoidance.

10

RESPONDING TO SEXUALLY RELATED BEHAVIOR

In clinical training it is often said that the easiest way to lose your license to practice is to have a romantic or sexually intimate relationship with your client. The rule is simple: If you want to continue being licensed to provide psychotherapy, do not sleep with your clients, do not touch your clients inappropriately, maintain clear boundaries, and so on. This is true for some time even after the therapy ends. The list of people to be romantically intimate with in the world is a long one, but for clear and important reasons, this list does not include your current or former psychotherapy clients.

The stakes are high when it comes to sexual behavior with psychotherapy clients. Allegations to a licensing board of sexually inappropriate behavior by a therapist, even if the therapist has not engaged in any such behavior, can have adverse consequences to the clinician in his or her clinic, agency, or institution. In addition, clients can initiate civil litigation in such circumstances. There usually are no eyewitnesses in individual psychotherapy,

http://dx.doi.org/10.1037/14752-010
Managing Therapy-Interfering Behavior: Strategies From Dialectical Behavior Therapy, by A. L. Chapman and M. Z. Rosenthal

making such claims challenging to refute. On top of this vulnerability, the nature of the therapy process, particularly with certain clients, can lead to the client feeling a deep and meaningful sense of intimate connection with the therapist. Neither sexual nor romantic, the therapeutic relationship brings moments that are shared as special and sometimes can be experienced as profoundly intimate. Sometimes, with some clients, the feelings of trust, validation, support, and empathy all can be experienced as love. For those clients with an impoverished history of feeling intimacy, understanding, and interest from others—or love—the therapeutic intimacy can be a somewhat new experience and one that can elicit feelings of affection or love toward the therapist. Many clinicians are trained to adhere to the American Psychological Association's "Ethical Principles of Psychologists and Code of Conduct" (2010) and are well-grounded in the ethical imperative to do no harm to clients. Indeed, engaging in any behavior that could be construed as part of a nontherapeutic relationship could potentially interfere with the psychologist's objectivity or risk exploitation or harm to the client. With all of this as a backdrop for the context of psychotherapy, it is no wonder clinicians can be nervous about inadvertently behaving in a way that could be experienced as inappropriate by our clients.

In this chapter, we review several dialectical behavior therapy (DBT) principles and techniques that can help clinicians respond to client sexual behavior. We discuss how to use behavioral principles (e.g., reinforcement, punishment, shaping, contingency management), cognitive acceptance and change, validation, and irreverence to address and reduce sexual behavior in clients. In addition, we illustrate ways to talk openly and honestly with clients about their feelings related to intimacy in therapy. We also highlight how to ignore when it may be effective to do so client behavior that could be interpreted as sexual. Throughout the chapter, we emphasize ways that therapists can use mindfulness as a set of skills from DBT to respond skillfully to clients' sexual behavior.

OBSERVING AND DEFINING SEXUALLY RELATED THERAPY-INTERFERING BEHAVIOR

Often, sexual therapy-interfering behaviors (TIBs) are obvious, but at times, they might be more subtle and hard to detect. Obvious examples include sexual propositions, discussions of posttherapy sexual relationships, physical advances, intimate questions about the therapist's sex life, and so on. Other less obvious examples might include the client wearing provocative clothing, sitting in unusual or provocative positions, displaying a lack of normative modesty regarding her or his body, talking frequently about sexual issues, and so on.

From the perspective of a DBT therapist, there is no such thing as sexually related behavior; there is only behavior. Some behavior is associated with romantic intimacy or sexuality. This means that some behavior on the part of the client may appear sexual to one therapist but not to another. Asking a therapist whether he or she is interested in being romantic or openly soliciting sexual intercourse in the session are clear examples. But as a therapist or counselor, how many times has a client been this direct with a sexual advance? If you are like most therapists and do not have the looks of a film star, it is unlikely that this has happened to you. That does not mean that it will not happen. The point is that sexually related TIB is a broader class of behavior than these most egregious examples.

As a category, type, kind, or class of behavior, sexually relevant TIB is more than a list of specific examples. As introduced earlier, this class of behavior is functional, not formal, which means that many topographically different behaviors can function as being sexual. The real question is whether the behavior in question is interfering with the therapeutic process. If it is, the behavior is TIB. The key point is that behavior is TIB when it functions to disrupt the process of therapy, even if it does not look superficially like sexual TIB. The following are some examples from our own experiences that illustrate the sometimes obvious and ambiguous nature of sexual TIBs.

MICHELLE AND JANE

Several years ago one of us was treating a client who had been an exotic dancer in local clubs. "Michelle" was a 23-year-old woman who was in treatment for problems with substance use. She had been using cocaine and opiates for the preceding 5 years and had been binge drinking and smoking pot since she was 15. She came to treatment because her life was rapidly spiraling out of control, and not just because of her substance dependence. Michelle also met full diagnostic criteria for major depressive disorder and borderline personality disorder (BPD). Even when she was not high, she was socially anxious, impulsive, and aggressive interpersonally. Sharp punches of negative affect hit her frequently and were intense. They came from all angles and wore her down most days. Irrespective of which emotion—shame, sadness, fear, or anxiety—her mostly likely response was anger. Her negative emotions had, over the years, become coupled with subsequent anger and hostility. Michelle described feeling most days like a caged animal, primed on the tips of her toes, ready to pounce. This left her generally moody and interpersonally prickly, with a history of violence and an arrest record. She also had a long list of life problems: having no job, no history of holding jobs, no college education, no vocational skills; being on probation; being a single parent of two girls; and so on. There was no shortage of treatment targets. Using DBT, we quickly established a treatment hierarchy to organize and put a structure to what we would target for change, when, and how.

Michelle was an attractive woman who entered a room with confidence. She carried herself in a way that was impossible not to notice. Boisterous and playful in the clinic lobby, Michelle was a loud and fast talker with a thick North Carolina accent. Many times she made the clinic staff laugh with her exuberance and charm. But this apparently confident public expression belied a profound inner paranoia and mistrust.

Michelle had made lots of money in the past by taking her clothes off in front of people seductively. The contingencies of her learning history had shaped her skills at using her physical appearance to get attention from others. Without a higher education or a technical skill, and with an expensive habit of polysubstance use, she had developed classes of behavior with men that functioned to elicit not only attention but also money. However, although she may have learned ways to capture the eyes and dollars of men, she did not trust them. Thus, it seemed somewhat surprising when Michelle openly shared her history as an exotic dancer early in treatment. Knowing her history, it did not take an expert psychologist to hypothesize that sexually inappropriate TIB could possibly occur. In the DBT consultation team, this possibility was discussed from the outset of treatment. A lot of time was spent exploring whether the door should be left open at each session, whether her behavior could be interpreted as flirtatious, and the pros and cons of her being seen by a male or female therapist. All of the psychotherapy sessions were video recorded. The team planned for how her TIB could affect both individual and group therapy; all focused on the potential that sexually relevant TIBs might occur frequently throughout treatment. The consultation team was ready for sexual behavior of some sort, though it was not quite clear what it would look like.

Michelle generally came to sessions dressed comfortably and casually, usually wearing jeans and a sweatshirt or hoodie. On occasion she dressed more provocatively, wearing tight-fitting shirts or pants. Sometimes she sat with her legs crossed while wearing shorts or would curl up in the therapy chair, cozy and comfortable, the way one might look at home on a couch in front of the TV or fireplace. Once or twice her shirt may have slipped to expose the top of her shoulder or bra strap. All in all, her comportment in therapy was different from the prototypical client. If 100 therapists watched a video of her DBT individual sessions with the sound muted, it is safe to bet that most would comment on how she seemed sometimes to behave in a sexually provocative manner.

It was clear that Michelle's history working in the exotic dance industry had shaped her generally flirtatious interpersonal style. We are all products of our learning history, and she was no exception. But the more interesting thing about Michelle was that this class of behavior did not, in any single instance, ever have the function of feeling flirtatious or seductive. The behaviors occurred, and not infrequently, but they never felt manipulative, strategic, or intentional. Instead, what could have been labeled pejoratively as sexual, flirtatious, or seductive seemed more genuinely to be overlearned, automatic, and unintentional behavior. Like those in any ordinary class of behavior, the behaviors in this class—habits, automatic responses, and interpersonal quirks—were conditioned and had over time generalized across contexts. Was this TIB? Let us consider another case example for comparison.

Another client one of us saw came to treatment for help with interpersonal problems and depression. "Jane" was in her mid-50s, divorced, and had no children. She was bright, clever, and well-educated. Well-off financially, Jane had not worked in a long time. She spent her days reading, shopping on the Internet, and trying to develop new hobbies. Although she had been in psychotherapy previously, she had never been treated by a male therapist. In one of the first sessions, Jane recognized her ambivalence about engaging in the therapy process. She insightfully highlighted how it would be hard for her to be vulnerable and authentic, to share her inner and most emotionally painful experiences with a man in a position of authority. Of course, this made sense: Here was a younger male therapist offering acceptance, validation, and encouraging hope to a lonely female client. The attention and understanding of her present emotional pain juxtaposed against the emotional abuse and neglect she had experienced by men in her past would engender a labile ambivalence about opening up and vulnerably entering into the therapeutic relationship.

Jane's primary problems centered on her interpersonal functioning. She was sweet and empathic one minute, hostile and dismissive the next. During sessions she swiftly moved from being endearing and gentle to being unlikable and aloof. One moment she was genuine and open, the next she could be sullen or coy or issue an ultimatum about how the particulars of the therapy process should play out. Sadly, an unfaithful husband and protracted divorce had left her irreparably disenfranchised from pursuing intimacy. Any time the therapy process elicited closeness, connection, or affiliative feelings, Jane lashed out with passive–aggressive behavior. Vulnerable therapeutic intimacy was a trigger for explosive interpersonal behavior that functioned to distance others from Jane. As others withdrew, it confirmed Jane's belief that she was not capable of finding intimacy. She declared defeat to this process, announcing once in a therapy session that she would never love again, never be loved, and never allow herself to get emotionally close enough to be hurt by others.

The trouble was that turning her back on love for others was profoundly incompatible with the depth and richness of emotion she privately experienced. Jane was a passionate woman who desperately wanted to be loved and in her heart had an abundance of love to share with others. In many ways Jane was like a lot of clients seen in private practices. She was depressed and lonely, grieving interpersonal loss, struggling to adjust developmentally to a new phase of her life. She was not suicidal or psychotic. She had never been violent or had used any drugs. She was difficult to get along with in contexts calling for trust, but she knew how to be perfectly if not extraordinarily pleasant in other social situations.

Like Michelle, Jane was an attractive woman with a commanding presence about her when she entered a room. With prodigiously flowing shiny black hair, large brown eyes, and fastidiously applied makeup, Jane's public demeanor was careful yet graceful. She walked slowly and deliberately, observant of others with the courtesy of a subtle nod and gentle eye contact. She did not behave in a sexual manner publicly. She dressed conservatively, hiding her figure with oversized clothes in neutral colors. She wore a gold crucifix on a chain around her neck and carried the Bible in her purse, speaking with conviction to strangers about her faith and subservience to a higher power. Jane projected a publicly Victorian persona, but when the door closed and therapy began, her repertoire of behavior changed.

Jane demonstrated sexually related TIB many times during therapy. When trying to work toward increasing skills use or reducing other TIBs, she might suddenly begin to opine about why psychotherapy clients would ever have a relationship with their therapist outside the therapeutic context. She would list all the reasons why she would never want to have a sexual relationship with a therapist, or she would ask questions about what would happen if clients had sex with their therapists. Significantly, the onset of her TIB would occur during moments requiring her to be vulnerable, talk about change, or engage in problem solving. When digging into the emotional barriers underlying her homework noncompliance, for example, she might declare that she could no longer continue the conversation because to do so would require becoming more emotionally intimate and that she was not ready to go to "the next base." Without provocation, this could then lead to her shamefully and angrily denouncing the idea of a relationship with the therapist outside of therapy as something she would never consider. This was TIB because it functioned to steer the therapy session away from the session goals and targets, distracting and slowing down the therapy process.

Some of Jane's behavior was explicitly sexually related TIB. Jane tangentially disclosed her favorite sexual positions and the ways in which her former sexual partners had selfishly failed to please her. In session she begged in gasps and tears to be understood as a woman who needed romantic intimacy to feel fulfilled. She asked question after limits-breaking question about the intricacies of the therapist's dating and romantic history. There was never any direct proposition for intimacy and never any inappropriate touching. Sadly, Jane's relationship history and emotional dysregulation led to many challenging sexually related TIBs. She was trapped by her history, stuck directly in her own way. Her TIB in treatment was the tip of the proverbial iceberg of what had kept her from living consistently within her most important values: meaningful and intimate relationships.

The core dialectic of acceptance and change is fundamental to understanding how to respond to sexually related TIB such as that exhibited in these examples. Is the TIB something to notice or for the therapist to tolerate without it arresting the process of the therapy session? Or should the TIB be immediately addressed and targeted for change? What should be changed, if anything—the client's behavior or perhaps their expectations, assumptions, or beliefs? As a basic premise in DBT, through radically seeking to understand the behavior that is therapy-interfering, the therapist also helps the client learn to change that which can be changed. Collaboratively and relationally, therapist and client together discern what makes sense and is valid, what is to be experienced without changing, and which in-session TIB can be changed to improve the client's life. In some moments it makes sense for the therapist to mindfully observe and let go of the truth of any thoughts related to TIB. In other moments the therapist and client may have to target ways the client can change how he or she responds to certain triggers associated with the onset of sexual TIB, such as feeling cared for, grateful, or attracted to the therapist.

All of this requires the therapist first to be mindful of his or her reaction to certain client behaviors. If the reaction evoked is one that is associated with intimacy, love, or sexual arousal, for example, the therapist has to further consider whether it is TIB. For now, let us assume there is such TIB and the client already has been oriented to this as a problem that has to be addressed as part of treatment. Let us assume the client agrees with being more effective interpersonally with others as a treatment goal and that developing real and lasting intimate relationships is an important value. In this context, we consider what the therapist might do if sexually related TIB appears to be occurring.

ADDRESSING SEXUAL THERAPY-INTERFERING BEHAVIOR

Several strategies can help therapists navigate the thorny terrain of sexually related TIB. As with most other TIBs, it is important for the therapist to start by observing, describing, and determining where the behavior falls in the target hierarchy. The key question is whether the apparently sexually related behavior is actually TIB. Another important step is to highlight or bring the behavior to the client's attention so that a collaborative discussion and assessment can occur. In terms of assessment, it is important to understand how and why the behavior functions as TIB and how the sexually related actions function both within and outside the therapy context.

Observing, Defining, and Prioritizing
Sexual Therapy-Interfering Behavior

Among the first steps in addressing sexual TIB is to assess and better understand how it functions both within and outside the therapeutic context. Even if the behavior is not interfering with treatment inside the clinic during therapy, this class of behavior may elicit different responses from people in the environment outside therapy. For Michelle, it is important to highlight how her apparently sexual behavior made sense in the therapeutic context but that it may not be effective in other contexts. The critical issue was that she had many TIBs, and sexually relevant behavior was not the primary target. Recall that she was aggressive with others, impulsive, depressed, anxious, using substances, needing to find a job, and so on. She also was chronically late to or did not show up for therapy appointments, was on the verge of homelessness, lied periodically, and did not complete psychotherapy homework. The DBT treatment hierarchy guides the therapist to focus on TIB, but it is up to the therapist and, in DBT, his or her consultation team to prioritize which of the various TIBs to attend to in any given session.

The first consideration a therapist has when a potentially sexually relevant behavior occurs is whether the behavior functions as TIB. Remember, Michelle was an exotic dancer who behaved provocatively, though the apparently sexual behavior did not function as TIB. It was easy to ignore and redirect her. She did not appear to be aware of how she could come across to others in a flirtatious way. She did not talk about her appearance, never initiated conversation about her sexuality, and unlike Jane, never talked about her romantic or intimacy needs. In addition, Michelle seemed unaware that her casual conversational habits might be interpreted as sexual, often calling her therapist or the clinic staff "honey" or "sweetie" in bidding farewell until the next appointment. Importantly, the extensive list of treatment targets meant that Michelle and the therapist both had bigger fish to fry than to spend time discussing how her behavior could be experienced by others as flirtatious. Staying out of jail, coming to therapy, doing her therapy homework, reducing addiction and anxiety, finding a job and stable income were all higher on the treatment target hierarchy. The potentially sexually relevant TIB did not interfere with treating those higher priority targets. Although the form of Michelle's behavior was often sexual, the function was not therapy-interfering. The opposite was true for Jane.

The key point is that form is not always function when it comes to potentially sexually related TIB. Take another example common to psychotherapy:

EXHIBIT 10.1
Steps to Decide Whether a Sexually Related Therapy-Interfering
Behavior Should Be Addressed

- What function does the behavior have on the clinician? Does it lead to a process that disrupts, slows, or otherwise interferes with the treatment process or outcomes?
- Is the behavior part of a broader class of behavior that is interfering with the client's life? For example, is the behavior functioning to increase others withdrawing?
- If the behavior functions to interfere with the process of therapy and is relevant to a treatment target in the client's life, is this a treatment target the client and therapist have collaboratively agreed is important?
- If the answer is yes to the second and third question, this is a therapy-interfering behavior that should be addressed.

The client yawns while stretching her or his arms high in the air, exposing a portion of his or her stomach. Is it important that the client exposed the skin, or is it a meaningless accident? Is this sexually related TIB? The answer depends on one's theoretical orientation; even within DBT it may or may not be conceptualized as TIB. To determine whether to consider this as TIB, the therapist has to understand the effect of the behavior on the therapist. Does it distract the therapist, change the topic, or lead to avoidance of emotionally difficult conversations? Does the behavior function to elicit client behavior of shame or self-loathing? Perhaps the behavior functions to increase therapist nurturance (e.g., "Oh wow, you look tired—are you getting the sleep you need lately?"). As a heuristic, Exhibit 10.1 can be used to help clinicians determine how to respond to a potentially sexually related TIB.

Highlighting and Talking to Clients About Sexually Related Therapy-Interfering Behavior

Orientation to sexually relevant behavior as possible TIB requires treating the client with the utmost gentle care without inadvertent fragilization. In DBT, the therapist attempts to be delicate about this kind of TIB without being overly cautious or apologetic. At the same time, the therapist has to be able to speak openly and irreverently about sexual TIB without in any way being judgmental of the client. This is a tricky balance to strike; it is like being a trapeze artist in a gust of wind. The client may become upset when the therapist observes and describes the sexual TIB, but shielding the client from negative emotions or embarrassment is only one of several competing goals in such moments. The communication style of being irreverent plays an important role in such considerations, allowing the therapist to talk about the things others are afraid to talk about with the client (e.g., being sexually suggestive or inappropriate) and to observe the behaviors that previous

TABLE 10.1
Dialectics When Orienting Clients to Sexually Related
Therapy-Interfering Behavior

Gentle	Matter-of-fact
Nonpejorative	Assess whether this was a problem in the past
Tentatively observe the behavior	Normalize the therapy-interfering behavior in the therapy context
Be willing to be wrong	Link to problem behaviors in client's life
Genuinely compassionate	Observe therapist limits

therapists might have noticed but chose to avoid. Table 10.1 offers dialectics associated with orienting the client to sexual TIB when it is relevant.

The exchange in the following transcript happened with a trainee one of us was supervising. The client was a young African American man in his mid-20s who was single and who had a history of brief romantic relationships. He was depressed, anxious, and highly ambivalent about beginning therapy. In the second session it became clear that he was attracted to his female therapist, who was trained in DBT. In the transcript, notice how the therapist balances being compassionate and gentle with being matter-of-fact. She neither avoids the topic nor says anything that could jeopardize the therapy. Instead, she orients the client to this as a possible problem, one they can return to as needed as they keep working together.

> *Client:* I don't know whether I can do this treatment.
>
> *Therapist:* Oh, you don't? Why wouldn't you be able to do this treatment?
>
> *Client:* [*pausing*] Well, you see, it's hard to say this, but I just don't know if I can work with you.
>
> *Therapist:* You don't know if you can work with me?
>
> *Client:* Right. I'm not sure if I can work with a therapist who is so good looking. There, I said it.
>
> *Therapist:* I can see how that might be difficult to say, and I appreciate you telling this to me.
>
> *Client:* Yeah, I didn't expect you to look like this, and it's going to be really hard for me to stay focused. Maybe we need to stop therapy. Maybe we could talk outside of therapy?
>
> *Therapist:* I totally get it. It's really hard when this happens, and you have to know that this kind of thing happens sometimes. You know, we've only just begun to work together, and we have a lot of time together in front of us if you decide to do this treatment. If you continued to find me attractive, you're

right that it could end up being a problem. On the other hand, it's possible that you won't find me attractive after we work together longer. Instead of us deciding right now to stop therapy, would you be willing to come in again for another session next week, so we can keep seeing whether this therapy might be a good fit for you?

Client: Um, I guess. I mean, I don't think it's going to work, but we can try.

Therapist: I think that would be a good idea. Sometimes when people start therapy they find things about their therapist that they imagine will be distracting or might get in the way of treatment. In this case you are finding me attractive, but in other cases clients sometimes find the therapist too old, too young, too calm, too excitable, or even too awkward interpersonally. Some African American clients only feel comfortable working with African American therapists. But for now, the thing that seems to be a problem is that you find me attractive. But we don't know yet whether this is a problem that needs to be solved by you finding a new therapist. It's possible that it does, but it's of course also possible that it does not. Time will tell, and we can come back to this along the way if we decide to work together.

Client: OK. But I want you to know that I think you are really kind of cute, and I wish we could have met before.

Therapist: I tell you what—let's agree that this could end up being a therapy-interfering problem and that we will keep our eyes on this to see whether in fact it becomes a problem? Deal?

Client: Deal.

As with any behavior, sexually related TIB has to be understood before it can be changed. If it is an ongoing class of behavior getting in the way of treatment, just like any other TIB, the contextual variables increasing the probability of the behavioral class have to be identified. And, like any other behavioral analysis designed to characterize the antecedents and consequences of problem behaviors, an analysis of sexually related TIB has to be done collaboratively with the client. This can feel uncomfortable to client and therapist alike when the topic is sexual TIB. Still, if the TIB is going to be understood and is relevant to the client's therapy goals, it has to be explored—not in a sterile and detached manner but, instead, in a sensitive and relationally focused way. An effective approach to these challenging psychotherapy moments is to be collaborative, caring, and kind in being client centered and supportive in a gently relentless pursuit of understanding. It simply is not reasonable to instantly shift treatment targets whenever these TIBs occur. Instead, the therapist must make a decision about whether, in any given moment, it is likely to be effective to target sexual behavior as TIB and when it may be more useful to ignore it.

When it comes to this decision, as noted earlier in this chapter, the DBT treatment target hierarchy is the therapist's best friend. To oversimplify, if the client and therapist are working on ways to prevent imminent self-injurious behavior and in the process of this discussion the client demonstrates sexually provocative behavior, there is little doubt about what the therapist would do. Because the TIB is lower on the hierarchy and, more important, because the therapist cannot help the client with TIB if he or she is dead or hospitalized, the therapist would prioritize targeting the self-injurious behavior. In this instance, the TIB would likely be ignored or, at most, observed as a problem that can be addressed another time after the problem of self-harm is solved. This is a straightforward situation.

Moving down the treatment hierarchy, if there are no treatment targets related to self-harm or harm to others, and if there are no egregious other TIBs (e.g., not showing up to treatment, being very late to appointments, refusing to talk), the issues being discussed are likely to be things interfering with the client's quality of life. If the client and therapist are working together to decrease depressive symptoms and increase the quality of relationships, for example, the therapist must decide, mindfully, whether it might be effective to weave into this discussion the observation about sexually related TIB. It may be that there is no clear link between these topics, so the therapist waits, ignoring the TIB, and later attends to it. Whenever the therapist ignores the sexual TIB, it is recommended that he or she consult with their treatment team or other trusted colleagues about this experience to stay ethically grounded and clinically responsible.

VALIDATION: BEING SURE ONLY TO VALIDATE THE VALID WHEN IT COMES TO SEXUAL THERAPY-INTERFERING BEHAVIOR

Validation is an essential skill in psychotherapy. DBT does not own and did not create validation, and all clinicians use it more or less skillfully. What DBT contributes is an operationalization of multiple levels of validation (see Chapters 2 and 3) as functional classes of behavior. Validation can take the form of therapist open-ended questions, affirmations, reflections, and summarizations, similar to other therapeutic modalities, such as motivational interviewing (Miller & Rollnick, 2002). Validation can include compassionate and curious attempts to understand the client's thoughts and feelings.

Validation also can include the therapist highlighting how past experiences or one's biology can help explain why thoughts, feelings, physiological sensations, or behaviors have occurred. Validation sometimes involves the therapist normalizing experiences as reasonable or common or as making sense given the current context the client is in, irrespective of their past. And validation in DBT can include efforts to be radically genuine, the therapist sharing his or her experience in an authentic and relationally mindful manner. Sometimes, but of course not always, this includes self-involving self-disclosures (disclosure of the therapist's ongoing reactions to the client's behavior) by the therapist.

Validation in DBT is functional, and as a result, it can take a host of different forms. On one hand, validation can be manifestly supportive and encouraging, the therapist agreeing with the client about this or that or encouraging the client to keep up certain behaviors. However, for the purposes of this chapter, it is especially important to highlight that validation is more than being nice, more than agreeing, and more than being an active and supportive listener. The art of validation is the therapist's ability to acknowledge what is present without inadvertently reinforcing dysfunction. This means that the therapist is mindful of the client's behavior and considers carefully what to confirm using validation and what to ignore or, if needed infrequently, what to disconfirm. For the therapist, validation is an active process requiring mindfulness, consideration of the case conceptualization, and decision making about what to confirm, what to attend to, and what to ignore or avoid. In the case of sexually inappropriate or related TIB, this active process of validation is a critical therapist skill.

The target for the therapist is to validate the valid. But in the case of sexually inappropriate behavior, where is the validity? A therapist might respond to this question by saying that there is always something to validate. When a client is behaving with sexual TIB, what might be possible to validate as being present in that moment, making sense, being legitimate, or being the result of the client's history or current circumstances? Expressions of sexual desire for or romantic interest in the therapist can be, from the perspective of a DBT therapist, validated. Feelings of emotional intimacy may be conflated with sexual or romantic experiences in the client's history. The therapist in this example could validate the feelings as making sense but disconfirm the option of sexual or romantic behavior.

Take the example of sexually provocative behavior that is distracting or that otherwise interferes with therapy. In the client's history, those behaviors may have been reinforced and may be effective at attaining or enhancing intimacy. The therapist in this case could simply acknowledge how the client's history makes the behavior understandable and, at the same time, observe limits about the therapeutic relationship. These are two general examples of how a therapist might mindfully balance validation of the valid with limit setting to reduce the probability of dysfunctional behavior being reinforced and to continue working with the client toward treatment goals. With this in mind, Table 10.2 provides an overview of how therapists might consider using levels of validation in response to sexual TIB. To make it concrete, imagine when reviewing this table that a client has expressed an interest in having a relationship with a clinician after therapy ends. Let us see what the therapist could do by using validation as a strategy with associated specific responses.

DIALECTICAL BEHAVIOR THERAPY STRATEGIES FOR HELPING CLIENTS WITH THOUGHTS AND EMOTIONS RELATED TO SEXUAL THERAPY-INTERFERING BEHAVIOR

So far in this chapter we have suggested that non–DBT therapists can borrow principles and strategies from DBT to be mindful of, orient clients to, and validate sexually related TIB. The ubiquitous dialectic of acceptance and change underlies all clinical considerations for how to respond to the client's TIB. A concrete translation of how to navigate this dialectic is to first use validation to understand and communicate understanding of what is valid about the TIB and then to set or observe limits. But what about all those thoughts related to the TIB? What can the therapist do when, for example, clients with BPD and chronic sexual trauma histories begin acting out sexually in the therapy room? After validation and observing limits, what does the therapist do?

In many instances, it may be effective to help the client learn ways to regulate emotions and cognitions associated with sexual TIB. As discussed earlier, this TIB should be mindfully considered and must be appropriate to target in light of other possible treatment goals. With that said, sexually inappropriate TIB often has to be attended to, not only because it is disruptive or uncomfortable for the therapist but also because it can be an exemplar from a class of highly ineffective behavior that is interfering with the client's life outside the therapy room—a *clinically relevant behavior* in functional analytic psychotherapy terms, as articulated by Kohlenberg and Tsai (1991). According to this model of psychotherapy, behavior that interferes with treatment may be conceptualized and targeted effectively when it is a similar functional class elicited by contingencies of the therapy process that are naturalistically relevant. In the case of sexual TIB, the behavior can be considered clinically relevant if it is similar in function to what the client does outside therapy.

In attending to sexual TIB, the therapist could use problem solving, chain analysis, or any standard behavior therapy or cognitive therapy

TABLE 10.2

Levels of Validation and Examples of Validating Responses
to Sexual Therapy-Interfering Behavior

Level	Type	Therapist response	Example of response
1	Paying attention	Listening without interrupting mindfully	"Tell me more about how you are feeling. I want to understand."
2	Active listening	Paraphrasing, reflecting, asking open-ended questions, summarizing	"You are noticing that I am interested in understanding you, you're feeling cared for by me, and this is leading to a lot of different feelings about our relationship."
3	Therapeutic mind reading	Stating the unstated, asking the client if he or she is experiencing X or Y on the basis of therapist familiarity and experience with this client	"We have worked together for a long time. I am wondering if right now you are feeling an especially close connection of intimacy."
4	Based on past or biology	Linking the client's therapy-interfering behavior (TIB) to his or her history to make sense of why the TIB may be occurring	"It's been a long time since you felt this close and vulnerable to someone. It would make sense if your mind was telling you that this means we should consider a relationship after therapy. The thought makes sense, even though the action will never happen."
5	Based on the present context	Linking the client's TIB to his or her current experiences or circumstances to make sense of why the TIB may be occurring	"This has been an especially emotional therapy session today. And I have shown you the kind of respect and understanding that you have not found easily with others. It would make sense if you felt a strong sense of connection with me in this today."
6	Radical genuineness	Authentically communicating without pretense in a humane way while observing limits	"Thank you for sharing this with me. To have a relationship with you after therapy ends would be ethically inappropriate and against my values. After therapy ends, we can stay in touch, but it will not be as a romantic relationship. I hope that makes sense and am open to talking more with you about this."

change-based technique. Problem-solving strategies were reviewed in Chapter 3 and could include using chain analyses to collaboratively discern what kinds of things typically increase the probability that the client will respond with certain kinds of sexually related TIBs. It may not be enough to validate why the sexually related TIB is occurring due to a history of sexual arousal being confounded with trusting or being emotionally vulnerable, as might happen in therapy. Instead, using chain analyses, the therapist and client together can examine the links in the chain leading up to and following sexually relevant TIB. Multiple hypotheses about what kinds of things could lead to these TIBs can be explored and solutions discussed openly about ways to change this pattern of responses.

For example, if a male client becomes highly flirtatious with his female therapist whenever she asks him to talk about his past relationships with women, the client and therapist could use a chain analysis to explore his reactions and identify possible solutions. It could be hypothesized that the flirtatious behavior is classically conditioned by the therapist's expressions of interest in his romantic relationship history. If chain analyses could not refute this hypothesis, a solution to explore might be to use mindfulness skills during the session before or shortly after asking about the client's romantic relationship history. Alternatively, it could be hypothesized that his flirtatious behavior is operantly maintained, whereby the probability of the behavior is driven by the likely immediate consequences of the TIB. An example of this could be whether the flirtations evoke observable behavior interpreted by the client as therapist discomfort, leading him to feel excited and sexually aroused. If the chain analyses supported this hypothesis, the solution might include experimenting with brief exposures to the cue, such as repeatedly talking about this topic in a structured and deliberate way, the therapist being mindful not to reinforce the behavior by appearing not to be distressed or uncomfortable, and may also include assessing changes in sexual arousal with successive exposures. In all cases of resolving the sexually related TIB, the therapist can follow guidelines from previous chapters for problem solving including, after using assessment strategies, analyzing candidate solutions, troubleshooting, and whenever possible, actively practicing the new response to change the TIB using such techniques as role playing, modeling, or rehearsal.

In addition to change-based problem-solving approaches to sexually related TIB, the DBT therapist uses acceptance-based techniques. These might include practicing acceptance-based mindfulness, emotion regulation, or distress tolerance skills when sexually related TIB occurs. These skills would be used so that the client could learn that the thoughts, feelings, and physiological sensations associated with the TIB can be experienced without adverse outcomes, other than possibly feeling temporary negative emotions. In addition, the therapist could help the client learn to allow him- or herself to experience without unskillfully responding to any number of internal experiences that historically have been associated with the onset of problem behaviors outside the therapy session. For example, the therapist could help the client accept the experience of sexually related thoughts without interpreting, judging, or trying to change these thoughts and without these thoughts having to lead to ineffective behavior that is inconsistent with the client's values. With all of these change- and acceptance-based tools at the disposal of therapists, there is one essential thing to remember: There is no one singular correct approach for helping clients manage their thoughts and emotions associated with sexual TIB. Table 10.3 presents examples of strategies that therapists across theoretical orientations can use to help in these situations.

Recall that we introduced earlier in the volume the concept in DBT of balancing the therapist communication style of reciprocal warmth with that of irreverence. The idea that a therapist might be irreverent in response to sexually inappropriate TIB might, at first blush, seem strange or worrisome. What does this mean and how can it be done?

In being irreverent, the therapist can be matter-of-fact, slightly unorthodox, or somewhat unpredictable. This is distinctly different from the colloquial notion of irreverence. The DBT strategy of irreverence does not take the form of criticisms, insults, or acts of unkindness. Further, it is unrelated to any traditional notions of religious irreverence, and it does not function as intended if the client experiences it as an aversive punishment. How could non–DBT therapists borrow the strategy of irreverence to help with sexually relevant TIB?

TABLE 10.3
Acceptance and Change Strategies to Help Clients Manage Thoughts
and Emotions Related to Sexual Therapy-Interfering Behavior

	Acceptance	Change
Thoughts	Awareness and experiencing of thoughts as only thoughts, and not as truth	Cognitive restructuring; examine the evidence for the truth of the thought and consider alternatives
Feelings	Observe and allow emotions to be present when they occur without escaping or avoiding them, but without acting on them	Eliciting specific emotions to learn how to reduce their intensity or duration by using emotion regulation skills
Physical sensations	Observing, labeling, and self-validating physical sensations associated with intimacy	Practice using emotion regulation skills to change patterns of reactions to sexually relevant sensations associated with the therapy

Irreverence in the case of sexually inappropriate behavior in DBT is probably most effective if it is matter-of-fact. This draws clear boundaries, observes reasonable and healthy therapist limits, and minimizes confusion about how thoughts and feelings resulting from therapeutic intimacy do not have to be conflated with romantic love or sexual behavior. Several years ago, one of us (MZR) treated a woman for posttraumatic stress disorder (PTSD) using cognitive processing therapy (e.g., Resick & Schnicke, 1992; Surís, Link-Malcolm, Chard, Ahn, & North, 2013). The client had a long history of sexual trauma, with an index trauma occurring when she was a teenage girl. A group of men had held her hostage and raped her repeatedly after a party many years before the therapy. After several months of focused treatment on her traumatic stress, the client's PTSD symptoms were significantly reduced. She elected to continue therapy, and we began to address relationship- and intimacy-related goals. She had been through 2 decades of PTSD symptoms unremitted until our therapy. She was divorced, single, and without avoidance of intimacy, finally. In one session she expressed her desires for sexual intimacy and romantic love. She sheepishly explained that she had feelings of love for her therapist. The response was validation, followed by irreverence:

> It makes sense that you have feelings like that. We have been through a lot together and you are finally free from avoidance and PTSD. Now we are working on you having healthy relationships with men. And I have been here with you the whole time, listening, understanding, and helping you. You trust me, and you don't trust a lot of men, for good reasons based on your history. So, I totally get the feelings you might be having. But here is the thing, and I will be matter-of-fact about this: There can never be a romantic relationship between us. It won't happen. So let's keep thinking about how to help you with these feelings while at the same time being clear, together, that our relationship is only going to be therapeutic, here in this office.

Notice first the validation from the heart, followed by concise and straight-shooting irreverence. There was no mincing of words. There would never be any nontherapeutic relationship; the feelings make sense, though the actions will never happen.

USING BEHAVIORAL PRINCIPLES TO HELP MANAGE SEXUALLY RELEVANT THERAPY-INTERFERING BEHAVIOR

In Chapters 2 and 3 we introduced ways in which DBT uses standard behavior therapy principles to change behavior. This includes concepts fundamental to behavior therapies old and new, such as reinforcement, punishment, shaping, and contingency management. When considering the use of validation and irreverence in response to sexual TIBs, the therapist is cognizant of how such responses might reinforce or punish certain behaviors. By definition, *reinforcement* and *punishment* refer to consequences that function to increase (reinforce) or decrease (punish) the probability of behavior. Positive reinforcement involves adding a pleasant stimulus to increase a behavior, whereas negative reinforcement involves removing an aversive stimulus to increase a behavior. Positive punishment refers to the addition of a stimulus to reduce the probability of a behavior, whereas negative punishment refers to the removal of a stimulus to reduce the likelihood of a behavior occurring. Table 10.4 provides examples of how reinforcement and punishment can be implemented when responding to client sexually inappropriate TIB.

Validation, when effective, can function to increase the probability of client behavior or to enhance client understanding of behavior. Irreverence can be used to observe and draw a client's attention to therapist limits concerning sexual TIB. Irreverence also can function to therefore increase or decrease the probability of certain behaviors. The result is that DBT strategies for managing sexually relevant TIB can be considered as ways to shape up new behavior, increase the probability of certain classes of behavior, or more generally manage the contingencies of the therapy session.

The use of shaping is fairly straightforward in psychotherapy. *Shaping* is used to gradually, over time, increase the probability of adaptive behavior to help the client meet their treatment goals. With sexually relevant TIB, the therapist can differentially reinforce adaptive behaviors in the therapy session until the TIB is less frequent, less dramatic and erratic, or generally

TABLE 10.4
Examples of How to Use Reinforcement and Punishment
With Sexual Therapy-Interfering Behavior

	Reinforcement	Punishment
Positive	Validate the reasonable and expected emotional reaction to feeling cared for, understood, or important	When the client asks if he or she can have a meeting with you outside therapy to talk about something personal, say clearly yet compassionately, "How about we talk about it in here instead?"
Negative	When sexual behavior begins to decrease in frequency or the client verbalizes the ability to predict and respond effectively to this therapy-interfering behavior, help the client feel less anxious or embarrassed	In response to sexual TIB, lean back in your chair and offer less warmth.

less dysfunctional. This requires therapist mindfulness about what to respond to in the moment. It is one technique that DBT therapists themselves are shaped over time to be good at, by virtue of working with multidiagnostic clients who meet criteria for BPD. Therapist mindfulness of the client enables effective responses to clients by helping the therapist be clear and open with the client about what he or she is responding to and why, what is valid and what may be less so, what to accept and what to change, and so on. The therapist is like an inspector at a manufacturing plant observing a seemingly endless stream of products as she or he moves along a conveyor belt. The task is to observe and respond effectively with precision and speed in order to be effective.

By being mindful of the client's behavior and how TIB relates to life-interfering behavior, the therapist is able to invite the client into a collaborative discussion about how certain behaviors have to be changed, why it might be helpful for the client given their values and goals, and how to begin making those changes right away in the session. Shaping behavior toward a shared endpoint, the therapist can use behavioral principles to try to increase or decrease classes of behavior. For sexual TIB, the therapist shapes the behavior by ignoring some behavior in order to attend differentially to other behavior, reinforcing and validating only the valid and punishing infrequently if needed. Accordingly, the therapist manages the contingencies of the therapy session. If the client engages in behavioral class X, the therapist manages his or her response mindfully to increase or decrease this class of behavior. This is done collaboratively, relationally, with the client's needs predominant. It may help to give a few more concrete examples.

One approach a therapist might use to respond to this kind of TIB could be to respond contingently with support and warmth to nonsexual expressions of emotional intimacy, gratitude, warmth, or other relationship-enhancing but nonsexual behaviors. Differentially reinforcing these behaviors could be a smart way to let the client learn experientially that the closeness and trust felt in psychotherapy does not have to be conflated with sexual intimacy, that nonsexual intimacy instead can be achieved. However, the therapist could contingently respond in a matter-of-fact way to observe limits and over time decrease sexually related actions urging the therapist to reconsider whether a post-therapy relationship is possible. The main point is this: When sexually related TIBs occur, it can be effective to manage them by planning to decrease specific behaviors and differentially reinforce alternative and more adaptive behaviors. In this way, contingency clarification and management strategies can be used to shape up more effective behavior that will help the client learn not only to be more effective during psychotherapy but also to enhance relationship functioning outside the therapeutic context.

GROUP PSYCHOTHERAPY AND SEXUAL BEHAVIOR

Thus far, we have considered TIB that is sexually related only in the context of individual therapy. But what about this kind of TIB in group therapy? Groups have all kinds of interesting dynamics, from outright flirtations to surreptitious winks; group therapy can be a fertile setting for sexually charged behavior. Whether the group therapy model is psychoeducational, cognitive behavioral, process oriented, or fellowship based (e.g., 12-step), and particularly when both men and women are in the group, sexually related TIBs may occur. What lessons can be learned from DBT about how to manage these TIBs in the group? To begin with, DBT provides clear limits set at the beginning of treatment about forming relationships in group therapy. Romantic relationships among group members are not permitted, as long as the group members are in DBT group skills training. This does not mean that two group members are not permitted to eventually become romantic or intimate outside the group. It simply means it is not possible until after they complete the skills training. If two group members graduate from group therapy, they can do whatever they please, but as long as they are in the group, they cannot form a relationship that is romantic or sexual outside the group. The rationale for this is that doing so would likely interfere with learning the skills in group—both for the client and for other group members.

You might be asking yourself how realistic it is to prevent any relationship from forming outside the group. After all, these are emotionally vulnerable people, sharing their struggles with each other and working hard to change their lives. It makes sense that, in this context, relationships outside the group might occur. A useful observation is that the relationship formed outside the group cannot be one that is private. In other words, anything that might be done or talked about outside the group between two group members has to be something they would be willing to do or talk about inside the group, with all group members. This dialectical synthesis allows group members to form relationships with each other, but not of the sexual or romantic type. All of this is articulated at the outset of group. If the client is unwilling to abide by this rule, he or she may not be permitted to begin group. The limit would be observed by the group therapist, problem solving would occur, and the client would either end therapy or return to group with a solution to the problem. The behavior could then be monitored and explored as needed thereafter, with an approach that is balanced by being compassionate and understanding on the one hand, while being firm and matter-of-fact on the other hand.

During group therapy, sexual behaviors observed by the DBT therapist are likely to be ignored unless they are egregious and demonstrably interfering with learning. If a client is flirting with another client, the therapist would immediately ask him- or herself whether this behavior is truly interfering with the group therapy. In DBT, the answer to this question hinges on whether the behavior in question interferes with learning. This is because DBT group is explicitly a context to acquire new skills. The assumption is that these skills—emotion regulation, interpersonal effectiveness, distress tolerance, and mindfulness—all have to be learned to help the client begin to live a life that is experienced as worth living.

MOVING FORWARD

This chapter has focused on ways to think about and respond to behavior that is sexually related and that interferes with therapy. A primary point we have made is that sexual behavior is a functional class of behavior that includes, but is not limited to, direct sexual advances or behaviors that some therapists might stereotypically believe are flirtatious or seductive. To reiterate: Form is less important than function when it comes to sexual TIB. Other underlying principles we have extracted from DBT to be used by practitioners not using DBT include the importance of balancing validation and acceptance with irreverence and limit setting and include the need to attend to sexual TIB mindfully without rupturing the therapeutic relationship. Indeed, these TIBs can be some of the most challenging and distressing for all therapists. We hope that some of what has been outlined can be borrowed from what DBT therapists do to help improve the way in which other therapists respond to these challenging situations.

11

ENDING THERAPY EFFECTIVELY

Therapy termination ideally can be considered a step along the path toward a more satisfying and rewarding life (Farmer & Chapman, 2008, 2016). For some, termination can be an exciting and empowering process, akin to graduation from school or promotions at work. The ending phase of therapy provides an opportunity to review the client's progress, the therapeutic relationship, the goals that the client has achieved or not yet achieved, and what was most and least helpful about therapy. Both the therapist and the client can learn from such discussions. When termination goes well, clients leave therapy feeling satisfied and proud of their progress. There is a plan to generalize and maintain gains, make further progress, and prevent relapse in important areas. The client may also have made a firm commitment for continual growth in ways that are consistent with her or his personal goals and values (Farmer & Chapman, 2008, 2016).

http://dx.doi.org/10.1037/14752-011
Managing Therapy-Interfering Behavior: Strategies From Dialectical Behavior Therapy, by A. L. Chapman and M. Z. Rosenthal

Alas, termination is not always such an ideal experience. For some clients, therapy termination is a frightening and daunting prospect. Some clients may have great difficulty contemplating the end of therapy and may even avoid discussions about therapy termination. Some clients may feel angry, rejected, or abandoned when therapy ends. In other cases, clinicians sometimes observe the worsening of symptoms or problem behaviors in the time leading up to termination. The client may decide to terminate therapy too early, before significant gains have been made, or at a particularly inopportune time, such as in a crisis or a period of suicide risk. Other clients may state intentions to quit therapy on a regular basis, making it difficult to move forward in a consistent manner. Sometimes, difficulties in the therapeutic relationship or a lack of progress may lead the therapist to desire termination or to terminate too early in a manner that is inappropriate or unethical. Moreover, in therapy, premature termination and dropouts are quite common (30%–50%; Baekeland & Lundwall, 1975; Barrett, Chua, Crits-Christoph, Gibbons, & Thompson, 2008; Chiesa, Wright, & Neeld, 2003; Kazdin & Mazurick, 1994; Wierzbicki & Pekarik, 1993).

In our clinics, we have seen and experienced both the ideal situations and the less fortunate ones. We have read extensively about termination and spoken and consulted with our colleagues, teammates, and consultants about these issues and concerns. In this chapter, we discuss strategies informed by dialectical behavior therapy (DBT) to maximize the effectiveness of therapy termination. We discuss ways to increase the likelihood that termination will proceed smoothly and effectively, strategies to prevent premature dropout, and ways to navigate common pitfalls associated with the process of termination.

KEY GOALS AND PRINCIPLES

There are several goals and principles to keep in mind when planning for successful termination. Having goals in mind regarding what constitutes successful termination will help the therapist and client organize their behavior in a way that maximizes the effectiveness of termination. The termination process also is an important part of therapy, and as such, the same principles (discussed in Chapter 2) apply to this phase of treatment as to the rest of therapy or to the management of therapy-interfering behavior (TIB).

Goals for Termination

Perhaps the first thing therapists should consider is what the specific goals are for successful and effective termination of therapy. Having a framework in mind and knowing these goals ahead of time can help therapists to proactively plan for termination, rather than to simply react to problems as they emerge. There are several potential goals for successful termination. First, termination is most effective when the client has been thoroughly oriented to the therapeutic process, the likely length and duration of therapy, and considerations regarding the decisions and timeframe for the end of therapy. Termination is less likely to proceed effectively when the client has little or no warning or opportunities for preparatory work, is unaware of the potentially time-limited nature of therapy, or does not know when or why therapy termination might be considered. Second, termination is most effective when the decision to terminate is collaborative. Decisions regarding the timing and process of termination, where possible, should be made collaboratively and with attention to the client's unique situation. Third, effective termination often involves the therapist and client deliberately and collaboratively planning for termination. This planning often involves relapse prevention, discussions of differences in the pre-therapy versus post-therapy relationship, and the troubleshooting of potential problems with termination (Farmer & Chapman, 2008, 2016). Fourth, it can also be helpful for the therapist and client to approach termination as an opportunity to reflect on progress, discuss any feedback the therapist or client may have for one another, and possibly to set future goals. Fifth, ideally, the client will leave therapy on a positive note, feeling empowered and as if she or he has made progress in important areas of life. Finally, successful termination involves a plan to maintain treatment gains and generalize what was learned in therapy to a variety of situations.

Dialectical Principles Applied to Termination

Several dialectics may arise in the course of therapy termination. Indeed, conflicts and polarities are built into the nature of this process, in that it is an unusual situation in which a close and emotionally intimate relationship develops; proceeds for a specified number of weeks, months, or years; and then ends. With regard to termination, one dialectic is that ending therapy is both painful for the client to even contemplate and in the client's best interest: The client needs therapy but needs to be free from therapy. The client's problems may be worsening, and at the same time, ending therapy may still be the most effective course of action. For clients with limited social support networks, therapy can both help her or him move forward in life and hold the client back at the same time (when the therapist is the primary source of social support).

A dialectic that arises when clients want to terminate prematurely is that the therapist may believe that remaining in therapy is in the client's best interest but he or she may also need to relinquish attachment to the client remaining in therapy. The therapist is both attached to the client's well-being and willing to let go of the attachment to the client being in therapy when or if necessary. Therapy is one way to develop a life worth living, but it is likely not the only way. This stance becomes particularly hard to maintain with intensely suicidal clients, when the therapist must both hold on (assess risk, try to ensure safety, encourage the client to stay in treatment, manage suicide risk effectively and ethically) and let go (accept that the client may kill her- or himself). Accepting that a client may quit therapy prematurely can help free the therapist from a narrow focus on keeping the client in treatment. Although we do our best to do this, the primary goal is not to keep the client in treatment; the goal is to work toward the client's best interests and well-being. Becoming focused on keeping the client in therapy is like becoming fixated on only one of many solutions to a larger problem. This is the trap into which some clients fall: There is some kind of problem, and the client focuses on quitting therapy (one of many possible solutions) before the dyad has really had a chance to better understand and try to consider a range of solutions to the problem.

ORIENTATION STRATEGIES

As discussed throughout this book, adequate orientation can help the therapeutic dyad to circumvent many potential problems or TIBs. Indeed, we have found that many therapeutic problems, as well as problems with supervisees, employees, and other individuals, are often failures of orientation. This is no less the case when it comes to therapy termination. It can be effective at the beginning of treatment to specify what the course of therapy might look like in terms of timing, frequency of sessions, and considerations regarding termination. Although it might seem premature to talk about termination at the beginning of therapy, some discussion of this can be helpful and can lay down a framework to prevent future problems.

Addressing the Time-Limited Nature of Therapy

Most forms of therapy are time-limited to some degree. As such (unless this is inconsistent with the therapist's theoretical or therapy orientation), it is helpful to convey at the beginning of treatment that therapy will end at some point. This type of orientation is also consistent with goal-setting theory and research (Fried & Slowik, 2004). If a student were in a course in which the instructor said that there would be a final exam at some point in the future, how much would we expect the student to study for this exam right now? What if the instructor said that the final exam would occur in 2 months? The student might not begin studying right away, but as the exam approaches, the student will put a fair amount of effort into studying, possibly in the week, or less ideally (and more commonly), in the hours prior to the test. Similarly, one function of the time-limited nature of therapy is that some time pressure can encourage consistent work. Indeed, DBT and cognitive behavior therapy (CBT), with their focus on the learning of new coping strategies, thinking patterns, and behaviors, require consistent work and practice. If both the therapist and the client know they have to use their time efficiently, they may be more likely to do so. This can be the case with both overall therapy duration and with session duration, as illustrated in the following clinical example.

We were recently seeing a client who had transferred to one of our therapists after working with another therapist in the community for the preceding 5 years. This individual struggled with severe generalized anxiety and worry and had a history of obsessive–compulsive disorder. In his previous treatment, therapy sessions were relatively open-ended, sometimes lasting an hour, sometimes 1 to 2 hours. When he began treatment, one goal of therapy was for him to embark on exposure-oriented treatment for social anxiety and worry. After the first several sessions, he was ready to start, and as is common among exposure-oriented treatments, the therapist scheduled 2-hour sessions to allow sufficient time for the exposure activities and for the client to return to emotional baseline prior to his departure from the session. After a few sessions, however, the therapist noticed increasing difficulty helping the client remain focused during the exposure interventions. It turned out that this client had been using marijuana more frequently than previously thought, and at times, this was interfering with his ability to concentrate in session. Compounding the problem, several life difficulties (breakup of relationships, conflict with his brother, loss of employment, and difficulties at school) made it difficult for him to want to prioritize exposure, and therapy sessions gradually began to involve more and more talk and less and less action. Moreover, he often engaged in marijuana use to manage the anxiety arising from these ongoing stressors. Approximately 70% of the therapy session involved the client verbalizing worries and ruminating about problems, while the therapist attempted to coach the client on how to use effective skills or to redirect him back to productive discussions. The therapist was feeling ineffective and demoralized, and the client commented that therapy did not seem to be working and stated that he wanted to quit.

After discussing this situation with the team, the therapist decided that the structure of the therapy sessions had to change. Specifically, as exposure therapy was on a temporary hiatus, the therapist decided to take the sessions back down to regular 50-minute sessions. The client agreed to this, and after a few weeks, the sessions were back down to about 50 minutes. Even this seemingly small structural change to treatment appeared to have a fairly dramatic effect. The client and therapist began to use their session time more efficiently, the client was easier to redirect from worry thoughts to effective coping skills and strategies, and the client began to work harder to reduce his drug use in anticipation of future exposure therapy sessions. There is nothing magical about a 50-minute session length or a 6- to 12-month treatment length, but the motivating effect of limited time can, at times, be magical.

Clarifying Contingencies

When providing initial orientation to the length and duration of therapy as well as issues around termination, it is important for therapists to attend to contingency management. In many settings, the contingency is such that the client receives more intense and immediate services when she or he is experiencing more clinically severe symptoms, such as the client who can only receive services through particular agencies when she or he is suicidal. Although greater clinical severity does often necessitate more immediate and intense treatment, it is important to balance this consideration with the types of behavior we would like to see increase (positive, effective coping) versus decrease (suicidality, nonsuicidal self-injury). If treatment providers withdraw support and care when clients show signs of improvement, the contingencies are the exact opposite of what might support ongoing progress. As a result, it can be helpful to convey to clients early in treatment that, as long as they are continuing to benefit from therapy, therapy will continue (Linehan, 1993a). If, however, problems are increasing or the client is not showing improvement, it might be important and ethically imperative to consider either discontinuation of therapy or modification of the therapeutic approach (American Psychological Association, 2010; Canadian Psychological Association, 2000).

Discussing the Logistics of Termination

Other important areas for orientation include providing clear expectations regarding the practical aspects of therapy discontinuation. This might involve briefly discussing the therapist's approach to relapse prevention and the maintenance of treatment gains. The therapist may also discuss whether therapy discontinuation involves an abrupt ending to treatment or a tapering schedule. Clients may sometimes feel anxious and worry that the ending of therapy will be much like a door closing and locking, when in fact the therapist may be willing to work collaboratively to devise a tapering schedule or to schedule booster sessions to provide continued support and maintain therapeutic gains. Some therapists might have an open door policy, whereby the clients may return at any time following therapy termination. Other therapists may decide that they prefer clients to take a break of a specific duration before returning to therapy or that clients return to therapy with someone else. We recommend that these types of decisions be made collaboratively and taking into account the client's unique set of presenting characteristics and problems.

Assessing Past Experiences With Termination

Either early or later in therapy, some assessment of clients' previous experiences with termination also can help to prevent future problems. If the client has had difficult or negative experiences with termination with other therapists, this is the time for the therapist to describe how treatment will be different. One of us (ALC), for example, saw a client whose previous therapist had told her that if she were to self-injure, he would discontinue therapy with her. On further assessment, this approach appeared to be a misguided attempt at contingency management or a rule based on the therapist's preference. The problem, however, was that the client would lose access to therapy if she were to continue to have the very problems that brought her to therapy in the first place. As a result, in her new therapy, the client was concerned about termination related issues and worried that she might be rejected by the therapist if she were to engage in self-injury, a behavior in which she still engaged regularly but was fully committed to working on and reducing. She often felt ashamed and reluctant to bring up self-injury, and she and I worked together to gradually build her trust and to reduce her shame and fear about therapeutic consequences of self-injury. In this case, it was critical for me to orient the client regarding this approach to self-injury and to termination.

BRINGING UP AND DISCUSSING TERMINATION

In addition to orientation, another way to prevent future problems is to begin to discuss and plan for therapy discontinuation well before it happens. During these initial discussions, the therapist and client may begin to review the progress that has been made so far and to define approximately when therapy might end. Other topics include when and how the client might know that she or he is ready for therapy to end, emotional reactions and thoughts about therapy discontinuation, and potential problems that might arise in the ensuing weeks or months. Attending to these issues relatively early in the process entails proactive coping (Aspinwall & Taylor, 1997), as described in the latest version of the DBT skills training manual (Linehan, 2015). An open discussion about problems and reactions the client might have regarding termination can help to maximize the chances of successful termination. Some of these challenges may include fears about the ending of therapy, concerns about the client's ability to cope and manage without therapeutic support, the worsening of symptoms prior to termination, anger and feelings of rejection, or demoralization and hopelessness, among others.

This proactive approach to termination can allow the therapist and client to collaboratively troubleshoot and address these problems ahead of time. Indeed, it can be helpful for the therapist to bring these potential problems up in a frank and open manner, even if the client may not actually be struggling with any of these issues. Highlighting common challenges with termination can normalize the client's potential reactions and facilitate disclosure and open discussion of concerns or worries about termination. For example, the therapist might say something such as the following:

> People have many different types of reactions to therapy ending. Some people are happy that therapy is over and see it as a sign of progress and moving on to the next step on the road to recovery. Others find themselves quite worried about termination, are not sure exactly how they might cope when therapy ends, or might feel as if therapy ending is a form of rejection. All these reactions are understandable. What are your thoughts on how you might react to therapy ending?

Ideally, these discussions should follow the flow of interventions discussed in Chapter 3, including assessment of potential problems with termination, problem solving, eliciting a commitment from the client to implement the solutions, and troubleshooting factors that might get in the way of the successful implementation of solutions. Another benefit of this proactive approach is that, once the stage is set through these discussions, the therapist can later remind the client of the plan they came up with should problems intensify as termination approaches.

MANAGING INTENSE EMOTIONAL REACTIONS TO TERMINATION

Clients may have a variety of intense emotional reactions to termination, including happiness, relief, anxiety, fear, anger, sadness, hurt, and so on. A few key therapeutic strategies and steps can help the therapist and client work effectively through a variety of potential reactions. First, it is important for the therapist to avoid pathologizing or judging the client's reactions. It can be easy to judge clients as overly dependent or as having poor boundaries when they fear the prospect of therapy ending. Sometimes these types of judgments stem from the therapist's own difficulty tolerating the client's emotional reactions. Life is easier when the client cooperates and is appreciative of therapy but is willing to let it go when the time comes. Therefore,

224 MANAGING THERAPY-INTERFERING BEHAVIOR

we recommend that therapists keep in mind the principle of spaciousness of mind discussed in Chapter 2, allowing and accepting the client's full range of emotions and behaviors, including intense reactions to the ending of therapy.

Second, one of the most important strategies in helping clients manage intense reactions to termination is to assess the essence of the problems or factors contributing to such reactions. A variety of factors may influence intense fear about termination, such as concerns that the client may not be able to cope effectively without therapeutic support, fear of the loss of an important relationship, concerns about the potential worsening of symptoms, and so on. In this way, the approach is similar to CBT approaches to other worries, fears, or intense emotional reactions. Understanding the nature of the worry or fear, the expected or feared event, and the client's beliefs regarding her or his ability to cope with it can facilitate effective interventions (Dugas & Robichaud, 2006). As discussed in Chapter 7 on anger, assessment also might address the possible *prompting events* for the emotional reactions (e.g., discussions or thoughts about termination, reminders that therapy is drawing to a close, or even progress), the client's specific *primary* (e.g., fear, sadness, hurt) and *secondary* (e.g., embarrassment or shame, anger) emotional reactions, *action urges* (e.g., to withdraw from the relationship, quit therapy first before it ends, avoid the therapist, yell), and thoughts or interpretations (e.g., thoughts that the therapist does not care, that it was just a professional but not a "real" relationship, thoughts that she or he will not be able to cope without therapy, concerns about loneliness and lack of support).

Third, it can be helpful to assist the client in observing and/or describing her or his emotional experiences. This is an excellent time for the skill of mindfulness of current emotion (Linehan, 1993b, 2015), whereby the client experiences, observes, and perhaps describes the sensations and action urges associated with an emotion. For clients who are sad or afraid about the ending of therapy, this might involve simply observing, experiencing, and watching the wave of the emotion come and go in the presence of a supportive, nonjudgmental therapist. Clients who feel overwhelmed by their emotions or who would otherwise have a hard time talking about their reactions may find that mindfulness of their current emotion allows them to "digest" their emotional reactions and increases their ability to work through them with the therapist.

Fourth, we recommend that therapists observe and look closely for the grain of truth or the validity in the client's reactions. Therapists might ask themselves, for example, "In what way does it make perfect sense that the client might be afraid of therapy ending?" Then, the task is to validate the valid and to avoid validating the invalid. The therapist might validate the sadness associated with the loss of the therapeutic relationship or the frustration about the fact that the therapeutic relationship may not continue as other relationships do but not the client's thoughts that the therapist does not care about her or him.

Fifth, once the client and therapist have achieved some clarity regarding the nature of the client's reactions, problem solving is a useful step. Recall that we reviewed the steps for problem solving using the acronym SOLVES in Chapter 3. These steps can be effectively applied to strong emotional reactions to therapy termination.

Fears About Termination

Fear and anxiety are among the most common emotional reactions to termination and in some cases are realistic. We have seen several clients for whom the therapeutic relationship was their primary source of social support. In these cases, the client's major concern was that she or he would be without any support when therapy ended. If this were the case, the therapist and client have an opportunity to identify the client's needs and goals and to begin to do some proactive problem solving to try to increase the chances that he or she would have adequate support when therapy is over. Other strategies might include coaching the client on distress tolerance skills to more effectively tolerate loneliness or to temporarily accept that limited support is available. The client and therapist might also agree to taper off sessions more slowly or to have regularly scheduled booster sessions.

For clients who have difficulty with fears of termination or of even talking about termination, exposure-oriented interventions may be appropriate. As an example, one of us (ALC) was seeing a client who was attached to therapy and the therapist and had tremendous difficulty contemplating termination. She had been thoroughly oriented at the beginning of treatment to the notion that therapy would end (and approximately when this may occur), ideally once she had met her goals and benefited from treatment. When treatment was approximately two thirds done and the client had made considerable progress (she had stopped self-injuring, made great progress on generalized anxiety and worry, stopped having panic attacks, and reduced drinking to a nonproblematic level, as well as improved her relationships with her husband and daughters), I briefly broached the topic of how she might know when it is time to plan for therapy termination. Although I stated that any decisions about therapy termination would be made collaboratively and proposed that it end soon, the client became extremely angry. Her face turned red, her muscles tightened up, and she raised her voice, saying, "Why are you talking about this?!" and she then criticized me for being so insensitive as to talk about therapy ending. She was so angry that it took about 15 to 20 minutes (and a number of relaxation and emotion regulation strategies) for her to become calm enough to talk further about it.

Afterward, and on further assessment of the essence of the problem, it was clear that her initial reaction was not anger; it was intense fear. She was afraid of how she would do without the therapist's support, and my bringing up termination posed, in her mind, a tremendous threat. She panicked and then became extremely angry. In this case, I could back off and say, "You're right, this is not something we really need to talk about now. Why don't we just leave it? We can always talk about it later when the time is right." This response, however, would likely help to keep the fear and anger alive, as well as provide negative reinforcement of confrontative behavior. In addition, my avoidance behavior would be negatively reinforced by the client's backing down and calming down. When termination became imminent and we really had to talk about it, I might have felt reluctant to bring it up, and/or the client might act and feel similarly at that point. Indeed, this is how clients can shape therapists into providing ineffective treatment.

The solution, instead of avoiding the discussion, was to use the principles of exposure therapy. First, I explained what might happen if we simply avoided discussing the ending of therapy, for example,

> You will stay afraid and probably angry, and I will feel reluctant to bring it up, even when it's really important to bring it up. This won't do you any good. You really don't want your therapist to avoid bringing important things up.

Second, I briefly described exposure therapy and how it works for anxiety and fear, for example,

> Sometimes the best way to become free from fear is to do the exact opposite of what you feel like doing when you're afraid. Instead of avoiding the discussion or thoughts about therapy ending, the opposite would be to jump in with both feet and talk about it, on purpose. It's a lot like getting over fears of anything, be it spiders, heights, snakes, etc.; the idea is to approach whatever you're afraid of, and over time, your brain will learn that it's safe.

Third, the client and I purposely had the discussion about termination several times over the next couple of sessions. Possibly because the client agreed to do this, the anger was greatly diminished during the first "trial," and the fear (and some sadness) was more salient. Over about three sessions of the client and I doing this for approximately 10 to 15 minutes each session, the client got to the point where she said she was bored of the discussion, that her fear was down to about 15/100, and that she did not think it was necessary to continue with the exposure. The fact that she went from panic and intense anger to boredom suggested that this intervention was successful. Moreover, several months later, the client brought up termination on her own, having decided that she had met many of her goals and was ready to start tapering the sessions.

Thoughts and Worries About Termination

When challenges regarding termination or fear of termination seem to be related primarily to the client's thoughts or worries, cognitive interventions may be helpful. In these cases, it can be helpful to attend to and assess the client's appraisals of the situation as well as her or his beliefs about the ability to cope with or manage the situation. The client may appraise termination as a threat or an overwhelming stressor, perceive termination as rejection or abandonment, or have low self-efficacy beliefs about her or his ability to function without therapy. It is not likely that the client only has these thoughts or challenges in the context of therapy termination; therefore, clarifying these thinking patterns provides the therapist and client with an opportunity to address important problem areas that may cut across other areas of life.

One approach to thoughts or worries about termination is to conduct behavioral experiments to test such thoughts. If the client is worried that time away from the therapist will be stressful and overwhelming, the therapist and client might decide to do brief behavioral experiments whereby the client avoids calling the therapist for the next week or two or a gap between sessions is purposely scheduled. The client's task would be to keep track of her or his emotions, thoughts, and actions during the intervening period, as well as to keep track of how she or he is coping with the situation. Behavioral experiments create win–win situations, in that even when situations are tremendously stressful and overwhelming, the client may find that he or she was able to cope with, or at least survive, the situation. Often, the client's experience might teach him or her that separation from therapy is not quite as stressful or overwhelming as initially thought. Even if the client both finds the situation overwhelming and copes ineffectively, the therapist and client have more information than they did before the behavioral experiment and will be able to do some planning for proactive coping.

WORSENING OF SYMPTOMS OR PROBLEMS
PRIOR TO TERMINATION

When a client demonstrates a worsening of symptoms or problems as termination draws nearer, it is tempting for the therapist to infer that she or he is purposely getting worse in order to stay in therapy. Other common assumptions are that the client is self-sabotaging, does not want to change or get better, or is indirectly expressing fear or stress regarding termination. Some of these assumptions may have a grain of truth, but within a dialectical framework, it is helpful to make assumptions that facilitate our effective functioning as therapists. The aforementioned assumptions are often dangerously close to assuming that the client is manipulating the therapist. Consistent with DBT, an alternative assumption is that clients are doing the best they can and want to change and have better lives. A related assumption is that most clients would prefer to end therapy gracefully, having learned new things about themselves and having learned effective strategies to deal with their emotions, solve problems, and improve their lives.

When clients seem to be getting worse in the time leading up to termination, a helpful first step is to assess and better understand what is happening. This requires behavioral specificity about the problem and clear, precise, objective assessment. In terms of behavioral specificity, the therapist might clearly define the ways in which the client is demonstrating a worsening of functioning. Has the client become more suicidal? Is the client engaging in less activity, reporting more sadness or emptiness or an increase in hallucinations, or exhibiting an escalation in angry behavior, no-shows, lateness, or other TIB? Are these changes in behavior different from what the therapist has observed throughout treatment? Indeed, some clients show a great degree of variability in their progress and difficulties throughout treatment, and what seems to be a flare-up related to termination may simply be part of the client's normal behavioral variability. Once the therapist is clear on the target, the core strategies we have already discussed can be helpful (e.g., highlighting and assessing the problem, collaborative problem solving, using core DBT or CBT strategies).

One common consideration is whether a worsening of symptoms may suggest the need to modify the timing or logistics of termination. This can be a challenging dilemma. Keeping behavioral principles in mind, the client would ideally receive more support and attention when she or he is displaying more effective behavior. The therapist continuing to see the client following a worsening of symptoms risks reinforcing some of the client's difficulties. At the same time, terminating when a client is going through a particularly difficult time, is in a crisis, or is acutely suicidal can be even more problematic. In times such as these, avoiding the reinforcement of problem behavior may be a lower priority than is the client's safety and well-being. A dialectical philosophy can help remind therapists to search for some kind of effective synthesis of these types of poles. One such synthesis might be to convey to the client that the therapist is willing to provide continued treatment, because it would be tremendously difficult for the client to lose an important source of support at such a time. At the same time, the therapist might make this extension of treatment time-limited and convey this to the client. In addition, the therapist might also help devise a plan to maximize the client's safety if the termination date approaches and the crisis or risk is still present. In these cases, it can also help to be transparent with clients about the rationale for continuing treatment, not continuing treatment, or modifying the schedule for termination.

CONSIDERATIONS REGARDING TAPERING SESSIONS

Therapists often consider some type of tapering arrangement to facilitate effective termination. There are a few important considerations regarding the schedule for how to end therapy. First, therapy can be a close, emotionally intimate relationship, an unusual relationship, compared with what the client might experience with other health professionals such as their primary care physician. For clients who become attached to their therapists, abrupt termination may be experienced as arbitrary and distressing. Other close relationships often are not time-limited, nor do they often end in an abrupt and final manner. It is not surprising, then, that TIB sometimes emerges toward the end of therapy. That said, there is tremendous value in the client learning how to navigate, understand, and manage the emotional reactions that arise in the context of the ending of the therapeutic relationship. If the tapering of sessions simply delays the inevitable and removes the client's opportunity and need to experience and work through such emotions, this may be a downside of tapering sessions.

A second consideration is that the client holding onto therapy and the therapist allowing this to happen by extending the termination phase may both be engaging in TIB. Sometimes the continued availability of therapy and the therapist maintains the client's problems. For clients with limited social networks, it would be important to assess whether the continued availability of the therapist following termination might actually reduce the chances that the client will work to develop her or his social support network. In her book on DBT, Marsha Linehan (1993a) uses the example of a client wandering the desert and periodically returning to the therapist to ask for small amounts of water. The client is temporarily satisfied and is able to survive on the small amount of water that the therapist can provide, but what she or he really needs is to find or develop a more consistent water source and then from there to build a home and a more sustainable living situation. The challenge is that sometimes those small amounts of water are critically needed, and at the same time, the client and therapist have to find a way to make sure that the client will continue working toward a sustainable life.

As another example of how continued therapy can maintain client difficulties, a therapist was seeing a client ("Bob") who made rapid and excellent progress in treatment over the first 4 to 6 months. When Bob came into therapy, he was suicidal, depressed, dissatisfied with his relationships, and he perceived little meaning in his life or in any of his activities. To Bob, his future seemed bleak, and he could not understand how it could be otherwise. After about six months or so, he was no longer suicidal, had made a career change that reinvigorated his interest in his profession, had improved his relationship with his partner, and had developed new friendships and improved relations with his family. He was happy with his life and hopeful about his future. Bob did not, however, want to quit therapy. He was afraid that if he was no longer meeting with the therapist, he would revert back to his old ways. Bob and his therapist continued, and the therapist made good use of the time by helping Bob to consolidate the skills he learned in therapy, learn to manage more minor daily life hassles, and plan to prevent relapse. Bob remained functioning well, and therapy continued to the point that the therapist was unsure of what to focus on each session (Bob was doing too well). When she brought this up, Bob's worries about quitting therapy became clear, and they finally had another target to work on: worry and fear. Over time, through behavioral experiments and the tapering of therapy sessions, Bob learned that he could function well without therapy.

STRATEGIES TO ADDRESS PREMATURE TERMINATION

Premature dropout or discontinuation of therapy is a common problem across settings and client populations. In the case of BPD, treatment studies have suggested a dropout rate of approximately 20% to 75% (Robins & Chapman, 2004; Stoffers et al., 2012). Across randomized trials comparing DBT with other control treatments, studies have consistently found lower dropout rates in DBT (Robins & Chapman, 2004; Stoffers et al., 2012). In addition, when examining the dropout rates for other outpatient treatments for persons with BPD, DBT still tends to have generally lower dropout rates (Robins & Chapman, 2004; Stoffers et al., 2012). Although these rates are still higher in DBT than we would like them to be, it is quite likely that we are doing something right in relation to clients who have the urge to quit therapy (see also Swift & Greenberg, 2015).

Therapist Assumptions

When it comes to clients quitting, having urges to quit, or talking about quitting, it is important for therapists to use an effective set of assumptions about therapy and their clients. Perhaps because DBT arose out of work with multiproblem, multidiagnostic, high-risk clients who often do not comply with standard treatment recommendations, one assumption is that therapists may need to go to extra lengths to help the clients stay in treatment. This is in contrast with the mind-set of clinicians working with less complex clients, when they may assume that clients who want to quit or drop out of therapy would be better off waiting until the "right time" to pursue treatment. For complex, high-risk clients, the right time for therapy is now, and the risks of losing or not receiving treatment are too high to ignore.

Often, the lives of individuals with BPD who are highly suicidal are unbearable and have to change (Linehan, 1993a). At the same time, these individuals do not have the skills to make their lives more worth living, and sometimes they also lack the motivation to do so. In addition, clients desperately want to change, but change itself is sometimes just as painful, if not more so, than is staying the same. On the road to recovery, clients become demoralized, experience doubts about themselves and about therapy, and react to problems in the therapeutic relationship by trying to escape this relationship. The therapist must essentially have faith that treatment will help as well as hope that the client's life can change in positive ways, if not right this moment, then over the long term. The therapist must have a strong conviction that a road to recovery involving therapy is the best path for the client. On the other end of the dialectic, therapists must also be willing to let go of clients who ultimately decide to drop out of therapy, who do not return phone calls, or who (as sometimes is the case) disappear off the face of the earth.

Ongoing Assessment, Self-Monitoring, and Prevention

The most common set of strategies to prevent dropout in DBT is a combination of self-monitoring and the use of a preventive approach. Each session, the client brings in a self-monitoring form called the *diary card* on which she or he has kept track of behaviors, events, thoughts, and feelings over the course of the week. Detailed discussion of the diary card is beyond the scope of this chapter, but we zero in on one section of the card that allows us to continually monitor dropout-related issues. Specifically, the client is asked to rate her or his urges to drop out of therapy prior to and following each therapy session. The therapist then reviews the diary card, and whether the client has reported urges to quit therapy, the therapist and client make this an important priority for discussion in their session.

This combination of self-monitoring and frank, open discussions of urges to quit therapy can help to normalize the experience of such urges. For clients experiencing multiple co-occurring problems, therapy is much like a challenging hike for which they do not know how to use the appropriate hiking gear. The weather may be challenging, with intense bouts of heat, cold, or driving rain. The therapist is there to help the client use her or his hiking gear effectively and to keep moving forward, but it would be natural for anyone in these circumstances to contemplate quitting periodically. Further, talking openly about the urge to quit can be disarming and can help the therapist demonstrate attachment to the client's well-being as well as a willingness to talk about and openly address concerns about therapy.

Another advantage of this approach is that the client and therapist will have the opportunity to address ongoing problems before they escalate to the point that the client actually does decide to quit. Clients may be reluctant to bring up problems in therapy or urges to quit until these problems become intolerable. Assessing, monitoring, highlighting, and addressing urges to quit before the problems become dire can be effective.

Managing Contingencies and Addressing the Problem

It can be challenging to navigate therapy with a client who frequently talks about quitting. We have seen clients who talk about quitting every few sessions; leave periodic voice, text, or e-mail messages saying that they are done with therapy; and so on. Most of these clients do not end up dropping out of therapy. From a behavioral perspective, it is important for the therapist to attend to all behaviors related to quitting, including the behavior of talking about quitting. Often, therapists assume that, if the client is talking about quitting, she or he has decided to end therapy and that it is a "done deal." They might, for example, assume the client has dropped out before she or he has actually done so, or they might start providing referrals and planning for termination. The problem with this is that the client's talking about quitting may reflect a firm decision to quit, or it may serve other functions altogether.

Either way, quitting therapy is both a problem (indeed, often a TIB) and a solution to another problem. Thoughts, urges, and discussion of quitting can be similar to thoughts, urges, and discussion of suicide. Suicide often is a solution to unbearable pain, and although suicide attempts themselves can become a problem, these behaviors are ultimately the client's attempt to solve a bigger problem in living—namely, that life is unbearably painful. Urges, thoughts, threats, and discussions about quitting can be conceptualized in a similar manner—as solutions to some problem. The problem might be that the client is having hopeless thoughts, is finding therapy to be stressful or distressing, is becoming demoralized with certain aspects of treatment or recovery, is having a hard time tolerating certain aspects of treatment (e.g., other group members' behaviors), or is encountering challenges in the therapeutic relationship. Thinking about quitting therapy may also serve to produce negative reinforcement in the form of temporary reductions in emotional distress, or it may serve to divert discussions away from painful topics. When this is the case, the therapist might focus on helping the client to tolerate discussions of these more painful topics or find other ways to manage emotions or relieve distress.

With this framework in mind, the therapist can broaden her or his view of the situation. It is important to both take the client's urges and statements about quitting seriously and to focus on the problem that the client may be trying to solve by quitting therapy. The solution may be to quit therapy, but the problem could be anything. Perhaps there is a poor fit of the therapist and client, the client is not making progress as quickly as she or he would like, the client feels hurt about something the therapist has said, the treatment itself is not working, or the client is becoming hopeless or demoralized. Quitting treatment or switching therapists is but one among many potential solutions to these problems.

MOVING FORWARD

Termination can be an empowering, successful experience or a challenging phase of treatment rife with potential pitfalls. It is important for the therapist to begin with clear goals for effective termination and principles to guide the effective navigation of this phase of therapy. In terms of principles, one common dialectic is that it is painful for the client to end therapy, and at the same time, termination may the best thing for the client's well-being. Awareness and effective navigation of this and other dialectics will help the ending phase of therapy proceed smoothly. As with other TIB-related issues, orientation can set the stage for effective termination and help to prevent problems. Interventions to facilitate termination sometimes involve helping the client manage intense reactions, fears, and worries about termination, addressing the worsening of functioning prior to termination, making sound clinical decisions about the logistics of termination, and so on. Finally, in addressing premature dropout or termination, we recommend that therapists approach this potential situation with an effective set of assumptions and with an eye toward focusing on the problem and effectively managing contingencies.

12

WHEN THE THERAPIST GETS IN THE WAY

Throughout this book, we have explored a wide range of topics related to how clients in psychotherapy can, in many ways, get in their own way through therapy noncompliance, hostility or passivity toward the therapist, being flirtatious, and so on. Each therapy-interfering behavior (TIB) brings difficult challenges to clinicians. With each different kind of TIB, we have made a central point over and over again. Client TIB is more the rule than the exception across psychotherapies. Dialectical behavior therapy (DBT) principles, strategies, and techniques to respond to TIB can help, even when the therapist is not treating the client with DBT. We have outlined practical solutions to help therapists respond to client TIB, whether one is a new clinician with little psychotherapy experience or a seasoned clinical psychologist with decades of practice.

http://dx.doi.org/10.1037/14752-012
Managing Therapy-Interfering Behavior: Strategies From Dialectical Behavior Therapy, by A. L. Chapman and M. Z. Rosenthal

However, therapists can get in their own way, too. Experts, trainees, and everyone between are all human and therefore are all fallible. There are many ways in which therapists can inadvertently engage in TIB. In this chapter, we explore how therapists across psychotherapies might find themselves saying or doing things that, despite their best intentions, interfere with the client's progress in treatment.

On the one hand, there are ways to circumvent some therapist TIB. On the other hand, it is impossible to prevent all therapist TIB. Because therapist TIB is inevitable, we suggest some straightforward ways to make the most of these circumstances. The therapist consultation team, mindfulness, and radical genuineness are discussed here as examples of approaches from DBT that can help any clinician minimize the frequency of therapist TIBs. We also provide examples of several strategies to use when therapist TIBs cannot be avoided or have already happened. In these ways, the sour lemons of therapist TIB can be turned into deliciously sweet psychotherapy lemonade!

DEFINING THERAPIST THERAPY-INTERFERING BEHAVIOR

For the purposes of this book, just as we have defined client TIB, *therapist TIB* is anything the therapist does that adversely affects the process or outcomes of psychotherapy or that has a negative impact on the therapeutic relationship. Behavior that interferes with the psychotherapy process can include the mistakes we therapists make, the things we say that backfire, the things we regret doing or not doing, and so on. Table 12.1 lists a few common examples of therapist TIB. It takes humility and an honest look in the mirror to assess one's own therapist TIB. With this in mind, we encourage you to consider whether any of these things have happened to you during psychotherapy. It does not matter whether you are a nervous graduate student therapist or a sagacious and smooth expert, the transactional process of psychotherapy ensures that if you treat clients long enough, at some point your actions or inactions will interfere with therapy.

Therapist TIB can be automatic and reflexive, a response in the process of therapy that is unplanned, possibly even something the therapist is unaware has happened. Examples might include forgetting something meaningful, interrupting the client when he or she is saying something important, or coming across as uncaring or patronizing. Therapist TIB can also be a planful, strategic, or intentional action with a purpose. For example, the therapist might arrive with an agenda and suggest at the beginning of the psychotherapy visit that the focus of the session may need to be about this or that clinical problem. The client may not take well to this directive target setting and might become emotionally detached throughout the rest of the

TABLE 12.1

Examples of Possible Therapist Therapy-Interfering
Behavior in Any Psychotherapy

Action	Inaction
Talking too long or being long-winded	Being silent too long or too often when the client is seeking direct suggestions, advice, or an intervention
Using too much therapist jargon or wording that does not resonate with the client	Assuming the client knows what the therapist is talking about
Expressing frustration in an intense, inappropriate, or generally ineffective manner	Not genuinely expressing emotions or appearing aloof, distant, or uninterested
Expressing unrealistic confidence in the likelihood or speed of a treatment working to solve a particular problem	Minimizing the magnitude of a client's problems or invalidating the client by suggesting simple solutions for complex, overwhelming problems
Changing or actively avoiding uncomfortable discussions or moments in psychotherapy	Not attending to client behavior that should be observed or explored even though it may feel uncomfortable to the therapist to do so
Rejecting, criticizing, or punishing client behavior	Being unwilling to disconfirm client behavior when it is appropriate to do so
Rigidly adhering to an agenda or rules dictating the content of the psychotherapy session without regard to the client's current wants, needs, or psychological state	Providing no clear plan, agenda, or orientation to the psychotherapy session structure or providing haphazard interventions
Describing treatment plans, case conceptualizations, or results from assessment findings in a manner that is unclear, inconsistent, or not reasonably associated with an empirical evidence base or theoretical account of the client's problems	Never informing the client about the diagnosis case conceptualization, treatment plan and/or rationale for selected treatment
Rigidly demanding unrealistic and/or perfectionistic expectations about what clients must do, such as never miss or be late to sessions, always complete all psychotherapy homework, or always remember to follow up on agreed-on tasks	Failing to attend to standard professional behavior, such as missing sessions, showing up late, forgetting or failing to do agreed-on tasks, and so on
Adhering to rigid and context insensitive rules about what is "right," "acceptable," or "appropriate" on the basis of ethical guidelines or principles when they do not prescribe or proscribe such specific mandates	Failing to reasonably adhere to ethical standards

session. Attempts to steer the conversation toward particular topics might be met with significant client unwillingness and irritation. It may not be a bad thing when this happens, but it could be conceptualized as therapist TIB if it functions to significantly and adversely affect the therapeutic relationship or treatment progress.

Of course, client negative emotional responses in psychotherapy are ordinary and may be expected responses to specific kinds of therapist behavior (e.g., asking questions in a certain way); these commonly are considered in the case conceptualization and can be exactly the kind of behavior to address with interventions in the treatment plan. In the earlier example, if responded to effectively, a detached emotional response from a client could be mined into profitable therapeutic gold, helping the client learn to relate better to others, decrease impulsive decisions, and/or improve the ability to experience and express emotions with others without needing to escape. This could be life-changing work. However, problems could occur if the therapist is inflexible, rigidly adheres to the agenda, or does not attend to the client's reactions. Sometimes, moving forward with an agenda the client does not like can still be effective. The trick is to supportively engage the client to move ahead with the treatment and attend to the in-session TIB. There is no need to frame this as an either–or kind of clinical decision.

It is important to highlight that it is not wise to simply use negative emotional reactions on the part of the client as an indicator of whether the therapist's actions were TIB. If it were this simple, then anytime clients came into psychological contact with unpleasant emotions or thoughts it would be therapy-interfering. Of course, this is not at all the case. Sometimes the most compassionate thing clinicians can do is to keep supportively motivating the client to move forward despite her or his emotional distress. The dialectical tension here is that, on one hand, clients may not want to feel unpleasant internal experiences in therapy, yet on the other hand, effective therapy commonly involves clients feeling unwanted and unpleasant internal experiences. This can be quite a conundrum. The resolution of this dialectical synthesis is to consider what is most likely to be effective, in the context of the TIB, to help the client get closer to his or her treatment goals. If the therapist is excessively directive, the client can become excessively resistant, avoidant, or disengaged. When fishing, if the fisherman reels a fish in too fast, the fish can get spooked and speed away. But to be effective the fisherman cannot just let go of the reel and allow the fish to swim forever. The synthesis is that the fisherman is mindful of the fish in context, aware of the need to allow the fish to swim a bit, while also attending to moments when it is most effective to reel the fish in without resistance. Similarly, the therapist has to avoid being excessively directive without flip-flopping to the other end of the extreme and providing no clear direction to relieve the client's suffering.

Therapists trying to direct the treatment with purpose and well-thought-out intent can engage in TIB when the client resists such actions. However, the opposite happens too. The therapist could decide that, to appease the client or help her or him feel comfortable, there will be no setting of targets or clearly identified goal for the session. The therapist could choose not to say a lot at the beginning or throughout the session, with the intention of helping the client learn to develop confidence and autonomy. In an effort to help the client learn to decide what he or she would like to talk about, therapist inaction in the form of silence could then lead the client to talk discursively about events of the past week without direction or structure. This, of course, could lead to the client feeling listened to, understood, or supported. Such experiences are vital to the development of trust, which is essential for the therapeutic relationship. However, as any therapist has experienced, sometimes the therapist's silence, slow nods, and empathic facial expressions do not function as intended. Instead of feeling understood and supported, sometimes clients feel ignored and embarrassed, uncertain about what to talk about, or unclear how they could be benefitting from this treatment approach.

Therapist silence and passivity can be therapy-interfering. From a DBT perspective, you can, as a clinician, listen your way into trouble by being excessively or noncontingently passive. Of course, there is no need to zero in on therapist passivity, because therapist activity also can function as TIB. Whether it is therapist words or silence, action or inaction, there may be a rationale for the therapist's behavior, and it may in fact be utterly reasonable. Still, the behavior can be therapy-interfering. This is not inherently problematic. What we believe often happens to make therapist TIB become a major problem is that therapists do not recognize or address such TIBs. Avoiding the management of their own TIBs can also be therapist TIB and can adversely affect the therapeutic relationship and treatment progress.

Another common therapist TIB occurs when clients engage in a significant TIB and the therapist does not attend to it. This can happen easily for any therapist, and we have had this happen to us many times. One client was in treatment recently for problems with anger and hostility. Early in treatment he began to express his hostility in session, complaining loudly and angrily that therapy was not going to help him, berating the clinic staff about problems with parking and check-in procedures, and expressing hopelessness that any therapist was skillful enough to help him. These behaviors occurred in the first session and in each of the next four sessions. They were unpleasant, and he was a client who was difficult to interrupt. He was angry about a lot of things, and attending to his hostility as TIB was extremely difficult. However, ignoring this behavior did not help the client. Not attending to his behavior might have been rationalized as being supportive, nondirective, and empathic, but it would not help the client if the therapist kept on avoiding noticing what he was doing. Avoidance of this TIB became therapist TIB. And this therapist TIB had to be changed if the client was ever going to learn to manage his anger more effectively.

Before considering how DBT principles and strategies can help, it may be useful to share another clinical example. The client was a young woman with borderline personality disorder who was substance dependent and was raising two young children alone. She had just begun DBT and was actively using crack cocaine. In the third session, she talked about how much she had used in the past week. She talked about her drug use in a cavalier manner, and as shown in the following transcript, the therapist decided to try to impress on her the consequences of drug use related to the two things that were the most important to the client.

> *Therapist:* Tell me more about what happened the other night.
>
> *Client:* I don't know, I just kept using. I didn't want to come home after I took that first hit. The shit was good, you know, and I wasn't thinking straight. I kept partying.
>
> *Therapist:* I get it. It's hard to stop once you get started. At any point in this process before you took that first hit did you consider coming home to be with your kids?
>
> *Client:* Nope.
>
> *Therapist:* You didn't think about the consequences of using?
>
> *Client:* Nope. You don't understand. It's not easy to just quit this stuff. It's got a hold on me.
>
> *Therapist:* It does seem to have a hold on you. I know from what you have told me so far that you truly, in your heart, want to stop using. It is tough to do, and wanting to stop is certainly important.
>
> *Client:* I do want to stop. I really want to change and get clean. But once I took that first hit, it was like . . . game over. You know? Forget it. No turning back. So I just said, "F it," and went with it, you know?
>
> *Therapist:* So the first hit is like stepping on a sheet of ice at the top of a steep hill. You lost your balance and then kept sliding, uncontrollably.
>
> *Client:* Yep. I lost it, man. Big time.
>
> *Therapist:* You know, if you keep using like this, staying out all night long, you could end up losing access to your kids?

Client: [*Pausing*] Oh, that's just cold. Not cool. Why do you have to go saying that? [*Silence, then starts to shake her head*]

Therapist: [*Silent at first*] I am trying to understand your experience throughout this situation. And trying to help you—I genuinely want to help you to realize the things you care about most in life are those two children.

Client: Yeah, but you just went too far. You need to back off of my shit. My kids are the most important thing in the world to me, and I know that my drug use is a problem. It's a problem for me, for them, for anyone around me. I come here to get help. I don't need you to remind me that my drug use makes me a bad mom. And you know what? I don't think I am a bad mom. I think I am pretty bad-ass mom. But I know I shouldn't be out using and should be home with my kids. They need a mom who doesn't use. I know. Jesus, I don't need you to give me shit about this.

Therapist: [*Leaning in*] I just went too far with you, and I apologize. Of course you already know the consequences of using. I didn't need to say that or to say it the way I did. I am sorry and didn't intend for you to feel this way.

Client: It's bullshit. I already told you I have problems trusting people. I told you I didn't know if I would come back to therapy after our first appointment. And now you go and do this. If I am going to do this therapy then I need you in my corner, OK? I can't have you telling me I am a bad mom. You understand?

In this example, the therapist TIB occurred when the therapist was matter-of-fact about the painful consequences of drug use. Nothing was illogical or incorrect about what the therapist said—it was the timing (too soon) and the way in which it was said (too direct). The client became angry, and the remainder of the session was spent picking up the pieces after the therapist TIB ruptured the therapeutic relationship. The client did, however, express appreciation that the therapist backed off and apologized. That was fortunate, too, because this client had a history of violence and anger problems.

From a DBT perspective, therapist TIB is as predictable as client TIB. It is not a matter of if, but a question of when the therapist's TIB will happen. If you are a clinician, you may be having a negative reaction to this premise. You, the therapist, with all your training and compassion and all your wisdom and selfless intentions, are likely to engage in TIB. Please take this as we mean it: It is a release from the need to be perfect. It is liberation from the shackles of idealization that clients (or you yourself) can place on you. You have a history, you have emotions, and you are not a blank slate. You cannot hide from what the psychoanalytic clinicians describe as *countertransference*.

You have thoughts, feelings, and physiological reactions to your clients. You have wants and hopes for them and for your therapy sessions. You have fantasies and you are sometimes attracted to clients and are sometimes repulsed by things they say or do. You have secret wishes, regrets, resentments, and so on. Therapists are not robots, and that is a good thing, but a hard part of this reality is that, in being human, therapist TIB happens and has to be attended to.

Sometimes therapists, especially those who are busy with large numbers of clients, can engage in TIBs that could have been avoided. They can be late for sessions, forget to follow through for clients on an agreement, become quickly frustrated with clients, and verbalize expectations for change that are unreasonable. There are also off-limits, egregious things therapists should never do: the *therapy destroying behaviors*. Exhibit 12.1 lists a few examples of these. Romantic or sexual advances toward the client are examples of what we mean by therapy-destroying behavior; these behaviors can destroy therapy in an instant. There are, of course, other examples of therapy-destroying behavior. Anything the therapist does that jeopardizes the client's safety could be therapy-destroying. Taking on a role that is not constrained to being a therapist can be therapy-destroying. One of us once had a client who was an entrepreneur and whose previous therapist had gone into business with him while they continued therapy. Neither the business nor the therapy ended well. Dual roles with your client can be therapy-destroying.

TIB is just behavior. Like any behavior, it is neither right nor wrong, neither good nor bad. There is no need to judge the TIB. It is interfering, and by definition, therefore, it is problematic. However, the fact that the TIB is a problem does not mean that it is a bad thing or that the therapist engaging in TIB has failed. As discussed next, this stance toward therapist TIB can be used to improve the therapeutic process and treatment outcomes. This stance includes a nonjudgmental and compassionate approach to preventing therapist TIB and can be accomplished by clinicians (a) expecting that this will happen, (b) accepting that it is OK and not evidence of any failure on their part, and (c) planning for ways to address therapist TIB when it does happen.

EXHIBIT 12.1
Examples of Therapy-Destroying Therapist Behavior

- Engaging in sexually inappropriate behavior
- Jeopardizing the client's safety
- Breaking confidentiality
- Conducting an intervention that is experienced as harmful by the client
- Taking on a nontherapeutic dual role

ADDRESSING THERAPIST THERAPY-INTERFERING BEHAVIOR

Several general strategies that are not unique to DBT can help to minimize the likelihood of therapist TIB, assuming that the steps of having adequate training, experience, and expertise for the therapeutic work being undertaken already are in place. Certainly, if any of these things are not true, the chances for therapist TIB occurring may increase. This is part of why it can be so challenging when first learning to be a therapist or when getting experience and gaining expertise providing a specific treatment or working with a specific clinical population. What are some approaches to mitigate therapist TIB?

First, therapists can prevent and identify problems by reflecting on their work. There are many ways to do this, including taking time after a session to think through how it went, what was effective or ineffective, and how the client responded to the interventions occurring during the session. Time is in preciously short supply for many clinicians, so it may be difficult to take time after sessions to reflect in order to identify therapist TIB. We recommend that therapists use the time when writing the psychotherapy note to reflect and consider whether any therapist TIB has occurred. The documentation for a psychotherapy session is something that is commonly done shortly after the session ends, and with intentionality the therapist can leverage this time to contemplate his or her TIB.

Second, it can be helpful to consult with and elicit feedback from others. Perhaps the first person to elicit feedback might be the client. Therapists could, for example, take time at the end of each session to inquire as to how the client experienced the session, what was most helpful and least helpful, and what she or he would like to focus on next time. This strategy can enhance the collaborative therapeutic alliance, allow the client an opportunity to bring up problems before they become more chronic and frustrating, and allow the therapist to model effective and nondefensive responses to constructive criticism.

Another way to receive feedback is to engage a regular network of peers, supervisors, or consultants with whom to consult about one's work. Even if a formal team is not possible, it can be invaluable to consult with and receive feedback and support from colleagues with relevant expertise. Over the years, we have found that it is not only professional peers but also our students and trainees who provide sage and useful feedback on our clinical work. Having session recordings available for such consultation can be valuable; otherwise, consultation relies solely on the therapist's potentially limited and biased memories of events. Even when problems are not apparent from the session recordings or from the therapist's description of what is happening, others may sometimes notice potential problems in the ways in which the therapist describes the client or her or his work.

DIALECTICAL BEHAVIOR THERAPY AND THERAPIST THERAPY-INTERFERING BEHAVIOR: THE ROLE OF THE CONSULTATION TEAM

What are some of the unique and specific ways in which DBT addresses therapist TIB? The primary structural mechanism is the consultation team. In the weekly meeting, the focus is on enhancing the therapist's skills, motivation, and competence, as well as providing support for therapists engaged in challenging clinical work. With a team of fellow DBT therapists helping each week, the therapist has a safe and recurring context to identify and conceptualize how therapist TIB can be prevented and managed. For example, the team members help each other be mindful of one another's reactions to clients, noticing when emotions seem to be present as the case is discussed. The team is a mechanism in DBT to hold the therapist accountable for therapist TIB (sometimes including the TIB of not addressing client TIB). In fact, at the beginning of each DBT consultation team meeting, as part of the agenda setting for the team meeting that week, each therapist identifies any therapist TIB he or she may have engaged in during the past week. As the cases are discussed, the team members help the therapist understand the TIB and consider ways to adjust the approach to prevent additional therapist TIB. The following vignette illustrates an example of the team process addressing this issue.

Team leader: OK, so let's turn now to helping Kirsten with her client Johanna. Kirsten, you are on the agenda as having therapist TIB with Johanna. How can the team help you?

Kirsten: Thanks. I have to admit I am a bit embarrassed about this, but I feel compelled to get help from the team about something that happened the other day with Johanna. You all know how difficult she can be at times, how people find her prickly and insensitive. In our last session she was talking about herself in this very grandiose way, talking about how attractive people find her, how much smarter she is than most people, and things like that. Here I am, 4 months after giving birth, clearly heavier than I used to be, totally exhausted and stressed to the max, and feeling sort of miserable. And Johanna, as you all know, is this petite, pretty woman who by all accounts is really smart. So she just keeps carrying on about herself in this narcissistic way, and I just kept getting more and more irritated.

Team Member 1:	I know how you feel. That kind of stuff just gets under my skin. It's hard to maintain empathy with clients who talk about themselves like that so much.
Team Member 2:	I feel the same way, but can I ask you a question? What was the TIB? What happened that interfered with the therapy?
Kirsten:	She's telling me about how her boss seems to be coming on to her at work and how she doesn't know what to do about it. But she has this smile on her face, like she is holding back what she is thinking. It's as though she is feeling pleased with herself recalling the story. She turns her head my way then asks if I have a mirror in the room. She wanted to check something out about the way she looked! That was it. I couldn't stand it anymore.
Team Member 3:	What did you do?
Kirsten:	I told her I didn't know if I had a mirror in the office. I dismissed her. She stood up and started to look around. I told her I didn't think she needed to look in the mirror. I said we needed to go back to understanding how she is getting her needs met with others. You should have seen the look on her face. She was not happy with me. After that she didn't look me in the eye the rest of the session, and let me tell you, as soon as we got near the end of the appointment time, she was out of there as fast as possible.
Team Member 1:	That is such a hard situation, Kirsten. I totally know how you feel.
Kirsten:	I think I was annoyed because I just didn't want to hear about this problem. It was the end of a long day.
Team leader:	I noticed you used the word *narcissistic* when describing this just now. Can you describe Johanna's behavior without using that term? Just be descriptive, behaviorally, with what you saw. Try to let go of any judgment of her or of you. Would you be willing to do that?
Kirsten:	Sure.
Team Member 2:	Before you do that, can I just notice that this reaction you had sounds a lot like how she has described other people reacting to her. This is one of her problems, right? She does things that come across as

	self-absorbed or self-indulgent at the expense of considering how others might feel.
Kirsten:	I think that is true, but I still should not have reacted the way I did.
Team Member 3:	It may be that there was no other way you could have reacted in that moment. This is what she does, and this is how people are likely to react to her. The thing I am wondering is whether you were aware of your reaction?
Kirsten:	I don't think so. I mean, well, not really.
Team leader:	So before we get any further, let's stop and ask you, Kirsten, how can the team help you with this?
Kirsten:	I think I just needed to say out loud what happened and get over feeling embarrassed about it. I know I need to be more mindful of my emotions when I am with Johanna. I know this is what she does and that I need to be ready for it so I can help her learn more effective ways of interacting with people.

In this example, Kirsten's TIB elicited an emotional response from Johanna, and because Kirsten was not aware of this process as it was happening, the client's response derailed the therapy session. When working with clients who tend to have what some would consider narcissistic behaviors, therapist TIB is likely to occur in situations similar to this example. In this case, the team consultation process helped Kirsten by providing a forum in which this was explicitly on the agenda to be discussed. By approaching her embarrassment rather than avoiding it, both Kirsten and the team helped increase the probability that the next time this happens, Kirsten will be more prepared and have a more skillful response.

THERAPIST MINDFULNESS CAN HELP REDUCE THERAPY-INTERFERING BEHAVIOR

Another key aspect of this example is the role that therapist mindfulness plays in addressing therapist TIB in DBT. Notice in the example how the team helped Kirsten come to her own conclusion that she had to be more mindful of her own emotions and thoughts when she is treating Johanna. This is important; therapist mindfulness in DBT is an essential element in preventing and responding effectively to therapist TIB.

Mindfulness is the core skill underlying all other skills in DBT. It is the springboard from which emotion regulation, distress tolerance, and interpersonal effectiveness skills arise. Mindfulness is taught repeatedly in the DBT skills training groups and is practiced each week in both in the client skills groups and the therapist consultation teams. Indeed, mindfulness is woven into the essence of DBT. DBT therapists commonly practice mindfulness with clients during individual therapy sessions. They assign mindfulness homework and give readings from books to help clients better understand and learn to cultivate a practice of mindfulness. And most germane to this chapter, DBT therapists practice mindfulness in their lives.

What does this mindfulness practice look like? Contemplative mindfulness practices can be found across Eastern and Western religious and spiritual traditions, and there is no single, specific, or "right way" to practice mindfulness as a therapist. However, because DBT incorporates many concepts from Zen Buddhism, it is common for DBT therapists to have experience with mindfulness practices from this tradition. DBT therapists practice what they teach, and as a result, the same skills we ask our clients to practice are the skills we practice ourselves. For mindfulness, this means that therapists using DBT practice observing and describing their experiences without judgment or evaluation, intentionally choose to one-mindfully do things with full attention each moment at a time, and aim to be effective with their actions by being sensitive to the context of each moment. In addition, DBT therapists work toward having moments of their life in which they can let go of the need to observe and describe experiences and instead fully participate without conscious awareness of each moment by fluidly responding effectively, as if they are in "the zone" that athletes find themselves in when at peak performance. Learning these DBT skills is hard for clients, and it can be equally hard for us as therapists.

Another important concept in DBT is Jon Kabat-Zinn's (1990, 1994) definition of *mindfulness* as the practice of paying attention in a particular way, without judgment, to one's experience as it is in the moment. This way of conceptualizing mindfulness is consistent with the Vipassana tradition of meditation and translates into a range of meditation techniques that are intended to cultivate insight and depth of contemplation and introspection, such as those that practice observing bodily sensations (e.g., breathing) or other internal experiences as they occur in real time without efforts to try to change such experiences. A common way of practicing such mindfulness exercises is to use *choiceless awareness*, a concept described by the Indian philosopher Krishnamurti (2001) wherein attention is paid to emergent internal experiences as they come and go, thoughts, feelings, and sensations honored as being present for the moments they are present, until they are gone and the next experiences arise, and so on. This form of mindfulness practice can be done briefly (e.g., for several minutes) or over extended periods of time. Whether using an insight-based meditation such as sitting for 45 minutes in the morning each day in silence using the choiceless awareness approach or whether the mindfulness practice is an active one involving observing and describing nonjudgmentally one's internal experiences as one goes through the moments of everyday life, the main point is this: Therapists may prevent therapist TIBs by using mindfulness practices.

Meditation and mindfulness can be used by any clinician. Where does this begin for the therapist without a history of practicing meditation? Remember, therapist mindfulness is a skill that has to be cultivated. It is an effective skill, but like any other complex skill, it takes time to develop and maintain. To catch yourself when you are allowing your own emotional reactions to get in your way as a clinician, we suggest you try several different mindfulness practices. We have been to multiple day-long or multi-day-long mindfulness retreats. These can be incredibly helpful in jump-starting or revitalizing your mindfulness practice. However, this is not the only path to take. There are many excellent books, websites, and online apps that have practices you can use. One of our colleagues at Duke University Medical Center, Dr. Jeff Brantley, has written extensively in his *Five Good Minutes* book series about ways to bring the practice of mindfulness into the business of everyday life (Brantley & Millstine, 2007, 2009). However you get there, therapist mindfulness is a required practice and skill to use in preventing and managing therapist TIB. Examples of how this might work appear in Exhibit 12.2.

In each of these examples, the practice of mindfulness can help bring to the therapist's awareness what she or he already is experiencing. By contacting your sadness or worry, feeling the pangs of embarrassment or anger, allowing into awareness the thoughts about your client or whatever else surfaces—by experiencing the present moment as it is and without judgment—therapists in DBT are prepared to prevent or respond effectively to their own TIB.

EXHIBIT 12.2
Ten Ways Therapists Can Use Mindfulness to
Prevent Therapist Therapy-Interfering Behavior

- Practice mindfulness meditation each day in the morning or at night
- Use brief mindfulness practices throughout the day
- Practice observing and describing thoughts and feelings before meeting with clients
- Use mindfulness at the beginning or end of each session with a particular client
- Eat mindfully throughout the day
- Walk mindfully throughout the day from your chair to the door or clinic waiting room
- Practice mindfulness in a consultation group of clinician colleagues
- Take several minutes to practice mindfulness before writing your therapy note
- Mindfully contemplate the daily life or history of one of your clients
- Practice mindful forgiveness and acceptance of clients that elicit frustration or other emotions

RADICAL GENUINENESS

Another DBT technique that can help prevent or reduce therapist TIB is *radical genuineness*. This is a term in DBT that refers to a form of client validation wherein the therapist acknowledges something that is present in the moment, such as a thought, feeling, or action, in a radically authentic manner. In this case, radical does not mean wild or on the fringe. Instead, the DBT conceptualization of radical genuineness invokes the mathematical notion of a radical—the root of being fully and deeply genuine with your client. It is the essence of authenticity.

To be radically genuine is to observe and describe what is as it is in the moment, without pretense. It is to be, at the core, honest and real. Clients often report that they experience therapeutic genuineness as humane and sometimes as quite different from their experience with other clinicians. Radical genuineness in DBT can take the form of simple and brief responses acknowledging something that is occurring in the moment that is ordinary, reasonable, or appropriate. As an example, a therapist might have limits for when they are able to have the next appointment with a client. The client might want to meet before or after the clinic closes, or even more challenging, the client could ask to meet on a day off for the therapist. Therapists need days off like everyone else who works, but if the client is highly distressed when making the request, the therapist may feel compelled to meet with the client as soon as possible. This could be quite a dilemma. If the therapist does not observe his or her limits and sets the appointment for his or her day off, the therapist could end up feeling resentful, regretful, or irritated, and this could lead to therapist TIB. However, the therapist could observe his or her limits and be left feeling guilty or anxious. What can therapists do in such situations?

Therapists could do a number of things, but one approach would be to be radically genuine with the client. It is ordinary and appropriate for all therapists to take a day off, and in fact, if the therapist takes time off to be restored and to generate a sense of work–life balance, she or he may be even more effective in helping the client. Or taking the day off might be necessary to deal with a stressful item on a to-do list. Taxes have to be done each year and having refrigerator repairmen visit and having deliveries made to the home can occur during wide windows of time. Sometimes days off are needed for any number of pedestrian reasons.

In this example, the inability to meet for a therapy session when the client wants to can be communicated compassionately in an authentic way by saying with radical genuineness,

> I can totally understand why meeting that day would be best for you. Unfortunately, I am not going to be working that day. It's a day off for me, and my days off are really useful to help me stay balanced and effective

in my work. Actually, on that day I am going to be waiting for the air-conditioning repairman to arrive, and he can be there anytime between 8 and 5. So, let's look at another day for our next appointment.

In this example, the therapist is being matter-of-fact and observing his or her limits. However, he or she might feel guilty about saying no to the client and, as a result, have to use emotion regulation, mindfulness, or distress tolerance skills to manage or experience any unjustified guilt. The therapist also could discuss this experience with the DBT consultation team. The critical point is that there is nothing particular to DBT about this radically genuine response. Therapeutic genuineness was central to the person-centered therapy developed by Carl Rogers in the 1940s and 1950s. All therapists could do this. The concept of radical genuineness can be borrowed by non–DBT therapists to help improve skillful responses in such situations by remaining authentic, preventing therapist negative emotions and TIB.

By being straightforward and authentic with compassion, radically genuine responses can help circumvent therapist TIB while simultaneously treating the client in a fair and respectful manner and avoiding infantilizing or fragilizing the client. The previous example involved the therapist being somewhat matter-of-fact while being authentic and observing a limit in order to prevent therapist TIB (and model an effective way to observe limits to the client, which for many clients is an important treatment target). The therapist in this example was not available on his or her day off, and it could be a simple matter of rescheduling. But what if the client responded by saying that he or she needed to meet that day with the therapist? What if there was something about that particular day (e.g., an important event was happening, and the client was extremely worried) that made the client feel strongly that he or she would benefit from a therapy session? To take it one step further, what if asking appropriately for what he or she wants was, in fact, therapeutic progress? In such a situation, the therapist could be radically genuine while still observing limits by highlighting the dialectic that, on one hand, the appointment could not happen on that day, though on the other hand, the client is saying he or she needs help from the therapist for that day. The resolution of these apparent contradictions could be that therapist and client work together to find a pragmatic way to plan for the client to be ready and skillful in response to his or her worries about the impending stressful event. For example, the dialectical synthesis could be a specific homework plan, planned set of skills to use, and/or brief telephone consultation or check-in with the therapist that day.

Radical genuineness is not always done in the form of being brief and matter-of-fact. In some clinical situations, therapists use radical genuineness to express heartfelt emotions, help motivate the client to make changes, or demonstrate how to use certain skills. Recently, I (MZR) was treating a depressed woman who was crying in the session, and in her distress, her emotional reasoning led her to proclaim she had no friends, no one who liked her, and that she had failed everywhere in her life. This was not a DBT case. However, to prevent therapist emotional reactions from leading to any therapist TIB, radical genuineness was used to remind the client, with emotional intensity and empathy, that these appraisals were a function of the emotional moment and need not be confused with the truth of her thoughts. We stayed with the emotion in the moment, disentangling affect from definitive cognitive appraisals. Rather than attempting to change these attributions using cognitive therapy techniques, being silent or supportive, or using an emotion regulation skill to change her emotions, radical genuineness was first used. This engaged and snapped the client out of the shell of her misery, opening her attention to hear what was being communicated, which allowed her to see a path forward and prepared her for a discussion about what she could do until the next session to reduce her depressive symptoms.

When trying to prevent therapist TIB, the key to radical genuineness is to be intentional, compassionate, and have the client's case conceptualization in mind when choosing to be radically genuine. Without such elements, radical genuineness can come across to clients as the therapist being self-centered, narcissistic, or even passive–aggressive. Good intentions and a nice therapist are insufficient in some situations, especially with more difficult-to-treat clients. A sound approach is to (a) be mindful of possible therapist TIBs that could occur, (b) consider carefully whether being radically genuine might help, and (c) ensure that the radically genuine communication can be done with the client's needs first and foremost.

When we teach radical genuineness to community clinicians, they often conflate this technique with the notion of therapist self-disclosure. These are not the same thing. Certainly, self-disclosure can be done in a radically genuine way. However, from a DBT perspective, self-disclosure can be done in many ways. Self-disclosures can be honest yet delivered ineffectively and then themselves become therapist TIBs. For self-disclosure to be radically genuine and help prevent therapist TIB, it has to be from the heart and authentic, yoked to the root of the therapist's experience, with the client's interests recognized. However, it does not have to be a soliloquy about a profoundly painful experience in the therapist's life. It could be, but does not have to be. In fact, what is probably more common and effective is the *routinely radically genuine response*. Several examples of this and how it can help reduce therapist TIB appear in Table 12.2.

TABLE 12.2
Ways That Therapist Radical Genuineness Can Help Reduce Therapist Therapy-Interfering Behavior

Example of therapist radical genuineness	How it can help reduce therapist therapy-interfering behavior
Connecting their private internal experiences of imperfection with client behavior (e.g., "Are you not feeling well? You seem like you are feeling sick. I hope you don't get what I had last week. It was going around.")	Acknowledging one's own ordinary vulnerability can help the therapist feel more comfortable acknowledging imperfection and allowing themselves to model effective self-awareness.
Communicating gently that the client is behaving in an unacceptable way that is highly ineffective (e.g., "I understand what you are asking for, can see why you might ask for it, and want you to know that it is not something I will be able to offer you. If I said yes to this request it could end up backfiring and making things worse. I don't want that to happen.")	This can help therapists with appropriate limit setting or observing of limits and can prevent therapist resentment or other negative emotions.
Observing that certain kinds of behavior are especially difficult or worrisome for the therapist (e.g., "Oh boy, this is one of those things that is really hard for me as a person and as a therapist. You know how we all have things that we get most nervous about? Well, this is one of those things I worry about a lot.")	This can prevent therapist therapy-interfering behavior by helping the client understand the therapist. As the client becomes more mindful of the perspective of the therapist, it can help increase client empathy and reduce client defensive emotional responses. This helps with the therapeutic relationship and enables the therapist to be comfortable expressing themselves authentically.
Acknowledging when a mistake has been made by the therapist (e.g., "I am so sorry. I didn't intend for you to feel hurt by my actions.")	This keeps the therapist from feeling unnecessary anxiety or guilt and models self-awareness.
Mindfully observing thoughts as thoughts and not the content of thoughts as literally being true, even when the content of the thoughts is painful to express (e.g., "I am having the thought that this treatment may not be working as well as we both want it to. And I'd like to notice this is only a thought; it may not be true, though I feel some sadness as I have the thought.")	This can keep the therapist from becoming stuck believing the truth of their own thoughts about the therapy process or client. For the client, it models the core dialectical behavior therapy skill of mindfulness and can elicit opportunities to practice mindfulness in the therapy session.

TABLE 12.2
Ways That Therapist Radical Genuineness Can Help Reduce Therapist Therapy-Interfering Behavior *(Continued)*

Example of therapist radical genuineness	How it can help reduce therapist therapy-interfering behavior
Verbalizing compassionately the dialectic of acceptance and change when the client is unwilling to change (e.g., "You know I fully understand how hard it will be to change how you live your life. If changing was an easy solution you would have done it long ago. I get it, and I might offer to you that the other side of this coin is acceptance. We could truly sit for a minute and experience the thoughts and feelings you are having, without trying to change them or do anything about them.")	This can allow the therapist to genuinely experience and help the client come into contact with the experience of acceptance. The idea is to shake up both the therapist and the client's notion of change as the only solution. The therapist can then radically consider what it would be like, step-by-step with the client, if the client let go of their agenda to change the way they are trying to make changes. This dialectic can yield a workable synthesis promoting a new approach to the client's problems and can help the therapist feel motivated and rewarded.

RECOVERING FROM THERAPIST THERAPY-INTERFERING BEHAVIOR

What can therapists do after therapist TIB occurs? To begin, we recommend responding to therapist TIB by being nonjudgmental and nondefensive. Therapist TIB happens to all therapists. We—the authors—cannot count the number of times we have seen ourselves engage in therapist TIB. Expecting and attending to therapist TIB can be done well with openness, vulnerability, and curiosity. From this introspective willingness can spring forth problem solving. Once the therapist TIB has been identified and the therapist is willing to try to understand what predicted it and how to effectively manage it in the future, the core DBT principles and strategies reviewed in Chapters 2 and 3 can be used.

Therapists can use chain analyses as a problem-solving tool to explore the antecedents and consequences of their own TIB. Perhaps the therapist was late to the session because the session before went long over the expected amount of time. Why was this? The chains in this analysis might reveal that the therapist was feeling afraid that the previous client would be upset if he or she was interrupted, and as the client kept talking it went over the allotted time. Or it could be that the therapist was late to the session after taking too long talking to a colleague on the phone, writing notes for another client, or reading something in the office. Using chain analysis, the therapist, working alone or with trusted colleagues, can consider ways to prevent this TIB from happening again.

EXHIBIT 12.3
General Process for Therapists Recovering from
Therapist Therapy-Interfering Behavior

- Observe therapist therapy-interfering behavior (TIB) nonjudgmentally and nondefensively.
- Approach the process of resolving therapist TIB with openness, vulnerability, and curiosity.
- Use problem-solving tools to explore the antecedents and consequences of the TIB.
- Consider multiple solutions without being attached to any one solution as being correct.
- When a candidate solution is identified, analyze the pros and cons of this solution.
- Refine the solution and troubleshoot how to implement it with an emphasis on ways to be pragmatic and effective, not on being right.
- Be mindful about when and how to use the solution and balance the need to follow up with the need to do so effectively when the context calls for it.

Once a candidate solution to the therapist TIB is identified, this plan becomes, from the perspective of a DBT therapist, something that needs to be reexamined. The solution to therapist TIB is analyzed and holes are poked in it until a revised and better solution is identified and the therapist is committed to implementing this solution. Naturally, there is no one solution to any specific therapist TIB. Instead, the process of problem solving is the key to yielding any number of possible solutions. The therapist could, for example, choose to practice mindfulness before each session with this client. However, he or she also could choose to use interpersonal effectiveness skills to ask whether the client is willing to come at a different time (if the time of the session was part of the problem) or to implement other solutions. Once the solutions are identified, the therapist can determine when and how to implement the solution. When the opportunity arises, the solution is implemented. Exhibit 12.3 lists several steps therapists can take to borrow approaches used in DBT to effectively manage the process of considering ways to move forward after therapist TIB occurs.

EVEN THE BEST PLANS CAN FAIL

Even the best plans for managing therapist TIB can backfire. It is OK when this happens, as long as this process is itself observed and attended to. Part of what drew us both to DBT is the openness and humility that therapists often have about themselves as imperfect clinicians. In that spirit, I (ALC) recently engaged in therapist TIB and developed what was thought to be a smart plan for how to recover after the TIB. An agreement with a client was made to provide a reminder call each week about attending group therapy, because the client was really depressed, alone and separated from her husband, and was having a hard time getting motivated. The plan had been the result of solving how to get the client to attend therapy more often and seemed like it truly would help. The first week, the reminder call never happened. The client came to session and received an apology with an honest and radically genuine explanation. I was traveling that week and forgot to make the reminder call. Unfortunately, after recommitting to this reminder call plan, I forgot again the following week. After following the steps listed earlier and overcorrecting for the therapist TIB (apologies given, validation of the client's emotions, reminder prompts put in the mobile phone), things changed for the positive.

MOVING FORWARD

It is normal for therapists to inadvertently do things that function as therapy-interfering. We are fallible. Our own complicated learning histories make us vulnerable to being ambushed by the vicissitudes of the present moment. Anything the therapist does that disrupts the therapeutic process in an adverse way can be TIB. Conventionally relegated to the psychodynamic concept of countertransference, the notion of therapist TIB in DBT is something that can be observed and discussed openly by clients and therapists collaboratively. Across structural elements of DBT (e.g., a weekly consultation team), techniques for managing therapeutic ruptures (e.g., mindfulness and radical genuineness), and principle-driven pragmatic processes (e.g., collaboratively and iteratively orienting, targeting, clarifying commitment to specific treatment goals), DBT provides therapists across a range of orientations with diverse client populations a menu of techniques to prevent and respond to therapist TIB.

REFERENCES

Abramowitz, J. S. (2013). The practice of exposure therapy: Relevance of cognitive–behavioral theory and extinction theory. *Behavior Therapy, 44*, 548–558. http://dx.doi.org/10.1016/j.beth.2013.03.003

Abramowitz, J. S., Deacon, B. J., & Whiteside, S. H. (2011). *Exposure therapy for anxiety: Principles and practice.* New York, NY: Guilford Press.

American Psychiatric Association. (2013). *Diagnostic and statistical manual of mental disorders* (5th ed.). Arlington, VA: Author.

American Psychological Association. (2010). *Ethical principles of psychologists and code of conduct (2002, Amended June 1, 2010).* Retrieved from http://www.apa.org/ethics/code/index.aspx

Aspinwall, L. G., & Taylor, S. E. (1997). A stitch in time: Self-regulation and proactive coping. *Psychological Bulletin, 121*, 417–436. http://dx.doi.org/10.1037/0033-2909.121.3.417

Baekeland, F., & Lundwall, L. (1975). Dropping out of treatment: A critical review. *Psychological Bulletin, 82*, 738–783. http://dx.doi.org/10.1037/h0077132

Baer, R. A. (2006). *Mindfulness-based treatment approaches: Clinician's guide to evidence base and applications.* San Diego, CA: Elsevier.

Barkham, M., Rees, A., Shapiro, D. A., Stiles, W. B., Agnew, R. M., Halstead, J., . . . Harrington, V. M. (1996). Outcomes of time-limited psychotherapy in applied settings: Replicating the Second Sheffield Psychotherapy Project. *Journal of Consulting and Clinical Psychology, 64*, 1079–1085. http://dx.doi.org/10.1037/0022-006X.64.5.1079

Barrett, M. S., Chua, W., Crits-Christoph, P., Gibbons, M. B., & Thompson, D. (2008). Early withdrawal from mental health treatment: Implications for psychotherapy practice. *Psychotherapy: Theory, Research, Practice, Training, 45*, 247–267. doi:10.1037/0033-3204.45.2.247

Bateman, A., & Fonagy, P. (2013). Mentalization-based treatment. *Psychoanalytic Inquiry, 33*, 595–613. http://dx.doi.org/10.1080/07351690.2013.835170

Beck, J. S. (2011). *Cognitive behavior therapy: Basics and beyond* (2nd ed.). New York, NY: Guilford Press.

Bongar, B., & Sullivan, G. R. (2013). Outpatient management and treatment of the suicidal patient. In B. Bongar & G. R. Sullivan (Eds.), *The suicidal patient: Clinical and legal standards of care* (3rd ed., pp. 157–199). Washington, DC: American Psychological Association. http://dx.doi.org/10.1037/14184-005

Bornas, X., Llabrés, J., Noguera, M., López, A., Tortella-Feliu, M., Fullana, M., . . . Vila, I. (2006). Changes in heart rate variability of flight phobics during a paced breathing task and exposure to fearful stimuli. *International Journal of Clinical and Health Psychology, 6*, 549–563.

Bouton, M. E. (1988). Context and ambiguity in the extinction of emotional learning: Implications for exposure therapy. *Behaviour Research and Therapy, 26,* 137–149. http://dx.doi.org/10.1016/0005-7967(88)90113-1

Brantley, J., & Millstine, W. (2007). *Five good minutes at work: 100 mindful practices to help you relieve stress and bring your best to work.* Oakland, CA: New Harbinger.

Brantley, J., & Millstine, W. (2009). *Five good minutes in your body: 100 mindful practices to help you accept yourself and feel at home in your body.* Oakland, CA: New Harbinger.

Brondolo, E., DiGiuseppe, R., & Tafrate, R. (1997). Exposure-based treatment for anger problems: Focus on the feeling. *Cognitive and Behavioral Practice, 4,* 75–98. http://dx.doi.org/10.1016/S1077-7229(97)80013-2

Canadian Psychological Association. (2000). *Canadian code of ethics for psychologists.* Retrieved from http://www.cpa.ca/docs/File/Ethics/cpa_code_2000_eng_jp_jan2014.pdf

Cavanaugh, M. M., Solomon, P., & Gelles, R. J. (2011). The Dialectical Psychoeducational Workshop (DPEW): The conceptual framework and curriculum for a preventative intervention for males at risk for IPV. *Violence Against Women, 17,* 970–989. http://dx.doi.org/10.1177/1077801211414266

Chapman, A. L., Dixon-Gordon, K. L., Layden, B. K., & Walters, K. N. (2010). Borderline personality features moderate the effect of a fear induction on impulsivity. *Personality Disorders: Theory, Research, and Treatment, 1,* 139–152. http://dx.doi.org/10.1037/a0019226

Chapman, A. L., Leung, D. W., & Lynch, T. R. (2008). Impulsivity and emotion dysregulation in borderline personality disorder. *Journal of Personality Disorders, 22,* 148–164. http://dx.doi.org/10.1521/pedi.2008.22.2.148

Chiesa, M., Wright, M., & Neeld, R. (2003). A description of an audit cycle of early dropouts from an inpatient psychotherapy unit. *Psychoanalytic Psychotherapy, 17,* 138–149. http://dx.doi.org/10.1080/14749730310001005294

Cloninger, C. R. (1986). A unified biosocial theory of personality and its role in the development of anxiety states. *Psychiatric Developments, 4,* 167–226.

Craske, M. G., & Barlow, D. H. (2007). *Mastery of your anxiety and panic—Therapist guide.* Oxford, England: Oxford University.

Craske, M. G., Kircanski, K., Zelikowsky, M., Mystkowski, J., Chowdhury, N., & Baker, A. (2008). Optimizing inhibitory learning during exposure therapy. *Behaviour Research and Therapy, 46,* 5–27. http://dx.doi.org/10.1016/j.brat.2007.10.003

Crowell, S. E., Beauchaine, T. P., & Linehan, M. M. (2009). A biosocial developmental model of borderline personality: Elaborating and extending Linehan's theory. *Psychological Bulletin, 135,* 495–510. http://dx.doi.org/10.1037/a0015616

Del Vecchio, T., & O'Leary, K. D. (2004). Effectiveness of anger treatments for specific anger problems: A meta-analytic review. *Clinical Psychology Review, 24,* 15–34. http://dx.doi.org/10.1016/j.cpr.2003.09.006

DiGiuseppe, R., & Tafrate, R. (2003). Anger treatment for adults: A meta-analytic review. *Clinical Psychology: Science and Practice, 10,* 70–84. http://dx.doi.org/10.1093/clipsy.10.1.70

Dugas, M. J., & Robichaud, M. (2006). *Cognitive–behavioral treatment for generalized anxiety disorder: From science to practice.* New York, NY: Routledge.

Esposito, C., Spirito, A., Boergers, J., & Donaldson, D. (2003). Affective, behavioral, and cognitive functioning in adolescents with multiple suicide attempts. *Suicide and Life-Threatening Behavior, 3,* 389–399. http://dx.doi.org/10.1521/suli.33.4.389.25231

Farmer, R. F., & Chapman, A. L. (2008). *Behavioral interventions in cognitive behavior therapy: Practical guidance for putting theory into action.* Washington, DC: American Psychological Association. http://dx.doi.org/10.1037/11664-000

Farmer, R. F., & Chapman, A. L. (2016). *Behavioral interventions in cognitive behavior therapy: Practical guidance for putting theory into action* (2nd ed.). Washington, DC: American Psychological Association.

Favazza, A. R. (1998). The coming of age of self-mutilation. *Journal of Nervous and Mental Disease, 186,* 259–268. http://dx.doi.org/10.1097/00005053-199805000-00001

Foa, E. B., & Rothbaum, B. (1998). *Treating the trauma of rape: Cognitive–behavioral therapy for PTSD.* New York, NY: Guilford Press.

Frank, E., Kupfer, D. J., Thase, M. E., Mallinger, A. G., Swartz, H. A., Eagiolini, A. M., & . . . Monk, T. (2005). Two-year outcomes for interpersonal and social rhythm therapy in individuals with bipolar I disorder. *Archives of General Psychiatry, 62,* 996–1004. http://dx.doi.org/10.1001/archpsyc.62.9.996

Freeman, A., & McCloskey, R. (2003). Impediments to effective psychotherapy. In R. L. Leahy (Ed.), *Roadblocks in cognitive-behavioral therapy: Transforming challenges into opportunities for change* (pp. 24–48). New York, NY: Guilford Press.

Fried, Y., & Slowik, L. (2004). Enriching goal-setting theory with time: An integrated approach. *The Academy of Management Review, 29,* 404–422.

Fruzzetti, A. E., Shenk, C., & Hoffman, P. D. (2005). Family interaction and the development of borderline personality disorder: A transactional model. *Development and Psychopathology, 17,* 1007–1030. http://dx.doi.org/10.1017/S0954579405050479

Goldfried, M. R., & Davison, G. C. (1976). *Clinical behavior therapy.* New York, NY: Holt, Rinehart & Winston.

Gottman, J. M., Driver, J., & Tabares, A. (2002). Building the sound marital house: An empirically derived couple therapy. In A. S. Gurman & N. S. Jacobson (Eds.), *Clinical handbook of couple therapy* (3rd ed., pp. 373–399). New York, NY: Guilford Press.

Gray, J. A. (1987). The neuropsychology of emotion and personality. In S. M. Stahl, S. D. Iversen, & E. C. Goodman (Eds.), *Cognitive neurochemistry* (pp. 171–190). New York, NY: Oxford University Press.

Greenberg, L. S. (2010). *Emotion-focused therapy*. Washington, DC: American Psychological Association. http://dx.doi.org/10.1037/e602962010-001

Gross, J. J. (1998). The emerging field of emotion regulation: An integrative review. *Review of General Psychology, 2*, 271–299. http://dx.doi.org/10.1037/1089-2680. 2.3.271

Harned, M. S., Korslund, K. E., & Linehan, M. M. (2014). A pilot randomized controlled trial of dialectical behavior therapy with and without the dialectical behavior therapy prolonged exposure protocol for suicidal and self-injuring women with borderline personality disorder and PTSD. *Behaviour Research and Therapy, 55*, 7–17. http://dx.doi.org/10.1016/j.brat.2014.01.008

Harnett, P., O'Donovan, A., & Lambert, M. J. (2010). The dose response relationship in psychotherapy: Implications for social policy. *Clinical Psychologist, 14*, 39–44. http://dx.doi.org/10.1080/13284207.2010.500309

Hayes, S. C., Brownstein, A. J., Zettle, R. D., Rosenfarb, I., & Korn, Z. (1986). Rule-governed behavior and sensitivity to changing consequences of responding. *Journal of the Experimental Analysis of Behavior, 45*, 237–256. http://dx.doi. org/10.1901/jeab.1986.45-237

Hayes, S. C., Wilson, K. G., Gifford, E. V., Follette, V. M., & Strosahl, K. (1996). Experimental avoidance and behavioral disorders: A functional dimensional approach to diagnosis and treatment. *Journal of Consulting and Clinical Psychology, 64*, 1152–1168. http://dx.doi.org/10.1037/0022-006X.64.6.1152

Hazlett-Stevens, H., & Craske, M. G. (2008). Breathing retraining and diaphragmatic breathing techniques. In W. T. O'Donohue & J. E. Fisher (Eds.), *Cognitive behavior therapy: Applying empirically supported techniques in your practice* (2nd ed., pp. 68–74). Hoboken, NJ: Wiley.

Herrnstein, R. J. (1961). Relative and absolute strength of response as a function of frequency of reinforcement. *Journal of the Experimental Analysis of Behavior, 4*, 267–272. http://dx.doi.org/10.1901/jeab.1961.4-267

Hopko, D. R., Lejuez, C. W., Ruggiero, K. J., & Eifert, G. H. (2003). Contemporary behavioral activation treatments for depression: Procedures, principles, and progress. *Clinical Psychology Review, 23*, 699–717. http://dx.doi.org/10.1016/ S0272-7358(03)00070-9

Howard, K. I., Moras, K., Brill, P. L., Martinovich, Z., & Lutz, W. (1996). Evaluation of psychotherapy: Efficacy, effectiveness, and patient progress. *American Psychologist, 51*, 1059–1064. http://dx.doi.org/10.1037/0003-066X.51.10.1059

Izard, C. E., & Kobak, R. (1991). Emotions system functioning and emotion regulation. In J. Garber & K. A. Dodge (Eds.), *The development of emotion regulation and dysregulation* (pp. 303–322). New York, NY: Cambridge University Press. http://dx.doi.org/10.1017/CBO9780511663963.014

Joiner, T. J., Conwell, Y., Fitzpatrick, K. K., Witte, T. K., Schmidt, N. B., Berlim, M. T., . . . Rudd, M. D. (2005). Four studies on how past and current suicidality relate even when "everything but the kitchen sink" is covaried. *Journal of Abnormal Psychology*, *114*, 291–303. http://dx.doi.org/10.1037/0021-843X.114.2.291

Kabat-Zinn, J. (1990). *Full catastrophe living: The program of the stress reduction clinic at the University of Massachusetts Medical Center*. New York, NY: Delta.

Kabat-Zinn, J. (1994). *Wherever you go, there you are: Mindfulness meditation in everyday life*. New York, NY: Hyperion.

Kabat-Zinn, J. (1996). Mindfulness meditation: What it is, what it isn't, and its role in health care and medicine. In Y. Haruki, Y. Ishii, & M. Suzuki (Eds.), *Comparative and psychological study on meditation* (pp. 161–169). Delft, the Netherlands: Eburon.

Kassinove, H. (Ed.). (1995). *Anger disorders: Assessment, diagnosis, and treatment*. Washington, DC: Taylor & Francis.

Kassinove, H., & Tafrate, R. (2002). *Anger management: The complete treatment guidebook for practitioners*. Atascadero, CA: Impact.

Kazantzis, N., Deane, F. P., & Ronan, K. R. (2000). Homework assignments in cognitive and behavioral therapy: A Meta-Analysis. *Clinical Psychology: Science and Practice*, *7*, 189–202. http://dx.doi.org/10.1093/clipsy.7.2.189

Kazdin, A. E., & Mazurick, J. L. (1994). Dropping out of child psychotherapy: Distinguishing early and late dropouts over the course of treatment. *Journal of Consulting and Clinical Psychology*, *62*, 1069–1074. http://dx.doi.org/10.1037/0022-006X.62.5.1069

Kohlenberg, R. J., & Tsai, M. (1991). *Functional analytic psychotherapy: Creating intense and curative therapeutic relationships*. New York, NY: Plenum Press. http://dx.doi.org/10.1007/978-0-387-70855-3

Kolden, G. G., Chisholm-Stockard, S. M., Strauman, T. J., Tierney, S. C., Mullen, E. A., & Schneider, K. L. (2006). Universal session-level change processes in an early session of psychotherapy: Path models. *Journal of Consulting and Clinical Psychology*, *74*, 327–336. http://dx.doi.org/10.1037/0022-006X.74.2.327

Koons, C. R., Robins, C. J., Tweed, J. L., Lynch, T. R., Gonzalez, A. M., Morse, J. Q., . . . Bastian, L. A. (2001). Efficacy of dialectical behavior therapy in women veterans with borderline personality disorder. *Behavior Therapy*, *32*, 371–390. http://dx.doi.org/10.1016/S0005-7894(01)80009-5

Krishnamurti, J. (2001). *The book of life: Daily meditations with Krishnamurti*. New Delhi, India: Penguin.

Leahy, R. L. (2003). *Cognitive therapy techniques: A practitioner's guide*. New York, NY: Guilford Press.

LeDoux, J. (2003). The emotional brain, fear, and the amygdala. *Cellular and Molecular Neurobiology*, *23*, 727–738. http://dx.doi.org/10.1023/A:1025048802629

Leibenluft, E., Gardner, D. L., & Cowdry, R. W. (1987). The inner experience of the borderline self-mutilator. *Journal of Personality Disorders*, *1*, 317–324.

Lemerise, E. A., & Dodge, K. A. (2008). The development of anger and hostile interactions. In M. Lewis, J. M. Haviland-Jones, & L. F. Barrett (Eds.), *Handbook of emotions* (3rd ed., pp. 730–741). New York, NY: Guilford Press.

Lewis, M. (2010). Self-conscious emotions: Embarrassment, pride, shame, and guilt. In M. Lewis, J. M. Haviland-Jones, & L. F. Barrett (Eds.), *Handbook of emotions* (3rd ed., pp. 742–756). New York, NY: Guilford Press.

Lewis, M., Sullivan, M. W., Ramsay, D. S., & Alessandri, S. M. (1992). Individual differences in anger and sad expressions during extinction: Antecedents and consequences. *Infant Behavior & Development, 15*, 443–452. http://dx.doi.org/10.1016/0163-6383(92)80012-J

Lieb, K., Zanarini, M. C., Schmahl, C., Linehan, M. M., & Bohus, M. (2004). Borderline personality disorder. *The Lancet, 364*, 453–461. http://dx.doi.org/10.1016/S0140-6736(04)16770-6

Linehan, M. M. (1993a). *Cognitive–behavioral treatment of borderline personality disorder.* New York, NY: Guilford Press.

Linehan, M. M. (1993b). *Skills training manual for treatment of borderline personality disorder.* New York, NY: Guilford Press.

Linehan, M. M. (1997). Validation and psychotherapy. In A. C. Bohart & L. S. Greenberg (Eds.), *Empathy reconsidered: New directions in psychotherapy* (pp. 353–392). Washington, DC: American Psychological Association. http://dx.doi.org/10.1037/10226-016

Linehan, M. M. (2008). Dialectical behavior therapy for borderline personality disorder. In H. Barlow (Ed.), *Clinical handbook of psychological disorders: A step-by-step treatment manual* (4th ed., pp. 365–420). New York, NY: Guilford Press.

Linehan, M. M. (2015). *DBT skills training manual* (2nd ed.). New York, NY: Guilford Press.

Linehan, M. M., Armstrong, H. E., Suarez, A., Allmon, D., & Heard, H. L. (1991). Cognitive-behavioral treatment of chronically parasuicidal borderline patients. *Archives of General Psychiatry, 48*, 1060–1064. http://dx.doi.org/10.1001/archpsyc.1991.01810360024003

Linehan, M. M., Bohus, M., & Lynch, T. R. (2007). Dialectical behavior therapy for pervasive emotion dysregulation: Theoretical and practical underpinnings. In J. J. Gross (Ed.), *Handbook of emotion regulation* (pp. 581–605). New York, NY: Guilford Press.

Linehan, M. M., Comtois, K. A., Murray, A. M., Brown, M. Z., Gallop, R. J., Heard, H. L., . . . Lindenboim, N. (2006). Two-year randomized controlled trial and follow-up of dialectical behavior therapy vs therapy by experts for suicidal behaviors and borderline personality disorder. *Archives of General Psychiatry, 63*, 757–766. http://dx.doi.org/10.1001/archpsyc.63.7.757

Linehan, M. M., Heard, H. L., & Armstrong, H. E. (1993). Naturalistic follow-up of a behavioral treatment for chronically parasuicidal borderline patients.

Archives of General Psychiatry, 50, 971–974. http://dx.doi.org/10.1001/
archpsyc.1993.01820240055007

Lynch, T. R., Chapman, A. L., Rosenthal, M. Z., Kuo, J. R., & Linehan, M. M.
(2006). Mechanisms of change in dialectical behavior therapy: Theoretical and
empirical observations. Journal of Clinical Psychology, 62, 459–480. http://dx.doi.
org/10.1002/jclp.20243

Malaffo, M. M., & Espie, C. A. (2007). Cognitive and behavioral treatments of primary insomnia: A review. Minerva Psichiatrica, 48, 313–327.

Marlatt, G. A., & Gordon, J. R. (1985). Relapse prevention: Maintenance strategies in
the treatment of addictive behaviors. New York, NY: Guilford Press.

McMain, S. F., Links, P. S., Gnam, W. H., Guimond, T., Cardish, R. J., Korman, L.,
& Streiner, D. L. (2009). A randomized trial of dialectical behavior therapy
versus general psychiatric management for borderline personality disorder. The
American Journal of Psychiatry, 166, 1365–1374. http://dx.doi.org/10.1176/appi.
ajp.2009.09010039

Miller, W. R., & Rollnick, S. (2002). Motivational interviewing: Preparing people for
change. New York, NY: Guilford Press.

Miller, W. R., & Rollnick, S. (2012). Meeting in the middle: Motivational interviewing and self-determination theory. The International Journal of Behavioral
Nutrition and Physical Activity, 9(25). http://dx.doi.org/10.1186/1479-5868-9-25

Miltenberger, R. G. (2011). Behavior modification: Principles and procedures (5th ed.).
Belmont, CA: Wadsworth.

Nezu, A. M., Maguth Nezu, C., & D'Zurilla, T. J. (2013). Problem-solving therapy:
A treatment manual. New York, NY: Springer.

Novaco, R. W., & Jarvis, K. L. (2002). Brief cognitive behavioral intervention for
anger. In F. Bond & W. Dryden (Eds.), Handbook of brief cognitive behavioral
therapy (pp. 281–296). London, England: Wiley.

Oatley, K., & Jenkins, J. M. (1996). Understanding emotions. Malden, MA: Blackwell.

Oldham, M., Kellett, S., Miles, E., & Sheeran, P. (2012). Interventions to increase
attendance at psychotherapy: A meta-analysis of randomized controlled trials. Journal of Consulting and Clinical Psychology, 80, 928–939. http://dx.doi.
org/10.1037/a0029630

Pepper, S. C. (1942). World hypotheses: A study in evidence. Los Angeles: University
of California.

Perlis, M. L., Junquist, C., Smith, M. T., & Posner, D. (2005). Cognitive behavioral
treatment of insomnia: A session-by-session guide. New York, NY: Springer.

Reese, R. J., Toland, M. D., & Hopkins, N. B. (2011). Replicating and extending the
good-enough level model of change: Considering session frequency. Psychotherapy Research, 21, 608–619. http://dx.doi.org/10.1080/10503307.2011.598580

Resick, P. A., & Schnicke, M. K. (1992). Cognitive processing therapy for sexual
assault victims. Journal of Consulting and Clinical Psychology, 60, 748–756. http://
dx.doi.org/10.1037/0022-006X.60.5.748

Rizvi, S. L., & Linehan, M. M. (2005). The treatment of maladaptive shame in borderline personality disorder: A pilot study of "opposite action." *Cognitive and Behavioral Practice, 12*, 437–447. http://dx.doi.org/10.1016/S1077-7229(05)80071-9

Rizvi, S. L., & Ritschel, L. A. (2014). Mastering the art of chain analysis in dialectical behavior therapy. *Cognitive and Behavioral Practice, 21*, 335–349. http://dx.doi.org/10.1016/j.cbpra.2013.09.002

Robins, C. J., & Chapman, A. L. (2004). Dialectical behavior therapy: Current status, recent developments, and future directions. *Journal of Personality Disorders, 18*, 73–89. http://dx.doi.org/10.1521/pedi.18.1.73.32771

Rosenthal, M. Z., Gratz, K. L., Kosson, D. S., Cheavens, J. S., Lejuez, C. W., & Lynch, T. R. (2008). Borderline personality disorder and emotional responding: A review of the research literature. *Clinical Psychology Review, 28*, 75–91. http://dx.doi.org/10.1016/j.cpr.2007.04.001

Sledge, W. H., Moras, K., Hartley, D., & Levine, M. (1990). Effect of time-limited psychotherapy on patient dropout rates. *The American Journal of Psychiatry, 147*, 1341–1347. http://dx.doi.org/10.1176/ajp.147.10.1341

Stoffers, J. M., Völlm, B. A., Rücker, G., Timmer, A., Huband, N., & Lieb, K. (2012). Psychological therapies for people with borderline personality disorder. *Cochrane Database of Systematic Reviews, 8*, CD005652.

Stulz, N., Lutz, W., Leach, C., Lucock, M., & Barkham, M. (2007). Shapes of early change in psychotherapy under routine outpatient conditions. *Journal of Consulting and Clinical Psychology, 75*, 864–874. http://dx.doi.org/10.1037/0022-006X.75.6.864

Sukhodolsky, D. G., Kassinove, H., & Gorman, B. S. (2004). Cognitive–behavioral therapy for anger in children and adolescents: A meta-analysis. *Aggression and Violent Behavior, 9*, 247–269. http://dx.doi.org/10.1016/j.avb.2003.08.005

Surís, A., Link-Malcolm, J., Chard, K., Ahn, C., & North, C. (2013). A randomized clinical trial of cognitive processing therapy for veterans with PTSD related to military sexual trauma. *Journal of Traumatic Stress, 26*, 28–37. http://dx.doi.org/10.1002/jts.21765

Suzuki, S. (1970). *Zen mind, beginner's mind.* New York, NY: Weatherhill.

Swift, J. K., & Greenberg, R. P. (2015). *Premature termination in psychotherapy: Strategies for engaging clients and improving outcomes.* Washington, DC: American Psychological Association.

Tafrate, R., & Kassinove, H. (1998). Anger control in men: Barb exposure with rational, irrational, and irrelevant self-statements. *Journal of Cognitive Psychotherapy, 12*, 187–211.

Tangney, J. P., & Dearing, R. (2002). *Shame and guilt in interpersonal relationships.* New York, NY: Guilford Press.

Teasdale, J. D., Segal, Z. V., Williams, J. G., Ridgeway, V. A., Soulsby, J. M., & Lau, M. A. (2000). Prevention of relapse/recurrence in major depression by mindfulness-based cognitive therapy. *Journal of Consulting and Clinical Psychology, 68*, 615–623. http://dx.doi.org/10.1037//0022-006X.68.4.615

Tompkins, M. A. (2004). *Using homework in psychotherapy: Strategies, guidelines, and forms*. New York, NY: Guilford Press.

Wierzbicki, M., & Pekarik, G. (1993). A meta-analysis of psychotherapy dropout. *Professional Psychology: Research and Practice, 24*, 190–195. http://dx.doi.org/10.1037/0735-7028.24.2.190

Yeomans, F. E., Levy, K. N., & Caligor, E. (2013). Transference-focused psychotherapy. *Psychotherapy, 50*, 449–453. http://dx.doi.org/10.1037/a0033417

INDEX

ABOUT THE AUTHORS

Alexander L. Chapman, PhD, RPsych, is a professor and coordinator of the clinical science area in the Department of Psychology at Simon Fraser University (SFU), a registered psychologist, and the president of the Dialectical Behavior Therapy (DBT) Centre of Vancouver. Dr. Chapman received his BA (1996) from the University of British Columbia and his MS (2000) and PhD (2003) in clinical psychology from Idaho State University, following an internship at Duke University Medical Center. He completed a 2-year postdoctoral fellowship with Dr. Marsha Linehan (founder of DBT) at the University of Washington. Dr. Chapman directs the Personality and Emotion Research Laboratory at SFU, where he studies the role of emotion regulation in borderline personality disorder (BPD), self-harm, impulsivity, and other behavioral problems. He has published numerous scientific articles and chapters on these and other topics and has given many scientific conference presentations on his research. Dr. Chapman also is on the editorial board for *Behavior Therapy*; *Personality Disorder: Theory, Research, and Treatment*; and *Journal of Personality Disorders*. He was recently designated Distinguished Reviewer by the editorial board of *Behavior Therapy*. He is a DBT trainer and consultant with Behavioral Tech, LLC, and is certified in cognitive behavior therapy by the Canadian Association of Cognitive and Behavioural Therapies. Dr. Chapman regularly gives local, national, and international workshops and invited talks on DBT and the treatment of BPD; has consulted with and trained clinicians in Canada, the United States, and the United Kingdom; and trains and supervises clinical psychology students. He has received the Young Investigator's Award of the National Education Alliance for Borderline Personality Disorder (2007), the Canadian Psychological Association's Early Career Scientist Practitioner Award (2011), and an 8-year Career Investigator Award from the Michael Smith Foundation for Health Research. He has coauthored eight books (five published, three in press). Three of his self-help books have won the Association for Behavioral and Cognitive Therapies Self-Help Book Seal of Merit award. In addition, Dr. Chapman is an assistant instructor at his local martial arts studio and has been practicing Zen and mindfulness meditation for several years. He enjoys cooking, hiking, skiing, cycling, and spending time with his wonderful wife and two young sons.

M. Zachary Rosenthal, PhD, is an associate professor with a joint appointment in the Department of Psychiatry and Behavioral Sciences at Duke University Medical Center and the Department of Psychology and Neuroscience at Duke University. He is the vice chair for clinical services within the Department of Psychiatry and Behavioral Sciences and the director of the Duke Cognitive Behavioral Research and Treatment Program. He is a clinician, educator, and researcher.